The
Lump
$um
Advisor

ANTHONY M. GALLEA

NEW YORK INSTITUTE OF FINANCE

NEW YORK • TORONTO • SYDNEY • TOKYO • SINGAPORE

Library of Congress Cataloging in Publication Data

Gallea, Anthony.
    The lump sum advisor : what to do whenever you receive a lump sum
distribution / Anthony M. Gallea.
       p. cm.
    Rev. ed. of: The lump sum handbook. c1993.
    Includes bibliographical references and index.
    ISBN 0-7352-0073-4
    1. Lump sum distributions (Pensions)—United States. 2. Old age pensions—
Taxation—United States. 3. Individual retirement accounts—United States.
4. Retirement income—United States. 5. Annuities—United States. 6. Investments—
United States.
    I. Gallea, Anthony. Lump sum handbook. II. Title.
    HD7105.35.U6G338   1999
    332.024'01—dc21   99-12188
                                                    CIP

This publication is designed to provide accurate and authoritative information in regard to
the subject matter covered. It is sold with the understanding that the publisher is not engaged
in rendering legal, accounting, or other professional services. If legal advice or other expert
assistance is required, the services of a competent professional person should be sought.

> *—From a Declaration of Principles jointly adopted by a Committee of the American*
> *Bar Association and a committee of Publishers and Associations.*

The views and opinions expressed in this book are solely those of the author, and have not
been approved or reviewed by his employer, Salomon Smith Barney, Inc.

Note: Portions of this book were published as *The Lump Sum Handbook,* Prentice Hall, 1993.

Printed in the United States of America
10 9 8 7 6 5 4 3 2 1

ISBN 0-7352-0073-4

ATTENTION: CORPORATIONS AND SCHOOLS
Prentice Hall books are available at quantity discounts with bulk purchase for educational, business, or sales promotional use. For information, please write to: Prentice Hall
Special Sales, 240 Frisch Court, Paramus, New Jersey 07652. Please supply: title of
book, ISBN, quantity, how the book will be used, date needed.

 NEW YORK INSTITUTE OF FINANCE
An Imprint of Prentice Hall Press
Paramus, NJ 07652

On the World Wide Web at http://www.phdirect.com

Preface

When I wrote *The Lump Sum Handbook* in 1990 and 1991, I did not imagine that seven years later, I would be writing a new work to replace the old.

I have always believed that the proper handling of a lump sum distribution is such an important subject, that many more works would have been published to add to and surpass my original work in this area. However, most IRA discussion is limited to a chapter or so in various financial planning books.

Seven years later, radical changes have taken place. An acceleration in corporate reorganizations has caused more and more people to receive lump sum distributions before they anticipated doing so. And, as concern continues about Social Security and the realization that it is not enough to provide a secure retirement, more and more Americans are seeking sound advice about how to fund retirement.

Recent changes in the tax law, especially in regard to the new Roth IRAs, have created new strategies and potential avenues for solution. Unfortunately, one of my great hopes—a more simplified tax code regulating IRAs—has not come to pass. If anything, the law has become more convoluted and more difficult.

I have rewritten the appropriate chapters having to do with tax issues to reflect the most recent knowledge at time of publication. However, readers are strongly encouraged to seek confirmation and advice from their own tax and legal advisors. While I can point the way and offer strategies and ideas, in the end, they must be specifically applied by his or her team of professionals. In addition, amendments and clarification of tax code are frequent and so, no book can claim to offer the final word on the subject.

With regard to investment advice, the reader will find essentially the same approach I outlined eight years ago. We live in an era where we constantly crave something new, but there is comfort in knowing that an investment strategy can stand the test of time.

Having learned my craft from over two decades of daily work, it appears that a few lessons have been worth learning.

A great deal, and very little, has changed in my life since my first book on retirement planning was published in 1992. Children who were in middle school or high school are now in high school or college. My wife of 22 years is now my wife of 29 years. A Team of six people has grown to fifteen, but our daily work remains essentially the same. Since 1992, our client base has more than quadrupled, no doubt due in part to the increased awareness of our work in the public domain.

Acknowledgments

I wish to thank several people who have helped me over the past few years to realize many of my personal and professional goals.

First, my wife Bonnie, without whom none of this would have happened. Throughout my professional career, she's been a friend, lover, and confidant. Too often, she had to shoulder alone the task of raising a family while her husband was giving a speech or a seminar in a faraway place. I have spent countless nights away from home tending to business, while she spent countless nights doling out cough medicine, or dealing with a contractor, or driving to soccer practice. No man was ever blessed with a finer companion.

My children, Chris, Shelle and Lisa have been an endless source of delight and as any parent can imagine, challenge. To watch them grow and deal with the transition from child to adult has been a pleasure and a joy. I couldn't be more proud of them and love them more for who they are and what they have each accomplished.

Admiring appreciation to my intern, Julie Parks from Yale University. Her unerring skill at editing my awkward writing and researching of current data contributed immensely to the readability of the text. Her talents are quite beyond her years, and I look forward to watching her career unfold in what will surely be a succession of success upon success.

This is my second book with Ellen Schneid Coleman as my editor and I can only say that I am most fortunate to be working with her again. Professional judgment aside, she makes writing and publishing fun, and the reader can be assured that any weakness in this book is, no doubt, the result of my stubbornness and not her good taste.

A deep bow to my partners on the Gallea Team at Salomon Smith Barney, who, as always, shouldered additional loads so I could write—Richard DiMarzo, Bonnie Lane, Tara Nemergut, Meredith Wilmot, Paul Beck, Donna Caufield, Darren Moran, Gina Buonono, Patty Davis and Sue Smith. You always were, and still are, the best.

I only wish that every executive in America was fortunate enough to report to my superior—Toni Elliott. And, to my branch manager, Jennifer Hartmann, my thanks for always plowing the road. Finally, to our operations staff, Geral Smith and Debbie DeBoard, thank you for your help and support.

A special mention to my accountant and friend, Harry Sealfon, for his vetting of the chapters having to do with income tax and tax calculation. He performed this duty with enthusiasm and care and it is all to the readers' benefit.

Kudos to Bill Patalon. Bill and I wrote *Contrarian Investing*, and he selflessly offered to help me with this manuscript. He sought no compensation nor public display for that effort. That is, Bill was being Bill. I am honored to count him among my closest friends and look forward to co-authoring with him again in the coming year on our second book.

Finally, I wish to thank our clients. It is difficult to communicate how much of a profoundly human experience it is to do the work I do. And, it is our clients who make it so.

If you can imagine being a part of the lives of 2000 families, helping thousands of parents, grandparents and children, you can begin to get the idea. As an intimate advisor, you see everything possible in the human condition—birth, death, illness, recovery, tragedy, soaring accomplishment. You see the traits of great-grandparents show up in great-grandchildren. You can follow family lines, and watch accomplishment and failure. Great dreams are born, some die and some are realized.

Imagine experiencing hundreds of everything—births, deaths, graduations, marriages, divorces, hirings, firings, retirements and rebirths. I have and it is wondrous to be part of that human parade.

All in all, it has been a wonderful experience to be part of all of this. It is the spirit of all of those families and the great energy they bring to life, that breathes life into this work.

Introduction

"Can I afford to retire?" Bill Johnson looked at me hopefully. I looked at his facts and figures.

"Well, that depends. What are you going to be doing?"

He stared at me thoughtfully for a few moments.

"Is that important to know right now?"

"Important? No. It's much more than that. It's the very reason why we're here."

I've spent the better part of a dozen years helping people like Bill Johnson. As a senior portfolio management director for one of the world's largest financial services firm, my day-to-day work revolves around serving people like Bill and his wife, Mary.

Most of my team's clients came into their wealth via a lump-sum distribution payment in cash of their retirement benefit from their employer. Our Team is responsible for over $800 million in client assets, much of it held by individuals in retirement accounts.

In 1981, when a Sylvania division was sold by GTE, I counseled several dozen Sylvania employees from four different locations in three states on how to handle their lump-sum distributions. It was my breakthrough into the lump-sum management business. At the time, it was the single largest transfer of retirement plan assets via IRA rollover that my firm had encountered. Since then, I've assisted retirees from Westinghouse, Eastman Kodak, Mobil, *US News and World Report*, General Signal, Xerox, Comsat, John Fluke, Delta Airlines, and many other organizations, large and small. Our clients live in two dozen states across the country, in various types of communities.

I've appeared on national television, radio, and in print, discussing the general topic of retirement planning and lump sum distributions. Of course, as the author of *The Lump Sum Handbook* and *Contrarian Investing*, my opinion or comment on retirement planning strategies is sought on a regular basis by the media and other professionals.

When you sit with an anxious couple in their fifties and try to help them make a retirement decision that will affect the rest of their lives, you realize how important it is to have sound knowledge. In working together, the three of us challenge the difficulties and problems at hand in order to come to the right decisions. These people simply want to enjoy a satisfying retirement. They want their retirement to be the capstone of their lives, their reward for all the years of sweat and toil, of sacrifice for their children and devotion to their parents and community.

Too often, poor planning, poor investment advice, and unexpected tax burden mar what should be the golden years of their lives. Sadly, most of it could be avoided.

I remember hearing an all-too-familiar story from one of my clients. A friend of his in Ohio had taken his pension lump sum and, rather than rolling it over to an IRA and investing for income, he tried to hit a financial home run. Unbelievable as it may seem, the individual chose to pay income taxes on the distribution ($100,000 tax bill) in order to invest the balance in a new sugar-beet-processing facility. He was blinded by promises of triple-digit returns on his investment. When mismanagement and strife between the partners had driven the company to bankruptcy, he actually considered having his wife sue his former employer; he would try claiming they should have protected her by not giving her husband the lump sum! I've seen just about all the bad things that people can do to themselves with a lump sum. I have heard about people losing their pension at the gaming tables, making disastrous investments, retiring too soon, and depleting their lump sum.

On a happier note, I've also seen a lot of the good things as well and these tend to be the overwhelming majority of experiences. People who were able to take a lump sum, triple it over time, and create real financial wealth for their families. Engineers retiring as millionaires. One of our clients took his lump sum, invested it in bonds, then took a real risk going to work for a small high-tech start-up; in old-time American fashion, the company was a big hit, and he retired a wealthy man. Clients have funded countless college educations for their grandchildren, helped out-of-work children through tough times, created scholarships for their alma mater, and donated countless dollars to charities, schools, and the needy.

I've gained priceless experience/education as a part of their lives. To be creative in devising strategies to solve problems. To invest with success and reduce taxes. In short, how to take a lump-sum distribution and use it as a tool to meet the needs of our clients. After working with over 2,000 families for nearly twenty years, I have some ideas and thoughts to share with you about what works and what doesn't to solve problems, invest with consistency, and keep the tax bite down.

This book offers the latest information about the lump-sum distribution. There is still no other book exclusively devoted to this subject despite the thousands of people every year faced with taking a lump sum distribution.

Whether you are an individual receiving a lump sum or a financial professional seeking to learn more about them, this book should be invaluable. This handbook covers all aspects of the lump sum, including tax and investment treatment. There is a case study presented at the end that offers an example of how the concepts and strategies discussed in the book can be applied.

You can read the book cover to cover, or if you have particular questions, you can use the Table of Contents and the Index to direct you to the section that provides the answer. For instance, you may want to know some basic facts about the bond market. You can turn to the chapter on bond investing and find a discussion of the subject along with comments about various portfolios you can create.

The book is generally written in the male voice. This was done for the sake of convenience and consistency. However, the lump-sum problem, and its potential profitable use is a subject that is gender neutral. Even if the lump sum is generated from a husband's employment, his wife will eventually inherit directly the problems it represents. In addition, women are forming an increasingly larger percentage of lump-sum recipients as their entry into the labor force many years ago begins to be reflected in their own employee benefits.

This book is the product of everyday experience gleaned from thousands of hours of meetings, seminars, and discussion. It is written by a working professional to provide practical solutions to the many issues surrounding the lump sum distribution. It is grounded in what actually works, not in abstract theory.

Contents

TO BONNIE AND CHRIS AND SHELLE AND LISA,
WITH ALL MY LOVE.

CHAPTER ONE

Overview:
Lump-Sum Basics

In 1974 Congress passed ERISA, the Employee Retirement Income Security Act. It represented a complete overhaul of federal pension law. This was in response to many abuses that had occurred in the administration of pension plans and in the payments of benefits promised to workers.

ERISA created a revolution in the management of retirement-plan assets in the United States. Among other provisions, this law allowed employers to offer the payment of benefits in a lump sum. Traditionally, a pension accrued over a worker's career was paid to him after retirement in the form of a monthly check, with optional payments to his spouse in the event of his death.

Under ERISA, employers could offer the retiree a single lump-sum payment in lieu of a monthly annuity. The retiree could then take advantage of certain tax breaks that would allow her to manage her own retirement plan. These new provisions created the need for individuals to learn more about the lump-sum distribution and how to manage it.

The effect on pensions in the United States was remarkable. From 1975 to 1997, total pension-plan assets increased by 1300 percent (see Figure 1.1). And the number of workers covered by pension plans increased by 90 percent.

At the same time as this was happening, American industry embarked on the greatest restructuring in history, with many of the largest corporations bought out and resized. Entire divisions were closed. Driven both by international competitive pressures and the increasing availability of funds to effect corporate takeovers, the pace accelerated throughout the 1980s. These changes triggered the termination of many benefit plans, since a change in corporate control has a direct effect on retirement plans. Hundreds of thousands of people had a lump-sum decision suddenly thrust upon them.

A side effect of becoming more competitive was the decision by many corporations to base retirement plans on the amount of annual contributions the corporation would make (known as defined-contribution plans). This was a complete change from the traditional plan where the employer promised the employee a specific benefit upon retirement, come hell or high water (defined-benefit plans). American managers schooled in the ruthless arena of competition were no

FIGURE 1.1   Private, State, and Local Government Pension Assets (in millions)

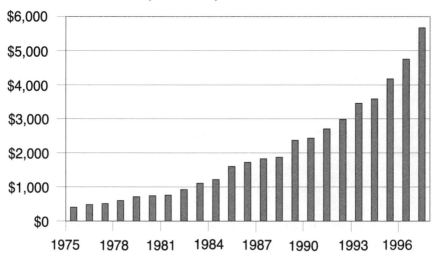

Source: U.S. Department of Labor

longer willing to commit the corporation to costly and permanent benefit programs.

From 1975 to 1994, the number of participants covered under defined-contribution plans soared by 260 percent, while those covered by defined-benefit plans barely budged (see Figure 1.2).

An increasing number of plans became structured, with the corporation's annual contribution tied to the performance of the company and the level of profitability. Since defined-contribution plans are typically paid out in a lump, the number of employees covered by lump-sum disbursing plans increased geometrically. Profit-sharing plans, 401(k) plans, and other similar-defined contribution plans became the benefit vehicles of choice for a growing number of employers.

And those still offering the traditional check-a-month-for-life plan began inserting provisions to let employees take benefits in one lump instead of as a monthly annuity.

As a result, the management of adequate income in retirement fell more and more on the shoulders of the individual. Today, fewer paternal corporations are willing to assume responsibility for seeing the retiree through his or her golden years. Hand in hand with this change is a greater willingness by more people to assume responsibility for taking control of their own retirement.

THE NEW INVESTORS

Investing awareness has increased tremendously during the past 20 years. Experience in making investment choices in 401(k) or other savings plans has made people comfortable with the concept of managing their own retirement funds.

In addition, workers are retiring at younger ages. In 1975, 75 percent of all men aged 61 and 62 were still in the work force. By 1997, that number had declined to 49 percent (average of ratios from 61 and 62 year olds).

The government has not been an idle observer in all this. In addition to ERISA, other pension legislation has been passed by a Congress eager to oversee the process. The Tax Reform Act of 1986, the Retirement Equity Act of 1984, the Tax Equity and Fiscal

FIGURE 1.2 Active Participants in Defined Benefit and Defined Contribution Plans (in thousands)

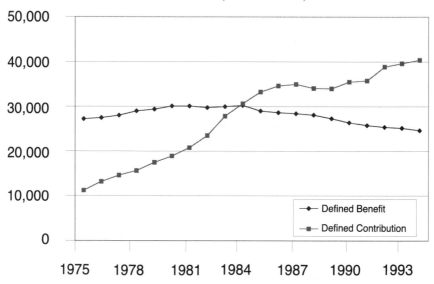

Source: U.S. Department of Labor

Responsibility Act of 1982, and others have clearly established government's abiding concern for the retirement-plan process. There is a national interest involved: To the extent that individuals can fend for themselves in retirement, demands on Social Security and other income safety nets are reduced. And with the number of Americans over 65 estimated to be one-fifth the total population (or 45 million) by the year 2000, government has a continuing need to oversee the retirement-income process.

NEW MONEY, NO ADVICE

When Individual Retirement Accounts (IRAs) allowed tax-deductible contributions, a flood of articles, books, and guides entered the market with advice on tax, investment, and planning. IRA experts showed us how we could become millionaires, and every bank, brokerage house, and mutual fund considered marketing for new IRAs an absolute must.

But then, in an effort to increase government revenues, the tax deductibility of IRAs was phased out through various benefit and income tests. The higher your income, the less deductible the contribution. Most workers lost the incentive to make an IRA contribution. Once tax deductibility was removed for most workers, the professional's interest in Individual Retirement Accounts waned, and there was very little new business in those tax-deductible IRAs. While hundreds of thousands of people were newly minted lump-sum recipients, advice on the subject was dwindling. Today most books on investment or retirement may carry a few paragraphs on the subject but little more than that.

This illustrates the basic problem with getting money in a lump sum: The recipients are often ill equipped to handle investing the money, to choose the right tax treatment, and to do the long-range planning necessary to get the most from their money. They are equally lost in judging the qualifications of others to handle it for them.

Consider a person who retires from a company and receives a lump-sum retirement distribution of $400,000. After saving for a home and putting three kids through college, he may never have had more than a few thousand dollars to invest during his entire working life. Yet he is now called upon to handle a large portfolio with complicated tax and planning issues.

Aside from lacking the proper technical skills, people also find it difficult to subdue their emotions while making financial decisions. We can all imagine a widow receiving her husband's life-insurance payment. In her grief she would be well advised to put the money in a money-market fund until her mind and emotions settle. Yet many immediately make investment decisions they later regret.

Most people getting lump-sum distributions focus on the money involved. Whether delighted, stunned, or simply overwhelmed by the responsibility, they find it easier to focus on readily quantified things such as rates of return or growth of capital. The numbers can be computed, and there is a seductive security to running computations and viewing the results.

This puts the cart before the horse. The first order of business is to understand yourself and what you want from a lump sum.

EXAMPLE   John Gowers was a high-level executive at a major American corporation. With an annual income running well into six figures, his responsibilities included hundreds of engineers and technicians in his role as director of research and development. Faced with an attractive early-retirement offer, he sought our advice as to whether he could afford to quit working. With liquid investment assets of well over $1 million in addition to a pension lump sum exceeding $900,000, I saw little difficulty in his taking the package and leaving his employer, "But," he said, "why don't you run the numbers." I said that I didn't have to, a quick take of his assets appeared to give him $80,000 per year in interest income, and with his modest expenses that provided adequate capital. He insisted that I run computer computations to satisfy his need to see numbers in black and white.

I asked him to leave the calculations for a moment and answer one question first. Since he was only 52, 1 asked, what did he intend to do with his life? Silence.

While he could produce reams of numbers covering every potential wiggle of inflation and interest rates, he didn't have the foggiest notion of what he was going to do with himself after he left his job. He had plenty of information about how much money he would have, but he hadn't given any thought to what he was going to do with it once he had it. What good are the computations, I suggested, if you don't know to what purpose the money will be put?

It was clear that what was needed was a life plan, before a financial plan could be set in place. Several weeks of discussion between him and his spouse followed. Only when the outline of their plans was in place did we proceed to their financial strategy.

LUMP-SUM REQUIREMENTS

A lump sum must be paid to you within one taxable year. You must receive the money because you have reached age 59-1/2, have separated from service, or have become disabled. Additionally, you must have been a participant in the plan for five years. If you are the beneficiary of a deceased employee, you, too, can receive a lump sum from your spouse's retirement plan, if he or she was eligible. A lump sum must be handled in a particular way to qualify for tax-favored treatment. If you are careful with it, you can defer and most likely reduce the federal income tax due.

Remember that "lump sum" has a specific meaning in the tax code. You need to meet the qualifications listed here. Simply because you get a chunk of cash in one check doesn't mean that it qualifies as a lump sum. If you get money from an employer's plan that doesn't qualify as a lump sum, it may be eligible for other favored tax treatment that will be discussed later in this chapter. So if you don't meet the lump-sum qualifications, don't panic!

Take It All in One Year

You must receive all the money from any plan during one taxable year. This means that if you accept any funds at all you must take every cent remaining in the plan before the tax year is over. You can't take a portion this year and another piece next year and still get lump-sum treatment.

If you have more than one plan, however, it may be that one will pay out immediately and another the next year, and both can qualify for lump-sum treatment. For instance, your pension plan may pay you on October 15. Your savings plan may not make a distribution to you until January 5 of the following year. Both would still qualify for lump-sum treatment. It's just that you can't take half of one plan now and the rest of it next year and still get lump-sum treatment.

You Have Reached Age 59-1/2

If you are still working for the company where you earned your benefits, you must be over age 59-1/2 to receive a lump-sum distribution. A major exception to this rule covers pension plans. You cannot receive a lump sum from your company pension if you have reached 59-1/2 and are still working,

If you are younger than 59-1/2, the law does not allow your employer to distribute any money to you out of your plan. However, you can receive a lump sum if your company was sold and the new owners terminate the old plan, but you keep working there.

You Have Separated from Service

This means you have quit, been laid off, fired, or have retired from the company where you earned your lump sum. Also, you are considered to be separated from service even if you go to work for someone else after leaving your old job. Separated from service refers to the employer who maintained the plan, not to your full retirement.

You Are on Disability

If you are disabled and can no longer work, you are eligible for a lump-sum payment, but only if you terminate employment. If you are still on your employer's payroll, you are not eligible. You are considered an active employee and so are not separated from service.

You Are the Beneficiary of a Deceased Employee

If you are the deceased employee's spouse, you have the same options open to you that your spouse had, which include taking a lump sum and rolling it over to an IRA. However, if you are a nonspouse beneficiary (a child, friend, or relative), you cannot roll it over to an IRA account. These beneficiary options are outlined in Table 1.1.

TABLE 1.1 Options Open to Lump-Sum Beneficiaries

Lump Sum Treatment	Spouse	Nonspouse
Roll over to an IRA?	Yes	No
Ten-year averaging?	Yes	Yes
Defer distributions?	Yes	No

SOURCES OF A LUMP SUM

Lump sums can come from your company pension fund, profit sharing, 401(k), SEP-IRA, Keogh (but not if you are self-employed), ESOP, TRASOP, or most other plans that enjoy tax-deferred status. These are often known as "qualified" plans because they qualify for special tax treatment from the IRS.

These plans defer any taxes on contributions or earnings until they are paid out to you. So most or all of the money in these plans will be immediately taxable to you if you don't treat them properly.

Your employer may maintain nonqualified plans. Distributions from them are not entitled to lump-sum treatment. They include certain types of deferred compensation plans. To be sure, check the status with your employer.

VESTING

Vesting means that the money in the plan is yours. In a plan such as a 401(k), all the money that goes in is yours from the time it is in the plan. You are fully vested. Pension plans have a vesting schedule that requires you to work for a number of years before the benefits are yours. This means that when an employee stays for only a year or two, the employer isn't obligated to give him or her any money from, say, the pension plan. Vesting allows the employer to reward long-term employees and ignore those who stay only a few months.

Vesting schedules vary from plan to plan, so you need to check yours for the details.

To be vested for a lump sum, you must have been a participant in the plan for at least five years. This is measured by the tax years of the employee, not by full calendar years. So an employee who was a participant from July 1992 until May 1996 is considered a five-year participant, even though he or she wasn't a participant for a full 60 months.

PLAN CATEGORIES

Federal law mandates vesting in a pension after five years. All plans fall into two categories—defined benefit and defind contribution. How the contributions are calculated and how the benefits are promised differentiate them.

Defined-Benefit Plans

A defined-benefit plan promises a specific retirement income to you. Your benefit is calculated using your years of service and your salary. Your employer hires an actuary to compute how much money must be set aside annually for each employee to provide the benefits promised upon retirement. If your employer enjoys good returns on the plan investments, he can use those profits to reduce the amount of money he must put in each year. But if the plan loses money on its investments, your employer must make up the difference with additional contributions. If the plan is current on its obligations and the amount of money it needs, it is called fully funded. If the plan is short, it is known as underfunded.

Once you retire, your employer will typically turn over a sum of money to an insurance company and purchase an annuity or a lifetime income stream that will guarantee the benefits to you and your spouse. Once she has done that, your employer is essentially out of the loop. Your checks come from the insurance company. However, an increasing number of employers are also offering direct payment in the form of a lump sum. A defined-benefit plan, then, promises a specific benefit to you in retirement, and your employer has varying contributions that she must make into the plan on your behalf each year. The benefit is fixed; the contributions are not.

Defined-Contribution Plans

A defined-contribution plan is the opposite. In this type of plan, the contribution formula is fixed each year, but no specific benefit is promised. The amount of the benefit will vary with the investment returns that the plan enjoys while you are a participant. Unlike a defined-benefit plan, your employer isn't responsible for making additional contributions if the investments perform poorly, nor can he reduce his contributions if the investments perform well.

Defined-contribution plans are typically savings or profit-sharing plans. Your 401(k) plan or your company profit-sharing plan is a defined-contribution plan. More companies are setting up defined contribution plans because a fixed benefit isn't provided to the employee and the employer's contributions can often be tied to profits. In this way the employer isn't on the hook to make contributions when business is bad, or to make good on specific benefits that have been promised in good times but can't be delivered. Many companies in steel and other heavy industries have found themselves in this position, although the problem has been greatly reduced over the past few years.

BASIC TYPES OF RETIREMENT PLANS

Whether defined benefit or defined contribution, your retirement plan falls into one of several types. Here are the most popular with a brief description of each.

Pension Plans

A pension plan is created to provide you with retirement income. Your employer makes annual contributions to the plan and often hires professional investment managers to handle the assets. The actuaries will tell your employer, each year, how much must be set aside.

Pension plans are usually defined-benefit plans. Defined-benefit pension plans are more prevalent in major corporations.

When you retire you will be offered several forms of payment. If you want to include your spouse in your pension in case you are the first to die, the amount you receive will be based on how much you want your spouse to have.

Your employer may also offer you a lump sum in lieu of the monthly check. Not all employers do this, and you have to check each plan to see if one is available. If you take the lump sum, your employer is washing her hands of her obligations to you under that particular plan, although her obligations on other plans continue.

TIP If you take a lump sum, you don't forfeit your rights to any of your other retirment benefits, such as medical or life insurance.

Profit-Sharing Plans

A profit-sharing plan is just what it sounds like. You are participating in the profits of the company. Profit sharing is a defined contribution; the plan document sets forth the formula that governs how much is contributed each year for you.

Since it is based on the profitability of the company, your employer will not be required to make contributions for you when the company loses money, and his contribution requirements will be considerably reduced in tough times. Employers like that flexibility, so profit-sharing plans are becoming more popular. And, since employees know that their retirement savings can depend on a profitable company, some employers believe that these plans help focus the work force on keeping costs down and earnings up.

Profit-sharing plans are usually paid as lump sum distributions, although annuity (check-a-month) options may be available to you.

401(k) Plans and 403B Plans

The 401(k) plan uses both employer and employee contributions. This defined contribution plan is primarily employee funded, although it is typical for employers to match some employee contributions. Contributions to 401(k) plans are made by the employee on pretax basis, which means, in effect, that you get a tax deduction for making the contribution.

EXAMPLE Tom earns $40,000 in wages and contributes $1,000 to his 401(k). He will pay income tax on $39,000 in earnings that year and won't be taxed on the 401(k) until he retires.

Funds from 401(k) plans are paid as lump-sum distributions to the employee.

A 403B plan is often used for teachers. Named for the tax-code section in which it is defined, a 403B plan is a defined-contribution plan, primarily employee funded. As with a 401(k), the employee is allowed to make pretax contributions. Generally offered through insurance companies, 403B plans pay out as either a lump sum or as an annuity purchased through the insurance company. Of course, if the annuity is elected, the lump sum is surrendered as payment for the contract.

Stock-Ownership Programs

ESOP (Employee Stock Ownership Plan) and ESOT (Employee Stock Ownership Trust) are defined-contribution plans that are funded with your employer's stock.

Because ESOP and ESOT plans are not diversified by investment, they are generally not used as primary retirement plans. Rather, they are supplemental plans. Employers will often set them up to make each employee a stockholder who will, it is hoped, take a greater interest in the profitability of the company.

In the case of employee-owned companies, the stock of the corporation is often placed in an ESOT or ESOP as the vehicle of ownership. If the company is sold, the plan typically will pay out a lump sum to the employees as former owners.

SPECIAL CIRCUMSTANCES

Sometimes your health, financial, or employment status creates complications.

Your Company Is Sold

If another company has bought out your company and you stay there under new management, have you separated from service? Most often the answer is "no," but there are exceptions. Because the rules are not clear, you can expect your employer to ask the IRS for a letter ruling on the issue. Letter rulings, by their nature, are answers to questions that are not obvious in reading the tax code. IRS personnel must research each request and arrive at a conclusion. A letter ruling requires preparation and time for the government to respond, so you may be in limbo for weeks or even months until the process is completed.

Your employer's attorneys will ask the IRS whether, given the circumstances of the buyout, a separation from service has taken place. Alternatively, your employer may decide to terminate the pension plan, and if your new employer has no plan that will take the money, the lump sum will be distributed to you. In either case, a ruling will be requested to define how the plan will be distributed, who will get the money, and what the tax rules will be.

Once the letter ruling has been issued, you can expect your former employer to obey it. If the IRS allows a distribution, however, it is up to your former employer to decide how it will be done. If the IRS does not allow you to take a lump-sum layout, your benefit will either be frozen with your prior employer or paid out upon your normal retirement under that plan or it will be rolled into your new employer's plan.

If you are considered separated from service, it usually takes a few weeks or months for the payout to be arranged. However, it cannot be unnecessarily delayed. Your employer will inform you of the various payment options available.

You Have Loans from Your Employer

If you have any outstanding loans from your plan, they must be paid off before you can receive your lump sum. You do not have the option of taking distribution, using a portion of it to pay off the loan, and keeping the balance. Doing that would constitute a taxable event and jeopardize your treatment of the distribution as a lump sum.

For example, let's say you have $100,000 in your 401(k) plan with a $10,000 outstanding loan. Your employer pays off the loan and distributes $90,000 to you. The $10,000 is considered to be taxable income, and the remaining $90,000, while eligible for rollover to an IRA, can't be treated as a lump sum for favorable tax treatment. The reason for this is easy to understand. Since you originally borrowed the $10,000 out of the plan and didn't pay taxes on it as a loan, paying it off with pretax dollars in your retirement plan means that you would get the $10,000 tax-free.

SUMMARY

Confused? Don't be discouraged. It is a confusing subject and many of the rules are vague or seem contradictory.

Most of the uncertainty will fall away once you clearly understand your tax position. And, understanding your tax situation is a matter of defining the type of distribution you are receiving. Your age, employment status, health, and the type of plan all need to be considered.

Many employers will offer a fairly complete explanation about how the distribution will be treated under the tax code, so check with your personnel department first.

If you can't get a clear explanation, you will need to hire an accountant or other professional advisor to help you. Whatever the case, be sure you understand exactly what kind of distribution you are receiving and the options open to you. Never take a distribution from your employer's retirement plan without first understanding your tax position.

CHAPTER TWO

Making the Decision: Annuity or Lump Sum?

Mark Severan was chief engineer in a group designing small motors for a major manufacturer. He had a spotless, 28-year career with his employer. He enjoyed his work and had the support and respect of his fellow engineers. Then, one Friday afternoon, Mark's supervising manager called him into his office. After assuring Mark of the company's deepest appreciation for his contributions, he asked if he would like to retire. After all, as Mark knew, the company was in a desperate fight to fend off foreign competition. By hiring new engineers at lower cost, the company could reduce the selling price of its product. At 52, Mark had enjoyed an excellent career, and while it might be tough to leave, the $300,000 pension lump sum could help grease the skids, couldn't it? Mark was speechless.

Mark isn't alone. Three million American workers retire each year, and many are offered an early-retirement package. The offer they receive often has nothing to do with their job performance. Many of us place a great deal of emphasis on our work. Indeed, for many of us, work defines who and what we are. I enjoy being a senior portfolio management director in a major company. I enjoy the respect and prestige it gives me. Frankly, I'm a bit afraid of the day when I'll have to shed the power and the title to become another retiree.

IS EARLY RETIREMENT RIGHT FOR YOU?

I've met with hundreds of people who are either contemplating early retirement or who have had it thrust upon them. If you're miserable at your job, if you hate walking in each morning, then the chance to retire is like a lifeline thrown to a drowning man. But if you like your work, early retirement can make you angry, hurt, and confused.

And yet, if you can walk away with a lump sum and go to another employer, even at a lower wage, it's probably worth it.

> **EXAMPLE**   Sam Cremona, at age 50, left his company with a $250,000 lump sum after 25 years as a production supervisor for a Fortune 500 company. If you had asked Sam why he was leaving, he would have listed boredom or burn-out as interchangeable reasons. While his new job at a small manufacturer paid $25,000 less than the $65,000 he had been earning, he knew that his lump sum could grow to $500,000 over ten years if he could just earn 7 percent per year. Sam and his wife were willing to take a short-term hit to their income to secure a better retirement income and to give Sam a chance to enjoy his remaining working years.
>
> Sam couldn't justify this move in strict dollars and cents. While his lump sum doubled, he also gave up $250,000 in wages to make the move. He considered this a worthwhile trade, however, his new job invigorated him ("These people really need my help," he would say), he is happy, and he feels that he has secured a comfortable retirement with investment of the lump sum. The thought of spending another ten years at a hateful job was too much to bear.

KNOW BEFORE YOU GO: WEIGHING MAJOR FACTORS

You need to carefully weigh medical insurance and other benefit differentials before deciding to leave your job. A good rule of thumb, however, is that if you are more than seven years away from retirement you can consider a career change as a reasonable move financially. Anything less than seven years and you're probably better off gutting it out.

The reasons lie in the mathematics of the move. If you have seven years to invest a lump sum, and assuming you can earn between 7 and 10 percent, you can increase it by between 60 percent and 100 percent. So a $200,000 lump sum becomes $320,000 or $400,000. This additional capital will compensate you for the lower wages a new job will entail. It is also enough time to let you earn benefits at your new employer.

Leaving your post for a new employer for a shorter time frame usually doesn't give you the time you need to replace the lost wages. Remember that the lump sum you leave on the shelf by staying with your employer will not grow at the rate you can make it grow in an IRA.

Warning! Don't assume you'll find another job. Beginning in your mid- to late forties, employment cannot be taken for granted. Have another job in hand before you leave. Don't feel guilty about this. If your employer wants you out, and a new job accomplishes that, you haven't betrayed anyone. And if you don't find another job, then early retirement would have been a mistake.

You Can't Go Home Again

Once you've done it, retirement is pretty hard to undo. Remember that at 55, it's reasonable to expect to live another 25 years. Most people view retirement as a time to suspend work and effort. Nothing could be farther from the truth. Successful retirees may slow down, but they don't stop. After a few months, you may find yourself restless. So when you face the retirement decision, ask yourself one question: Retire to what? If you don't have a ready answer, postpone the decision if you can.

OK, BUT HOW DO I PAY FOR IT?

The old rule of thumb was that you needed to replace 70 percent of your working income in order to retire. More and more people are using 80 percent as a replacement figure, and I agree. Not only are retirees much more active, and, as a result, spend more money, but the reality of inflation means that you need more of a hedge than people did in generations past.

> **EXAMPLE**   Bonnie Stamford was the executive assistant to a senior vice president in a company making plastic auto parts. Her expenses of $20,000 per year when she retired reflected a lifestyle fueled by her final salary of $30,000. After 10 years of retirement, inflation has pushed her expenses to nearly $27,000. Although Social Security, a monthly pension, and income from her IRA (she rolled over her company savings plan) served to meet her expenses, she was eventually forced to sell her home, rent an apartment, and use the proceeds from the home for expenses.

What appears to be perfectly adequate income today may be insufficient in a few years. As you get older, your value as a worker will diminish—so you can't count on reentering the work force if things don't work out.

You have to be concerned as much with lower interest rates as with higher inflation. For instance, if you've bought 30-year bonds to lock in your retirement income, what will happen if inflation takes off and you're locked in lower yielding investments?

If you can't come close to 80 percent of your working income as retirement income, it's too early to quit. Continue working until you can hit this figure. Or, you must downsize your lifestyle.

> **EXAMPLE**   Charlie Kraft earns $75,000 a year as a manager in a Fortune 500 manufacturing company. His retirement income appears to be around $45,000, or 60 percent of his current salary. His budget confirms that he needs nearly $60,000 to make retirement work. He and his wife decide to sell their home, worth $225,000. They purchase a condominium in Florida for $100,000 and invest the remaining $125,000 in bonds at 7 percent. The additional income of $8,500, plus the reduction in state income taxes and lower utility bills, nearly closes the gap. To completely fill the gap, they decide to spend the $125,000 in principal over their joint

life expectancies. And, the federal exclusion for capital gains on the house sale preserves their funds for investment.

Charlie wanted to retire. He found a way to make it possible.

You need to temper the following advice. For instance, if you have been saving $10,000 a year from your salary, you can eliminate that from the calculation. It would be a much different scenario.

EXAMPLE   Charlie Evans is earning $75,000 per year. After paying his income taxes and expenses, he is saving $10,000. To save that $10,000, of course, he needs $14,000 in pretax wages. (After paying taxes on $14,000, he has $ 10,000 left to invest.) So Charlie is actually living on $61,000, not $75,000. Put another way, he needs $61,000 in pretax income to meet his expenses. Using the 80-percent-income rule, he needs about $49,000 in retirement income to compare to 80 percent of his actual pretax needs while working (80 percent of $61,000 is $49,000). He is very close to the income he needs. Perhaps a part-time job will close the gap.

Also, if you have had a very high level of expense because your job requires a lot of traveling or a great deal of entertainment, you can eliminate all those job-related expenses.

So you need to take a look at your sources of income and your budget for expenses.

EARLY RETIREMENT WRAP-UP

Taking the early retirement offer is a complex decision. Many financial and emotional issues have to be carefully considered and examined. The best way to approach the question is to do as thorough an analysis of your income and expenses as possible. All other questions aside, the first question that must be answered is: "Can I afford to take this offer?"

Your planning must be comprehensive. It should include a budget, estimate of income, medical and life insurance, investment strategy, and contingency plans. Don't simply look at the income you'll be receiving. That's important, but so are these other issues.

Your planning must be done with your spouse. You'll both have to live with the decision, so you both need to make it. Make sure you're jointly committed to this new life.

Few people change their style in retirement. If you've always had modest desires, that will continue. If you've enjoyed the good life, with plenty of nights out and trips abroad, you'll probably want more of the same. It is very difficult to change our habits as we get older, so don't plan on a radical restructuring of your life when you retire. It probably won't happen.

Don't be blinded by the money. If you take a lump sum, you will invest it and live from the income it produces. A $500,000 lump sum means that at 7 percent, you'll receive $35,000 per year from it. That is its value to you. Almost no one spends the principal. You will cling to that principal as your primary source of security. Certainly the inheritance it could provide for your children is important, but that should not be a primary consideration in deciding whether to accept it and retire early.

ANNUITY VS. LUMP SUM

Before we compare the advantages and disadvantages of taking a lump sum, we need to understand how a lump sum is computed and what assumptions are used in generating the amount of the alternative monthly check.

In a defined benefit pension plan, your employer makes a contribution to the plan each year and invests the money. A specialist called an actuary computes how much money needs to be set aside in order to provide a pension to you on retirement.

> **EXAMPLE**   You join your employer at age 40. To provide a pension for you at 65, money needs to be set aside. The actuary takes into account your salary, your years of service, and your life expectancy in order to advise your employer that she needs to contribute $1,000 to the pension plan for you that year. The actuary assumes the plan will earn 6 percent per year.

Each year the actuary makes the computation, and another amount is contributed on your behalf. If the plan earns more money than the actuary assumed, less money has to be contributed in the future. And if the investment experience is lower than anticipated, more money has to be set aside.

If your employer is current on her entire pension funding, the plan is considered to be fully funded, and if not, underfunded. By the time you have reached retirement age, the pension plan has $100,000 or $200,000 or $400,000 that has been earmarked for your pension. The amount varies, of course, with the pension you have earned.

On your retirement, your employer will send a check to an insurance company that will, in turn, promise to pay you and your spouse a specific amount of money each month for the rest of your lives. If you live longer than they estimated, the insurance company must continue payments. And if you die earlier than expected, the insurance company keeps the money your employer sent to them. By sending over the check, your employer has purchased a lifetime annuity for you and your spouse, but everyone refers to this annuity as your pension. (Sometimes, your employer will keep the money in the plan and pay you directly.)

If you are offered a lump sum, your employer is giving you the option of creating your own annuity. Instead of the insurance company getting the money, you do. Once the lump sum is paid to you, all your employer's obligations to you under the pension cease. But don't confuse a lump sum with your other retirement benefits. Paying you a lump sum from the pension plan is simply another form of payment; it does not affect the other benefits you have: medical insurance, life insurance, and so forth.

ANNUITY PAYMENT CHOICES

Since the amount of the pension depends to a great extent on your life expectancy, your options will include variations that take life expectancy into account. Here are the most popular options. The amounts of money are taken from an actual pension computation and are shown to illustrate the relative amounts of each.

1. *Single Life:* Your pension is paid monthly for the rest of your life. When you pass away, all benefits cease. Your spouse receives nothing.

2. *Fifty percent Joint and Survivor:* $2,000 to you, $1,000 to your spouse. Your pension of $2,000 is paid until your death. Then your spouse will receive 50 percent of your pension, or $1,000 for the rest of her life.

3. *One hundred percent Joint and Survivor:* $1,600 to you and the same amount to your spouse after your death.

4. *Ten-year Certain:* $1,800 guaranteed for at least 10 years. Should you pass away before 10 years have passed, your spouse will receive this amount until the tenth year after your pension began. After the tenth year, all benefits cease.

There are other variations on these basic payment methods. For instance, there are 75 percent joint and survivor benefits. You can see that the amounts of the pension vary, depending on how many lives are being covered and for what period of time.

If you are single or married you can name another person as your pension beneficiary. The life expectancy calculations will take into account any age differentials. You are not limited to naming a spouse as your beneficiary.

When you select a pension option, you are making assumptions about your joint life expectancies:

EXAMPLE   Your spouse is in poor health. Since the single-life pension offers you the maximum pension, you take it, assuming that your spouse will not survive you.

EXAMPLE   You are in poor health. You select the 100 percent joint and survivor, assuming that your early death would otherwise penalize your spouse's pension benefit. This option offers your spouse the greatest pension benefit.

The Advantages of the Monthly Annuity

1. There is one overriding advantage to the monthly check: It is guaranteed and predictable. Once the payments begin, you can count on

them. The insurance company is taking the risk of having enough money to meet the obligation to you.

2. If the markets are poor, if interest rates fall, the insurance company has to wrestle with this. You're off the hook. Your monthly check arrives without interruption and without change.

3. Your financial planning is greatly simplified, as is your tax planning. The predictability of the check insures that.

4. You have no need for investment advisors.

5. The pension has no real effect on your estate planning since there is no residual inheritance to pass to the family.

6. You will pay quarterly estimated taxes on the pension, and they will be just as predictable as the amount of your pension.

The Disadvantages of the Monthly Annuity

1. *The monthly annuity has no cost-of-living adjustment.* Generally, pensions are fixed when you retire. If you retire at age 60, you can reasonably expect to live another 20 to 25 years. At an annual inflation rate of 3 percent, the purchasing power of your money is cut nearly in half in 20 years. And if inflation accelerates you'll have to bear the brunt of that.

Figure 2.1 shows the effect of 4 percent inflation over time on $40,000. The numbers in the right-hand column show how much money will be needed in the future to equal $40,000 annual income in today's dollars assuming 4 percent annual inflation. A real eye-opener!

FIGURE 2.1 Effect of 4 percent Inflation

Year	Dollars Needed to Equal $40,000 Today
2003	$ 48,000
2008	$ 59,000
2013	$ 72,000
2018	$ 87,000
2023	$106,000
2028	$129,000

2. *If you do not reach a full life expectancy, your family is shortchanged.* You may have worked for 40 years to build your pension benefit, but if you die the month after your retirement, your family will have received one monthly check as a benefit.

3. *There is no residual.* Once you and your spouse are gone, there is no further obligation to your family under the plan. Payments stop.

4. *Selecting the payment option is irrevocable.* Once you have selected the method of payment, it can't be changed. So, if health or financial circumstances change down the road, you can't go back and adjust your pension benefit.

5. *A monthly pension is not entirely risk-free.* If the insurance company goes broke and if you are not able to go after your employer for your pension, government insurance will step in. However, this insurance has limits. You might not get your entire pension.

THE LUMP SUM

Remember that a lump sum is an optional form of pension payment. So, in addition to the options we listed earlier, you have the option of taking your pension in a single lump sum. Once this is paid to you, all obligations to you cease. Your employer will give this check either to you or to the insurance company. In either case he is washing his hands of the problem.

The Advantages of Taking the Lump Sum

1. *You are in full control of your finances and income.* With a lump sum, you can generally decide how to invest it, when to take your income, and when to pay your taxes.

2. *A lump sum allows for growth over time.* If you don't need the income or growth from your lump sum, you can reinvest it. This will increase the size of the lump sum and the income it generates.

3. *A lump sum means that your spouse will earn the same retirement income that you earn.* Most couples living on a monthly pension check face the difficult reality of a reduced monthly income once the breadwinner passes away. With a lump sum the same income is available to the surviving spouse.

4. *A lump sum creates a new source of wealth for the family.* Once the recipient passes away, the lump sum can be passed to his or her spouse. And on the spouse's death, the balance can be paid to the children or to any other beneficiary. This can create a significant inheritance where none existed before.

5. *A lump sum provides a source for emergency funds.* A catastrophe can be met with funds from a lump sum. In a bind, extra money can be spent to rebuild a house, pay medical bills, or send a grandchild to college.

The Disadvantages of Taking the Lump Sum

1. *Life becomes more complicated.* Decisions must regularly be made about investment and tax questions. The burden of properly handling the lump sum falls on your shoulders. And while qualified professionals can make the job much easier, all they can do is advise. The decision is always up to you.

2. *You must deal with investment risk.* With a lump sum, you have to invest the money and accept whatever returns you earn. Again, while qualified advisors can help with the process, they can't control the markets, so returns can be unpredictable.

3. *You have to rely on other people for help.* This may not be much of a problem when you are younger, but once you reach your mid- to late seventies, your mental faculties may begin to fail. So it is important that you have advisors, especially investment advisors, whom you can trust.

Should the Beneficiary of a Deceased Employee Take a Lump Sum

The death of the employee often casts into doubt the treatment of his or her beneficiaries in relation to retirement-plan distributions. Generally, beneficiaries are divided into two groups for purposes of defining the treatment that can be used: The spouse and everyone else.

The spouse-beneficiary of a deceased employee can get a lump sum. All the options that were available to the deceased employee are available to the spouse-beneficiary, including the right to roll over the money to an IRA. All other beneficiaries must pay income tax on the lump sum according to the income distribution rules set out in the code.

For this reason a nonspouse beneficiary may elect to take a lifetime annuity, if available. Federal and state income tax on a large lump sum can exceed 40 percent. It may make more sense to take an annuity that is based on the entire pretax amount.

WEIGHING THE OPTIONS

For some, the decision is a simple one. In others the choice elicits anxiety and fear. If you find yourself having difficulty making this decision, you should know that this is not unusual. Not only is this one of life's major financial decisions, but it is one in which you don't have complete information to make the right decision. You can't divine the future. Will interest rates remain attractive for a lump-sum investment? Will inflation strip the value of an annuity payout? Over time, I've developed some basic guidelines to help you make the right decision.

1. *If your health is poor, take the lump sum.* Your monthly pension is based on a normal life expectancy. If your health makes that doubtful, take the lump sum. Your spouse, instead of facing a reduced pension, will have full advantage of the lump sum—the amount on which your pension was based.

2. *If you have no immediate need for the income, take the lump sum.* You can invest the money and make it grow. Whether you are going on to another job or have alternative sources of income, a lump sum allows you to postpone unwanted income and income taxes to enhance your position. A $200,000 lump sum grows to $280,000 at 7 percent over five years. This increases your income base by 40 percent!

   Rule of Thumb: If you can grow the lump sum by 25 percent to 30 percent over this time frame, it is a much better deal than the monthly annuity. A 25-percent-larger lump sum will allow you to live strictly from the interest and have the same pension as the single life monthly annuity. Your family is left with the lump sum as a new source of wealth, regardless of your life span.

3. *If you are a poor manager of money, take the annuity.* If your investment history is a disaster, if your spending frequently careens out of control, if you have a gambling problem, take the annuity. A lump sum in the wrong hands is a loaded gun. If you blow the money, there is nowhere else to turn. You're much better off with a monthly pension: It inculcates discipline by doling out the money to you a small piece at a time. And, no matter what you do with each month's check, there will be another one behind it.

4. *If you're heavily in debt, take the annuity.* Debtors often view the lump sum as their chance to "get clean." They reason that they can take the lump sum, pay down their debts, and invest the balance. This rarely works. First, in order to pay a creditor $1, you need to take $1.30 or $1.40 from the lump sum because there are taxes to be paid first. So this is very expensive money. Second, by paying down debt you haven't addressed the root problem: your spending habits. People near retirement who are heavily in debt have either faced a catastrophic illness, can't say no to their kids, or can't control their spending. Budgeting out of the monthly annuity can pay debt due to illness. If you take the lump sum and you fail as an investor, you won't have the money to pay down the debt, AND you'll be short monthly income. What a disaster! Take the annuity and get some debt counseling.

5. *If you are unsure, hire your advisors first, then make the decision.* If you can negotiate a successful hunt for an accountant and investment advisor, you are well on your way to a good lump-sum experience. Your accountant should be the primary source of advice here, since his or her view is generally unbiased. Your investment advisor has a built-in bias toward the lump sum, although good ones will give you a straight and honest opinion. If your accountant feels it makes sense, ask your investment advisor for an investment game plan: how will the money be invested, and how will the income flow out? Armed with this information, the decision is much easier to make. If you can't find advisors, or if you can't formulate an investment strategy, you may be forced to the annuity payout.

6. *Don't be blinded by the size of the lump sum.* Yes, $300,000 is a lot of money, but at 7 percent, it means simply $21,000 per year of income. If you can live on $21,000, then by all means take the lump sum. You will have secured an inheritance for your kids, and you can dip into the $300,000 for emergencies. But don't let the amount of money blind you. Most people prefer to live off the income generated by the lump sum and are very reluctant to spend any of the principal.

7. *Don't underestimate the effects of inflation.* That monthly check may look princely today, but year after year of inflation will take its toll. A lump sum will give you the opportunity to fight inflation with wise investment. Think about people who retired in the late 1960s on a pension of a few hundred dollars a month. That was a generous pension then, but hardly adequate today.

8. *The decision must be a joint one.* In most families, one spouse does the financial wheeling and dealing. Don't ignore your spouse in this decision. He or she may have to live with it for a lot longer than you do. Investing may be your hobby but it may not be your spouse's. You may feel that the monthly pension is adequate, but your spouse will have to live with the effect of decades of inflation. You may not care to leave an inheritance to your children; your spouse may. This decision is too important not to discuss. Each party should have an equal vote, and each should be committed to the decision reached.

9. *Don't shortchange your spouse's pension.* In looking at the monthly annuity, you may feel that the money you'll receive is adequate. Don't be selfish and lock your spouse into a reduced pension. Your spouse won't stay home and sit in a chair once you're gone. And the expenses of running a house go on and on. Think very hard before you select a 50 percent joint and survivor pension.

   EXAMPLE   You take a $2,000-per-month pension, with your wife receiving $1,000 per month on your death. In ten years, you die. Your wife's pension of $1,000 is now worth only $744 in today's dollars after ten years of 3 percent annual inflation. Inadvertently, you may be condemning your loved one to an income level of impoverishment.

10. *The primary purpose of a pension is to provide income to you in retirement.* All other considerations are secondary. You may feel a strong desire to provide an inheritance for your kids. This is a noble and worthwhile goal, but it shouldn't be the primary consideration. If you can't put together a viable financial and investment plan for the lump sum, you shouldn't take it. Don't let secondary considerations overly influence your decision. If it is a close call, then let them be the deciding factors.

A CASE STUDY

Art Fowler has been employed at ABC Widgets for 32 years as a marketing manager. His wife, Sally, looks forward to having him around the house. They're eager to work on their golf game, visit their two children and five grandchildren, and take that long trip out West that they've planned for many years. Art enjoys his work, but feels that since they're both 60, it's a good time to get out and smell the flowers. Their financial situation is relatively simple.

House	$200,000 (no mortgage)
CDs	$50,000
Debt	$10,000 (primarily an auto loan)
401(k) Plan	$ 75,000
Pension:	$280,000 lump sum or
	$2,250 per month, zero for Sally, or
	$1,900 per month, $950 for Sally, or
	$1,500 per month, $1,500 for Sally
Social Security	$800 per month

ABC Widgets will provide medical insurance until Art reaches 62, then Medicare will take over. There is also $50,000 in company-sponsored life insurance with a death benefit that reduces by $10,000 per year.

How should Art and Sally structure their retirement?

The first calculation that has to be made is whether or not Art should pay the taxes on his 401(k) and pension lump sums and then roll the money over into a Roth IRA. If he is willing to pay his taxes up front, he can enjoy tax-free growth and tax-free withdrawal from the Roth later on. And, if he has other funds, he can replenish the taxes paid to roll over the entire pretax equivalent amounts into a Roth IRA.

Since their adjusted gross income is under $100,000, he does qualify for a Roth IRA. A quick computation shows that he would pay about $140,000 in income taxes on his $355,000 rollovers, leaving him with $215,000 in his Roth IRA. Since it will take them about six years to earn back the taxes paid, assuming an 8 percent return, Art is doubtful. Once they realize that they need income right away from the IRA, the idea of losing funds that could otherwise generate income seals the decision. If they take the lump sum, they won't use a Roth.

The 401(k) should be rolled over to an IRA. By deferring current income tax, the full amount of the lump sum can be invested for income, or can simply grow untouched. Art has to be very careful: If he decides to leave the 401(k) in his employer's care, he must continue to invest it himself.

Art should start Social Security as soon as possible, at age 62. (It is generally not wise to wait until 65. You can take a reduced benefit at 62 and invest the money until 65. By then you've earned enough to overcome the reduced Social Security benefit.) Since his insurance benefits are locked in, there is little to do there.

The big decision is the pension plan. Art and Sally start by adding up their sources of income, and since 6 percent is a reasonable risk-free return, they use it as a planning number. (You can generally use 6 percent to 8 percent and be safe.)

$50,000 CDs at 6 percent	$3,000 per year interest
$75,000 IRA rollover	$4,500 per year interest
Total	$7,500 per year

It's a short list, but they can add in a couple of items.

Social Security at 62	$9,600 per year
Monthly pension	$18,000 to $27,000 per year
Total Pensions	$27,600 to $36,600 per year

Grand Totals

Savings	$7,500 (CDs and 401(k) rollover)
Social Security	$9,600
Pension	$18,000 to $27,000
Total	$35,100 to $44,100 annual gross income

They now add up their monthly budget and find that their expenses run about $1,800 per month, or $21,600 per year. After checking the tax tables, they estimate that they'll need to bring in around $26,000 per year pretax to meet expenses. Should they take the lump sum or the monthly annuity?

The monthly annuity appears to meet their needs. In analyzing it, they discard the maximum pension of $2,250 since it would leave Sally with nothing on Art's death. They consider but abandon the 50 percent joint-and-survivor option. Sally can't make ends meet with a monthly pension of $950. So they eliminate all monthly options except for the 100 percent joint and survivor: $1,500 per month.

Their insurance agent suggests that Art take the maximum pension of $2,250 per month and invest $750 per month in an insurance policy for Sally's benefit. On his death the policy will pay her a lump sum that will allow her to create her own pension plan, replacing Art's income, which would disappear. The numbers seem to add up and make sense, but Sally is uncomfortable with the thought of finding people to help her manage the money many years from now and without Art to help her.

Now they can more accurately target their income at $35,100 per year. This is still enough to meet their bills, but they are concerned that a few years of inflation will wipe out the cushion they currently enjoy. Although Social Security will give them cost-of-living increases, they feel that a fixed pension will necessitate spending their savings to make ends meet.

They turn to analyzing the lump sum. The amount of $280,000 rolled over to an IRA and invested in bonds will earn $19,600 per year (they can get 7 percent on the money) in interest income. Their accountant assures them that they can buy good quality bonds and lock in that income for 10 or 20 or 30 years if they want. And they will still have the $280,000 as a nest egg.

The right course of action becomes clear: They will take the lump sum, roll it over, and buy a portfolio of corporate bonds, with maturities running from 8 to 15 years. Their average yield is a bit below 7 percent, but they like the idea of being able to reinvest as they go along in case inflation does take off. (Sally notes that if inflation becomes a problem, they can earn higher interest rates as bonds are rolled over at maturity and can even buy income-producing inflation hedges such as oil stocks if necessary.)

Because they haven't had a lot of investment experience, they limit their account to better quality bonds; they are willing to take less income for a greater degree of safety. The IRA is invested in longer-term bonds, so they set up their savings CDs in five pieces, with $10,000 rolling over every six months. (They buy a ladder of 6-month, 1-year, 1-1/2-years, 2-years, and 2-1/2-years CDs.) This gives them some cash to use every six months if they run a bit short.

Since Social Security doesn't start for two years, they find that their current income of $27,100 is barely ahead of their expenses, but they want to travel while their health is good. They decide to tap their savings for $4,000 per year for the next two years. Then, when Social Security kicks in they will let the interest on their savings compound to rebuild the principal spent.

Art names Sally as beneficiary of the IRA (which holds his 401(k) and lump-sum pension distribution). They agree that on Art's death, Sally will roll over the IRA to her own name and designate their two children as equal beneficiaries.

They are satisfied that they have taken care of their income needs, with a substantial cash cushion for emergencies, but have also helped secure the future of their children and grandchildren with an impressive inheritance. A visit with their attorney confirms that since their entire estate is less than $600,000, there will be no estate taxes due on their deaths. He does suggest a living trust for their savings to avoid probate expense and delay on that amount.

You can see that Art and Sally kept their assumptions and planning simple. They used the risk-free interest rate on U.S. Treasuries to structure their plan, and when the numbers made sense, they used bonds as investments. It is important to note that they didn't use overly conservative or aggressive rates of return as assumptions—4 percent or 12 percent, for instance. They used what was available to them when the lump sum was available. They didn't assume rates would be any higher, or any lower, and then they locked in the rate for a reasonable period of time. Nothing fancy. But it is a plan that will work and will serve them well. Had Art not needed the income from the IRA, he could have let the account grow and could have begun a higher income stream in the future.

Art goes on to consult for two years. His IRA grows to $406,000 from $355,000. His annual interest income at 7 percent is now $28,420 per year, or $2,368 per month. Since Social Security is providing nearly $10,000 per year, Art takes only $16,000 per year from the IRA, allowing it to continue to grow, although at a slower pace.

Since Art is consulting and has income from his work, he avoids paying taxes on a monthly pension that he neither needs nor wants. The IRA provids tax-deferred buildup of his benefits.

A final note: If Art and Sally had done their computations and found that their retirement income was short of their needs, there would be little they could do. Art would have to keep working to age 65, or later, to save enough and build additional retirement benefits. Retirement planning can never begin too soon.

SUMMARY

Making the retirement decision can be overwhelming. There are a host of personal and financial issues that need to be properly addressed before the decision can be made.

The best advice is to go slowly and work with reasonable assumptions. Wishful thinking about earning 12 percent per year is as dangerous as not planning your post-employment lifestyle.

Engage your spouse actively in the discussions, seek educated opinions, and then put your plan in place.

CHAPTER THREE

What Can You Do with a Lump Sum?

When you take a lump sum, you have three choices:

1. Pay income taxes on the lump sum when you file your tax return.
2. Roll over the lump sum to an IRA rollover account.
3. Roll over the lump sum to your new employer's plan.

PAY TAXES ON YOUR LUMP SUM NOW

Your lump sum came from a "qualified plan." This means that none of the money has been taxed except for any after-tax employee contributions. Both federal and state governments allowed a tax-deferred buildup since its purpose was to help fund your retirement. The government considers that a goal worthy of a tax break.

Once you take the money, all the income taxes become due. So if you don't roll over the money to another plan, you have to settle with the government. You do this by claiming the lump sum as additional income when you file your tax return.

There are several ways to compute the tax. Generally, paying current income taxes is not a good strategy to follow. The reason is simple: By deferring the taxes, you get to invest the tax money and earn income on it.

Only if you have an immediate or foreseeable use for the money should you consider paying the current tax—and then only if you can apply favorable income-averaging treatment. Keep in mind that with amounts over $400,000, income-averaging, while available, carry heavy tax treatment. (Thia is a reminder that the 1997 tax law repealed the old 15 percent excess tax on large IRA accumulations or distributions.)

> **EXAMPLE**   You receive a lump sum distribution of $100,000. You elect to pay taxes on it. After tax you have $70,000. At 7 percent, this earns $4,900 per year before tax. Had you rolled over the $100,000, you would be earning $7,000 per year tax-deferred.

You should not underestimate the power of this tax-deferred compounding.

Figure 3.1 shows the effect of rolling over $100,000 to an IRA and enjoying 7 percent tax-deferred growth, versus paying taxes and investing the remaining $70,000 at 5.25 percent tax-free. After 12 years, you have over $65,000 in additional capital by rolling over. Granted, the tax hasn't been paid on the IRA, but the additional capital will more than make up for that tax, especially since you'll most likely take your IRA income over many years.

As a rule of thumb, there is only one circumstance that should cause you to pay current taxes on the lump sum. You can take advantage of special tax rules that allow you to pay a tax so low that it overcomes the disadvantage of sending the government a check.

MAKE SURE YOU HAVE A QUALIFYING LUMP-SUM DISTRIBUTION

In order to qualify for favorable tax treatment, you need to make sure that you have a qualifying lump-sum distribution. There are several conditions that must be met. If your distribution meets them, then you can take a look at special income-averaging tax breaks. If you don't

FIGURE 3.1 Tax-Deferred vs. Tax After-Tax Growth

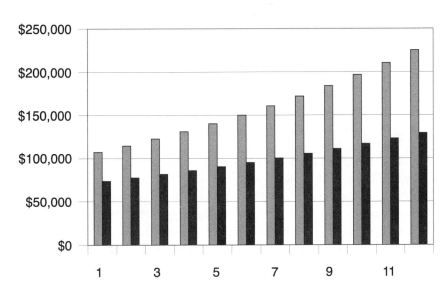

meet these qualifications, favorable income-averaging tax breaks are not available. (You may still be able to roll over to an IRA, however.)

1. The distribution must come from a qualified plan. Typically, this would mean your pension, profit-sharing, 401(k), or stock bonus plan.

2. You must be separated from service, become disabled, die, or have attained age 59-1/2.

3. You must have participated in the plan for five years, except in the case of death.

4. You are receiving your entire account balance in one tax year.

If you are unsure about these qualifications, your company's personnel department should be able to clarify them for you.

Once you have established that your distribution is a qualifying lump-sum distribution, you need only to look at your date of birth to determine what tax break you can get. However, keep in mind the magic of age 55. If you are under 55, any amounts not rolled over are subject to a 10 percent tax penalty in addition to the ordinary income tax. Amounts not rolled over after you have reached age 59-1/2 are simply claimed on your return as ordinary income. No penalty applies. If you're over 59-1/2, you may be able to take advantage of certain tax breaks.

And you can roll over any amount you wish. For instance, you could keep 40 percent of your distribution, pay tax on it, and roll over the remaining 60 percent.

If You Were Born Before January 1, 1936

You can pay tax on your distribution using several different tax rates. The one you choose is strictly up to you.

1. *You can pay ordinary income tax.* This is generally the least attractive alternative. If you elect this option, you add the amount of the lump sum onto your tax return and pay the taxes due when you file your return.

   EXAMPLE   Your income from wages for the year is $42,000. You receive a lump sum of $3,000, which you don't roll over. Your adjusted gross income for the year is $45,000.

   You must pay ordinary tax if you decide to roll over a portion of your distribution. Since a partial rollover takes away any income-averaging possibilities, you have to apply ordinary income rates. Sometimes this can be useful.

   EXAMPLE   You receive a $100,000 lump-sum distribution. You decide to keep $3,000 for a vacation and roll over $97,000. You will pay ordinary income tax only on the $3,000 you keep.

2. *You can pay tax under ten-year forward averaging.* Under this formula, you pay tax at a reduced tax rate. If you elect averaging, you cannot roll over any of your distribution. You must pay tax on all of it. You still pay the tax in one year when you file your tax return. (It isn't a tax that you pay over ten years.)

   In this calculation you are allowed to assume that you were a single taxpayer (even if married) receiving the lump sum in equal installments over ten years. This way, your tax bracket on the lump sum will be much lower than your normal ordinary income tax rates. An important point to remember is that the ten-year averaging tax is applied independent of your other income.

EXAMPLE　John and Mary each receive a lump sum of $10,000. John has earned $50,000 from his job and Mary has earned $165,000. The tax on the $10,000 lump sum will be the same for each.

Many people get quite excited about ten-year averaging, but, as Table 3.1 shows, on larger lump-sum amounts it isn't very attractive.

TABLE 3.1 Approximate Tax Rates on Various Lump-Sum Amounts as a Percentage of the Entire Lump Sum

Amount of Lump Sum	10-Year Averaging Tax
$ 25,000	7.2 percent
$ 40,000	10.5 percent
$ 50,000	11.8 percent
$ 100,000	14.5 percent
$ 200,000	18.5 percent
$ 250,000	20.3 percent
$ 300,000	22.1 percent
$ 400,000	25.7 percent
$ 500,000	28.7 percent
$ 750,000	34.6 percent
$1,000,000	38.2 percent

You can see that the "favorable" tax rate can be quite high. Tax-deferred compounding is the overwhelming treatment of choice for lump-sum recipients.

You may elect ten-year averaging on IRS Form 4972. However, there are some other requirements to be met.

- If you elect averaging on one lump sum, you must income-average all the lump sums you receive that year.

- Ten-year averaging is a once-in-a-lifetime election. If you take it for your current lump sum, you lose, forever, the right to use it again. Think carefully about using it if you are going on to another employer. You may make better use of it in the future.

- Ten-year averaging is based on 1986 tax rates, not current ones. Don't apply the wrong tax table.

- Income averaging could be repealed by Congress. You can't take it for granted.

- You can treat the pre-1974 benefit as a capital gain subject to a flat 20 percent tax rate, with the balance taxed as ordinary income under the 5 or 10 year averaging rules. You will probably not find this advantageous.

- Ten-year averaging benefits extend to beneficiaries if the deceased employee was born before 1936, and, in a twist, the employee need not have been a participant in the plan for five years. Note that the age of the employee is the determining factor, not the age of the beneficiary.

- A distribution from an IRA is not considered a qualifying lump-sum distribution, so income averaging can't be applied to it.

Remember that five-year averaging will be available only until January 1, 2000. Finally, don't forget the effects of state income taxes. They are in addition to any applicable federal income tax.

If You Were Born After December 31, 1935

1. *You can pay ordinary income tax on the distribution.* An additional 10 percent tax penalty is applied to the distribution if you're under 55. The added tax burden makes this option unattractive. There are, however, exceptions to this penalty. They include total disability, large payments for medical expenses, and court-ordered payments under a divorce decree, among others. The best advice here is that if you want to take the money and pay tax on it the services of a Certified Public Accountant are a must. The issues become too complicated for the layman to work through with certainty. Even if you think you have a handle on it, you need to have your assumptions checked by a pro.

Finally, keep in mind that if you are under age 59-1/2 you must either roll over the distribution to an IRA or pay ordinary tax. There are no other choices. The various lump-sum-distribution income-tax options, based on birth date and age, are summarized in Table 3.2, but don't forget the Roth income test.

TABLE 3.2 Summary of the Income-Tax Options

Treatment	Born Before 1/1/36	Born After 12/31/35	Under Age 50
Roth Conversion?	YES	YES	YES
IRA Rollover?	YES	YES	YES
10-Year Averaging?	YES	NO	NO
10 Percent Tax Penalty If Not Rolled?	NO	YES, if under 55	YES

ROLL THE LUMP SUM INTO AN IRA ROLLOVER ACCOUNT

This is the course nearly all people choose to follow.

You need to think about how you are going to use the money. If you intend to invest to create an income stream, rolling over is usually the best alternative. The investment of the tax money is a powerful benefit to you.

Even if you intend to buy a retirement home, you may find it makes more sense to roll over your distribution and take a mortgage on the property, using your IRA income to make the payments.

When in doubt, roll over the money. Nearly 100 percent of my clients have chosen this option. At least you will have postponed payment of the income tax, kept the distribution intact, and can enjoy tax-deferred growth. Later on, you can always convert to a Roth, if you should wish to.

By rolling over the money to an IRA, you can continue to defer taxes due until you pull the money out. Think of the IRA rollover account as your own pension plan. Like your employer's plan, an IRA enjoys tax-deferred treatment of the income received as long as it remains in the account. All the money remains intact for you to invest and use.

Since you can compound your investment using the government's tax money, an IRA rollover is a strong vehicle to use. There are many other benefits, and they are covered later on.

EXECUTING THE ROLLOVER

The best way to execute the rollover is to have your employer send the funds directly to your IRA custodian. If you receive the funds, your employer must withhold 20 percent of the payout for income taxes. If you decide to roll over the distribution, you need to replace the 20 percent withheld out of your own funds. You will then receive a refund when you file your tax return.

> **EXAMPLE**   You have a lump sum of $100,000. Your employer sends you the check, having first withheld $20,000. You roll over the $80,000 and take an additional $20,000 out of your savings account to complete the $100,000 rollover. Next April, you apply for a refund based on the $20,000 withholding as an over-withholding.

It can be pretty tough to replace that 20 percent. Worse, if you do not replace it when you execute your rollover, it will be considered a distribution from the lump sum and a 10 percent tax penalty will be applied to it as well if you are under 55!

> **EXAMPLE**   You don't have the money to replace the $20,000 withholding, and you roll over only $80,000. The $20,000 is considered a distribution, and if you are under 55, you owe an additional $2,000 as a 10 percent tax penalty!

It is quite clear that your employer should send the money directly to your IRA custodian. If she does so, no withholding applies.

Dates Are Important

If you receive the check, however, copies should be made of both the check and the envelope in which it came. A 60-day clock starts ticking upon receipt, so you need proof of distribution. The IRS lets you roll over a lump sum to an IRA to avoid current income tax, but you must do so within 60 days of receipt. If you don't roll it over within the 60-day window, you lose, forever, the right to roll over the distribution, and you will have to pay current tax on it.

> **TIP**   Constructive receipt (the day you receive the money) begins the clock ticking. In my experience, in 99 percent of all cases the money arrives in plenty of time to use the employer's statement as the date of distribution.

If you miss the 60-day window, don't ask your custodian to fudge his records. It's against the law.

There will be several dates to consider: the date shown on the distribution statement, the date of the check, the postmark on the envelope. Why copy the envelope?

> **EXAMPLE**   A lump-sum distribution check is drawn on March 31. But it is misplaced in the personnel office and isn't actually mailed until July 3, long past the 60-day rollover window. The postmark on the envelope is the only proof that the distribution wasn't actually made until July 3—despite the earlier dates on the distribution statement and the check. A copy of the envelope can be shown to the IRS in case of audit. Copies of the check should be retained, along with any stubs attached to the check. If there is any dispute later on with the company over the amount of the distribution, a copy of the actual check will help speed the inquiry. In addition, any future audit by the IRS will certainly be easier to handle if a copy of the original check is in your folder.

As a matter of course, make copies of the check and the envelope for your files. Check to make sure that you do not inadvertently go over the 60-day window. Once the 60-day window is violated there are no exceptions. The rollover is disallowed. And consider this: When an audit occurs it almost certainly will be after the year of distribution. If the IRS denies the rollover two years later, for instance, two years of taxes plus interest and penalties have accumulated. That's a very expensive mistake.

If your distribution comes to you in more than one piece, the 60-day window begins ticking after receipt of each separate distribution.

A 60-Day Strategy

After receiving the payout, you may wish to earn interest on the funds up to the sixtieth day and then roll over the money. This depends on whether you need additional funds for current income. The money will be earning interest somewhere during the 60 days. It's simply a choice between earning it inside or outside the IRA.

If outside, funds can be put in a money market fund or a very short-term CD. Then the principal is rolled over to the IRA upon maturity and the interest is left behind. Since you must keep the interest, it will be treated as income in the year you earned it. Do not roll over the interest you earn outside the IRA.

Statements and Deposits

Save each monthly statement. The first statement is especially important because it shows the amount and date of the lump-sum deposit into the IRA account.

Make your deposit in the form of the original check, your personal check for the same amount, or a wire transfer from your bank. The form of the deposit isn't important. If securities and cash are going in, deposit the check, your replacement money for the tax withholding, and the stock certificates, if any, that were distributed.

This can be a tricky maneuver since people are often confused by how many shares to roll over. Analyze the distribution statement you receive. The company statement will list all aspects of the lump-sum distribution, pretax employer contributions, pretax employee contributions, after-tax employee contributions, and value of the distribution, as well as a breakdown by cash and stock amount. Focus on the taxable portion: This is the amount eligible for rollover (see Table 3.3). It is the combination of all the pretax portions of the distribution, employer pretax contributions, employee pretax contributions, and the tax-deferred growth of the account.

TABLE 3.3 Portions of Distribution Eligible for IRA Rollover

Item	Roll Over?
Employer Pretax	Yes
Employee Pretax	Yes
Tax-Deferred Growth	Yes
Employee After-Tax	No

The nontaxable portion is the sum of all after-tax contributions to the plan. The nontaxable portion may not be rolled over. If the distribution is entirely in cash, it is a simple matter to roll over only the pretax amount.

If, however, part of the distribution is in the form of company stock, the calculation becomes more difficult and confusing.

> **EXAMPLE** You receive a lump-sum distribution of $98,000. The distribution is in the form of a check for $80,000 and 1,000 shares of your employer's stock.
>
> Stock cost to the plan: $16.00
>
> Stock price on date of distribution: $18.00
>
> Stock price on day you roll over: $19.00
>
> The check for $80,000 should be rolled over, as are the 1,000 shares of stock. Market value on the date of rollover is irrelevant. The stock need not be sold to effect the rollover. Deposit the certificate in the IRA account and hold or sell the stock, depending on your outlook for it as an investment.

IF YOU DON'T ROLL OVER THE STOCK

Keep in mind that if you don't roll over the stock, you have to pay tax on the amount of your employer's pretax contribution to the purchase of the stock. In this case, you would have $16,000 in taxable income on which to pay tax, assuming that the stock was purchased only with employer's contributions. The Form 1099-R that your employer sends you will break out these figures for you, in addition to the statement you receive on the distribution from the plan. You do not pay tax on the gain until you sell it. Once you have paid the tax on stock not rolled over you have a new cost basis of $16. Stock not rolled over into an IRA is still subject to the 10 percent pre-55 tax penalty.

> **EXAMPLE** You decide to keep the stock and roll over only the cash. You must pay income tax on $16,000 in income (1,000 shares times the acquisition cost of $16). Two years later, you sell the stock for $21. You have a capital gain of $5,000 on which tax must be paid.

REPORTING REQUIREMENTS FOR IRA ACCOUNTS

Any distributions you take from your IRA will be reported to you and to the IRS on Form 1099-R. So if your IRA income doesn't appear on your tax return, the IRS will question you. They know you have it. If you roll over the lump sum, you won't be claiming it as income on your tax return.

> **TIP** Don't be surprised if the IRS sends you a letter a year or two later asking about the lump sum. Usually, a letter in reply with copies of your supporting statements showing timely rollover is sufficient. Be aware that the receipt of a lump sum can create a heightened interest in your tax situation.

TO ROTH OR NOT TO ROTH

The Taxpayer Relief Act of 1997 introduced new IRA options and complications, among them, the Roth IRA. Named after Senator William Roth, chairman of the Senate Finance Committee who steered the legislation through the Senate, a Roth IRA can accept a rollover from a Traditional IRA.

You simply direct your IRA custodian to transfer your old IRA into a new Roth IRA. Only ordinary income taxes are due, and the 10 percent tax penalty is waived for a Roth conversion. If you do not have enough other savings to pay the taxes, they can be paid from your old IRA and the remainder rolled over.

Your eligibility to use a Roth IRA is determined by your adjusted gross income in the year you convert. Of course, although your IRA is added into your income for the year, it is not included in the income test. Generally, single taxpayers below $100,000 adjusted gross income and married couples with AGI of less than $100,000 are eligible.

Since you are paying all the income taxes on the IRA now, all future earnings can grow tax-deferred and can be withdrawn, tax-free if you have had the Roth IRA for five years, *and* you have attained age 59-1/2. In addition, you can withdraw the money tax-free if you are under age 59-1/2 if you have had the Roth for five years *and* you are using the money for the first time purchase of a home, *or* you have become disabled.

Finally, the minimum distribution rules that apply to Traditional IRAs at age 70-1/2 do not apply to Roth IRAs.

EXAMPLE OF CONVERSION TO A ROTH   Bill Dawkins is 56. He has a Traditional IRA rollover in which his original pension lump sum of $200,000 was rolled four years ago. It is now worth $300,000. Bill and his wife will have an adjusted gross income of $82,000 this year and so he is eligible to convert his Traditional IRA into a Roth IRA. With a combined tax bracket of 40 percent, Bill would have to pay $120,000 in income taxes and transfer the remaining $180,000 to a Roth.

He notes that assuming an 8 percent rate of return, his traditional IRA would be worth $600,000 in nine years, while his Roth would be worth $360,000. If he took 7 percent of his account each year as income, the Traditional IRA would produce $42,000 per year, or about $25,000 per year, after income taxes. Taking 7 percent from his Roth would generate about $25,000 per year, tax-free.

Since there is no significant advantage to the Roth, he decides to keep the Traditional IRA, preferring to have the earnings power of the additional $120,000 working for him.

As you can see, giving up 40 percent of the funds in taxes doesn't really buy Bill any real advantage over time.

Yes, but what if Bill can *replace* the $120,000 in taxes and put the full $300,000 in a Roth?

EXAMPLE   Bill's twin brother, Jim, has an identical situation, except that he also has $120,000 in a separate investment account, for a total of $420,000. Jim asks his custodian to transfer the entire $300,000 Traditional IRA to a Roth IRA, and when he files his income tax return, pays the taxes due from his investment account, leaving him with the $300,000 Roth. Assuming all his investments earn 8 percent on a taxable or tax-deferred basis, was this a good move?

Again assuming at 8 percent return, if he had kept his Traditional IRA and investment account, in nine years his funds would have grown to $820,000 (We assume $20,000 in taxes were paid on his investment account). His conversion to a Roth would have also doubled to $600,000. However, the taxes due on his Traditional IRA (now worth $600,000) would be $240,000, leaving him with $360,000 after tax on the Traditional IRA, and around $220,000 in his investment account since taxes were paid as he went on the gains in the investment account.

Jim is ahead by about $20,000.

Yes, there is an advantage in replenishing the taxes from another source and keeping the IRA intact. However, it must also be said that uneven investment returns and the negative effect of low investment returns can mitigate the Roth decision. Only a careful analysis of your tax situation can determine the correct answer. Since there are tens of thousands of dollars in tax payments at risk, a Certified Public Accountant should be retained to compute the calculations for you.

Having said that, I can also tell you that I have found a mixed opinion among professionals on this conversion question. Although I have looked at dozens of situations for potential Roth conversion, I have found very few that made sense for older people. My sense is that there is a cut-off somewhere around age 50-55. Below 50, a Roth would be the account of choice, and above 55, a Roth might not make sense again assuming you are taking large income distributions. Whether or not a Roth will work for you depends on many other factors in your personal and financial situation. Again, I can only repeat that qualified assistance should be retained to compute the various IRA options in your particular situation.

ROLLING OVER THE LUMP SUM TO YOUR NEW EMPLOYER'S PLAN

If you have moved on to a new job, you can sometimes roll over your lump sum to your new employer's retirement plan. Not all plans accept rollovers from other plans, so you have to check with the personnel department of your new employer in order to get the facts.

By rolling the lump sum to a new plan, you add it to the retirement money that you'll be earning at your new job. The money you roll over will fall under the rules of the new plan so you have to be careful.

For instance, if you want to withdraw the money someday as a lump sum, you need to be sure that the new plan allows this, especially in the case of a pension plan. Also remember that once the money is rolled over you can't pull it out until you once again meet the rules for a lump sum, that is, until you reach age 59-1/2, separate from service, become disabled, or are the beneficiary of a deceased employee.

Since these restrictions do not exist in an IRA rollover account, most people tend to roll over the lump sum to an IRA and not to an employer's plan. If you want the option of being able to roll over your distribution into a future employer's plan don't contaminate this lump sum with any other contributions in your IRA rollover account.

The Conduit IRA

By isolating the IRA to contain only the distribution from your employer, you have established what's known as a conduit IRA. This is a holding tank between two employer plans. Once you have established a conduit you can at some later date roll those funds over to a new employer's plan. So if you have an existing IRA, open another one for your lump sum. You can have multiple IRAs.

While I am sure people do roll over their lump sum to a new employer's plan, I haven't seen too many examples of it. Once you obtain control of the distribution you won't want to give it up. I'm sure that the massive layoffs and corporate restructuring we've seen in our country have contributed to this attitude: People want the security of managing their own funds and their own future.

When to Roll to a New Employer's Plan

There are two strong reasons, however, why you would consider rolling to your new employer:

1. One is if the new plan has very attractive investment vehicles. Your employer may have a guaranteed interest-rate account that you find compelling. Or there may be several low-cost investment vehicles you wish to use.

2. By rolling over to a new employer's plan, you preserve the right to use special income-averaging rules.

Keep in mind that you can execute a rollover from IRA to IRA only once in a 12-month period.

> **TIP**   Rolling to your new employer's plan can be advantageous from a cost perspective. If your lump sum is less than $20,000, you should consider your new employer's plan. The expense of running an IRA rollover account can be relatively high for smaller accounts. So you should explore fees before making a decision on where to roll the distribution.

Don't forget that once you have made the rollover it is an irrevocable decision. You can't execute a rollover and then change your mind later in the year. Be careful before you do it and explore all the facts first.

GUIDELINES FOR SUCCESSFUL INVESTING

I believe there are certain time-honored rules that, if followed, can form the basis for a successful investment strategy. Whether very conservative or very aggressive, I believe all investors can follow these guidelines. These guidelines will keep you out of a lot of difficulty and trouble. They form a basic test that you can apply to a contemplated investment strategy to weigh the merits of that strategy. If it passes muster, then it could be a viable solution to your investment problem.

For the lump-sum investor, an investment strategy should meet all of these rules. If it does, then you need to ascertain the risk of the strategy. If the risk is acceptable and the investment selection reasonably constructed, you can consider the strategy.

You need to remember that whatever investment strategy you select should be in harmony with your values and your personality. For instance, I am a contrarian investor. I enjoy buying assets at a discount and I have the patience to wait, years if necessary, for those investments to pan out. Others with a shorter time frame might find this approach uncomfortable and difficult.

Just because I believe in a contrarian approach doesn't make it appropriate for everyone. And so, when you hear about a particular philosophy or way of investing, feel free to reject it if it doesn't feel right to you. Don't find yourself slaving away at a strategy just because an expert has had success with it. We can all arrive at investment success by taking different paths and approaches.

Rule 1: If You Can't Sell It Any Time You Want, Don't Buy It

Liquidity is the ease with which an investment is turned into cash. A good investment should have an active market that assures an ability to sell. Almost anything can be converted into cash, but the real question is, at what price? No matter what the asset, there comes a time to sell. Why sell?

- Because you think the investment has peaked and you want to avoid a loss. (Sometimes this is irrational fear, but it is a realistic reason, nonetheless.)
- Because even though you like the investment, you have a more profitable use for the money.
- Because you have to raise cash for expenses.

All three are good reasons to sell. And when you want out, you don't want to wait. If you need the money, the lack of a ready market can be devastating.

When you can't sell an investment, there are many negative repercussions. First, you can't get your money. Lack of liquidity may force you to sell a better investment. This lowers your overall portfolio return by forcing you to keep the bad and sell the good.

It puts additional psychological pressure on you. If you want to sell something and can't, the fear of loss remains. You can't relieve the concern by selling, and therefore you have to live with it.

When you buy an investment, examine its liquidity closely. The following investments offer the best liquidity:

1. Publicly traded common stocks
2. Government bonds
3. Certificates of deposit
4. Highly rated corporate bonds (minimum rating A-)
5. Government-insured mortgages from Ginnie Mae, Freddie Mac, and Fannie Mae
6. Individual municipal bonds
7. Mutual funds

You know that you can generally put your portfolio into cash within 15 minutes if you have to. You want to know that when you make an investment, you can get out when you want and at a fair price. This enables you to invest with confidence. Since there is a ready market, you can get in and out of these holdings easily.

Rule 2: Buy Only Investments of Good Quality

Avoid the lure of "getting seemingly high returns from penny stocks and junk bonds. Buy only quality: blue-chip stocks, investment-grade bonds. I am convinced that over time, you will make more money.

It is rare for a blue chip such as General Electric or McDonald's to slide into bankruptcy. It is a stunning event when an investment-grade credit such as Xerox or J. P. Morgan defaults on its debt. By avoiding a major catastrophe that takes such a toll on capital and psyche, you improve your performance. You eliminate the big disasters that come when you swing for the fences.

I know that high-quality stocks and bonds can give up some appreciation potential compared with small stocks and higher-risk bonds. But to keep liquid, and to control risk, you have to move to higher quality. The wisdom of this proves itself time and time again.

A strategy of investing in high-risk, high-growth stocks for higher returns, while good advice in a vacuum, is not suitable for most investors, especially those investing with their IRA. The ride is usually too bumpy for most of them.

In bad times it is much easier to sleep at night knowing that when the markets and the economy right themselves, the positions you hold will recover as well. There is no guarantee, of course, but you limit investment to companies that have stood the test of time.

When you look for quality, you tend to eliminate a lot of problems. You don't want stocks with company-wrecking lawsuits pending, or those breaking under a mountain of debt. Yes, such securities offer tremendous potential for gain if you're right and the problems work out. But for the vast majority of investors, those stocks are not suitable for their temperament or their portfolios.

This same logic holds true in the bond market. You should be more inclined to earn 7 percent on a government-insured mortgage than 9 percent on a below-investment-grade bond. If you want more than a relatively risk-free return on your money, you should invest in common stocks where you can earn 25 percent or 50 percent or more if you're correct.

Why take the risk in guessing the future of a dicey bond for a mere 2 percent extra return? If you're wrong on the bond and it collapses, you could have a loss of 100 percent of your investment. To earn 2 percent and risk 100 percent is a poor trade-off.

The bond market will allow you a rate of return that exceeds inflation. You can't expect to do much more than that over time.

When you decide to buy bonds, you buy quality that assures you of getting your interest on time and your principal back too. Try not to make it any more complicated than that.

Rule 3: Keep Your Investment Strategy Simple

The best investment strategies are easy to explain and simple to understand. Many investors think that a good investment strategy has to be complex and sophisticated to work. Actually, the opposite is true. I never was happy with an investment strategy or idea unless I could explain it on the back of a napkin, or summarize it in three sentences or less. Why is this so?

I believe that simple strategies, because they don't require a lot of manipulation, work in all kinds of markets. Simple strategies play on large themes that have proven themselves over time. Let's take an example:

You could construct a very good stock investment system by deciding to buy stocks only when they report dividend increases and higher earnings within the last three months. And you would sell when earnings declined, or when the dividend was cut, again within the last three months. Over long periods of time, this system would work very well, for the following reasons:

- A dividend increase shows confidence by the board of directors in the earnings growth of the company; the board is asserting that a higher level of dividend payments to stockholders will be sustained by better earnings. And better earnings and higher dividends generally result in higher stock prices.

- An earnings increase shows positive momentum in the company's affairs and therefore attracts investors. It may not be accompanied by an increase in the dividend, but if you're looking for gains, the dividend isn't as much of a concern as is a rising earnings stream. This rising earnings stream will in turn drive the price of the stock.

- By selling on an earnings decline, or dividend cut, you are working on the opposite side of your buy discipline. Poor earnings drive investors away from individual stocks. While it is true that stocks often decline in advance of poor earnings announcements, it is also true that greater declines follow the actual announcement, in most cases.

Our simple system buys stocks when the earnings and dividend news is favorable, and avoids them when the news is less than favorable. Over time, you'll stay in better stocks and get out of losers. This simple system would make money for anyone over time.

Compare this to a system that requires 10 or 20 variables to generate buy-or-sell decisions. The odds increase greatly that something won't be just right.

Ask a football coach how many players he wants handling the ball on any particular offensive play. The more players involved, the greater the risk of fumble.

Another reason simple systems work best is because they don't take a tremendous amount of effort to update. You have to recognize that our daily lives make it very difficult to devote large amounts of time to any task, so a complicated system that takes an hour a day to run will fail over time because vacations, illness, and boredom will break it down.

Rule 4: Have Patience and Stick to Your Discipline

Most people have good reasons for the investments they make. Given time, their investment strategies would generally work very well. The problem is that people lose patience. Good investment takes years of constant work and attention. Sometimes the solution takes much longer than anticipated.

An avalanche of financial advice that comes to us every day tends to make us jittery. Today you are told to buy bonds. Tomorrow go for the gold. No! Another expert says you've got to get into the stock market. If you aren't making money RIGHT NOW you feel that the boat has left the dock without you.

Do you know why real estate was such a good investment for so many Americans over the years? It's simple: They bought their houses and then held them for 30 years. Inflation took care of the rest. They showed patience with the investment. Of course, they had the patience because they lived there, and holding the house came naturally.

You can't do quite the same thing with a stock, but you certainly don't have to sell after 90 days because things aren't moving fast enough.

Once you have developed a good investment strategy, give it time to work. How long? A fair test is three to five years. In the stock market, a complete cycle, from bottom to top and then back to bottom takes about three to five years. If you enter a strategy and then abandon it after a year, all you've proven is that your strategy was not effective for that particular year. It hasn't proven a thing about the longer-term value of your discipline. Patience, patience, patience!

Rule 5: Realize That No Strategy Is Perfect

In investing, it's enough to be right a little more than half the time. (I know some traders who are right only a third of the time, but it is still enough to create significant profits.) You don't need perfection, and you can't get it. If anyone achieved investment perfection, he or she would eventually have all the money in the world. It will never happen, so don't expect to be perfect. Accept your losses as part of the deal and be realistic.

The very nature of risk means that losses will occur. If you have a good system and the patience to see it through, the market will give you a fair opportunity to make your share of profits.

Rule 6: Admit Your Mistakes

You are not going to be right 100 percent of the time. You will make mistakes. When you make one, admit it to yourself quickly and rectify the situation.

Whenever you find yourself hoping instead of thinking, you've got a mistake on your hands. Sell it. Whenever you tell yourself that the world is wrong and that other people just can't see what you see, you've got a mistake on your hands. Get rid of it. When the markets move decisively against you, you've made a mistake. Change what you're doing.

Stubbornness and the inability to admit you're wrong can cost you more than any single thing. We all hate to admit that we goofed. And when you're keeping score with something as emotionally charged as money, it's even harder.

Rule 7: Set a Limit on Your Losses

Any pro will tell you that the first loss is the easiest one to take. Selling a stock at $44 that cost you $50 is much easier than selling it at $35.

Keep the losses manageable and reasonable. As a rule of thumb, don't let any loss grow beyond 15 percent. You can always handle a loss like that. It's the 50 percent and the 100 percent losses that cripple. They're tough for two reasons: First, you must sustain the loss. Second, your capital is tied up in a loser and is not working productively. The numbers are very difficult when it comes to making up losses. A 50 percent loss requires a 100 percent profit to recoup ($10,000 becomes $5,000; you need a doubling to get back to $10,000).

Executing this rule requires a mastery of Rule 6. You need to admit your mistake, set a limit on it, and get out of it. Remember, the markets will be there tomorrow. There is always another investment to make.

Rule 8: Diversify Your Investments

Don't ever put all your eggs in one basket. If you invest in common stocks, buy smaller amounts of each but have at least 10 different positions. If mutual funds are your choice, have at least three working for you. Don't put more than 5 percent of your account in any bond not backed by the government. Don't put all your money in common stocks. Diversifying your portfolio is the best way to reduce your risk.

Rule 9: Hedge Your Bets

If you have a lot of money in short-term bonds, buy some long-term bonds. If your account is invested in common stocks, buy some bonds. If you own a lot of long-term bonds, buy a bit of gold.

Have an assortment of investments that will move in opposite directions from each other. This will certainly clip off some high returns, but it will also temper some of the losses. Put another way, never bet the ranch on any idea, no matter how good.

Rule 10: Recognize That All Markets and All Investment Are Cyclical

High fliers eventually return to earth, and last year's ducks can be this year's swans. Look hard at stocks that are down. If basic quality is there, they will recover. When interest rates have risen and bonds are trading at a discount, buy some. Rates will eventually fall. When others chase today's hot stock, sell yours. If you get in the habit of buying when prices are down and then holding with patience, you'll find your returns improving. You can do this when you remember that most markets and most investments eventually turn.

SUMMARY

Every investor needs a set of guiding principals when investing. I have presented one set that I believe has timeless value. I try to keep these in mind whenever I am considering a specific investment strategy or am unsure as to my course of action. Over time, I have learned to appreciate their value.

None of the ten are original thoughts. Some were learned the hard way, and others were absorbed quickly.

When reading the story of any investment debacle, I can usually trace the problem to a violation of one of the principals. Perhaps it was lack of diversification that caused a devastating loss. Or, an inability to admit a mistake and cut a loss short. Whatever the cause, you can probably find the answer here.

1. If you can't sell it, don't buy it.
2. Buy quality.
3. Keep your strategy simple.
4. Have patience.
5. Realize that no strategy is perfect.
6. Admit your mistakes.
7. Cut your losses short.
8. Diversify your investments.
9. Hedge your bets.
10. Remember that all markets and all investments are cyclical.

CHAPTER FOUR

Managing Your Lump Sum

There are few subjects in personal finance as complicated as the lump sum. An individual who takes a lump sum is responsible for understanding a long list of tax, investment, retirement-planning, and estate-planning issues. It is not a process that can be successfully negotiated alone. And the larger the distribution, the more complicated the situation.

When you take a lump-sum distribution and roll it over to an IRA, you are creating your own pension plan. If you are considering a Roth IRA, the contemplated taxes could be several hundred thousand dollars. You have decided to assume the task of investing, reporting, and following changes in legislation as they affect your rollover account.

But ask yourself: Am I qualified to do this? If not, can I get the help I need? You no longer have the security of a paycheck to see you through a difficult period. Can you find qualified help? The answer is most certainly yes. And the help you get will have a great deal to do with the quality of your retirement.

Some investors need very little support. Some know absolutely nothing about investing money and need a great deal. Some use professionals simply to okay decisions they make on their own. They arrive at a course of action and run it by their advisors to get an opinion. Others need to rely on professionals for all their investment work; they have no particular interest in investing, or they feel inadequate for the job.

In too many cases a husband handles all the financial affairs of the family. On his death, his survivors feel left completely in the dark.

I raise these issues to illustrate that there are many questions to be answered: those related and unrelated to taxes and investment. Taking a lump-sum distribution may make perfect tax and investment sense. But the personal issues may call into doubt the wisdom of that course of action.

When your pension is paid to you in a monthly check, tax and investment problems are minimal: You take each distribution and pay the tax. This is a far cry from managing a tax-sheltered distribution that can amount to hundreds of thousands of dollars.

Considering the size of the distribution, professional help usually is a must. Although you may be capable of managing the money, it is difficult to believe that a competent professional can't add value to the process. And if your spouse is not inclined toward investment and tax work, then professional assistance is inevitable.

You have to carefully consider how your rollover will work and how it will be handled when your spouse controls it as your beneficiary. You have to make provisions for your children, too.

GET THE PROFESSIONAL ADVANTAGE

There are so many good professionals available today, and at reasonable cost, that it is difficult to understand why people choose to go unassisted. Consider the fact that after age 70-1/2, the tax penalty for under-distributing from the IRA account is a full 50 percent of the difference between the amount that was required to be paid out and the amount actually paid out. This can easily amount to several thousand dollars.

It is also worth noting that the deferred tax bill on these distributions also can run into the tens and hundreds of thousands of dollars. Why not take every precaution to protect this capital?

A few hundred dollars spent working with a competent accountant can avoid much grief. In the same way, a good attorney can draft an estate plan that can save thousands in estate taxes. A professional investment advisor can increase investment returns.

An individual with a lump sum may find all these subjects of great interest. He or she may be relatively competent in one or two of these areas, but can we imagine an individual competent in all? Typically, individuals who have a great interest in investing will attempt to handle the lump sum alone. After all, they reason, they know how to invest as wisely as the next person. Although this may be true they overlook the fact that someday their spouse may have to take the reins.

With the death of the account holder, the survivor must now seek professional help. Often this individual has no basis for picking among those offering services. Instead of putting into place a team of advisors that can carry on after your death, you have left your spouse in the position of finding professionals to advise without the benefit of your knowledge. Admittedly, he or she will have little basis other than "gut feel" for picking the people needed. This is a notoriously unreliable way to do it.

You and your spouse would be better served if you established a team of professional advisors. Wealthy individuals are quite used to doing this—they try to manage a process instead of managing each investment.

If you enjoy investing on your own, you can split your IRA among two custodians. Have a broker help you purchase a good bond portfolio, and you can manage some equities in mutual funds if you wish. Or you can buy and sell your own bonds and seek help with your equities. In any case, you are bringing aboard an investment professional who can carry the ball for your family once you are gone.

The benefits don't accrue only to your heirs. After all, a good professional will add a lot in the form of good research, investment, and financial advice.

You may enjoy the money you save doing your own tax return, and you may be perfectly competent to do so. However, once you have to deal with the complexities of the IRA distribution rules, especially prior to age 59-1/2 and after age 70-1/2, a good accountant can save a lot of grief. Consider that next to investment loss, the Internal Revenue Service is the biggest threat to your existing capital. (See

Table 4.1 for approximate federal estate tax due on estates on varying sizes.) Don't try to do it alone.

The same goes for a good attorney. You don't need a litigator or a real-estate attorney. You need a good estate-planning specialist. Unlike an investment advisor or an accountant, an attorney isn't visited annually. Generally, you will have your estate plan rewritten after receipt of a large lump sum. The addition of a lump sum can balloon your estate into significant estate-tax liability. A sound estate plan can help mitigate the effects of that tax.

TABLE 4.1 **Federal Estate Tax**

Net Estate	*Approximate Federal Estate Tax Due*
$ 600,000	$ 0
$ 750,000	$ 55,500
$1,000,000	$153,000
$1,250,000	$255,500
$1,500,000	$363,000
$2,000,000	$588,000

Together, your investment advisor, accountant, and attorney form your first line of defense against unnecessary taxes and poor investment performance. All this translates into more money for you and your family and a better retirement experience.

Let's look at how to find each of these professionals. It's better to quarterback a good team than to try winning the game alone.

FINDING A GOOD ACCOUNTANT

I have found that of all the financial professions, accountancy has the highest consistency of good-quality practitioners. If you hire a Certified Public Accountant (CPA), the odds of getting poor advice are relatively small.

Accountants come in two basic varieties: tax and audit. Tax accountants do what you would expect; they advise their clients about paying taxes. In addition to working on your tax returns, you can expect to call your accountant any time during the year when you have a tax-related question. And your accountant can often give you good advice on other financial questions as well.

There are accountants who specialize in auditing work for corporations and other institutions. It is their job to check corporate management's figures about sales, profits, inventories, and other matters reported to the public. They provide a seal of approval for the corporation's financial statements.

As an individual, you will hire a tax accountant, although she or her firm may provide audit services as well.

In seeking out a CPA, you are retaining an individual who has earned that license from her state of residence. She has passed rigorous examinations in accountancy and represents the highest standards of her profession. Your individual tax return will be well within her abilities.

A personal referral is always the best way to start. Ask people you know whom they use. Small-business owners are an excellent referral source. When you get a large lump sum, it is not unlike starting and running a small business of your own. Your needs will be more complex than those of the average person.

Get two or three names from people whose judgment you respect and ask them about the service. Are they treated well? Is their tax work completed on time? Does their accountant give them ideas or simply fill out tax forms? Will they continue to use their accountant? Do they think their accountant is too busy to take on another client? Keep in mind that good practitioners attract new clients. They rarely have a lot of time on their hands, so you want to be sure that their level of service has kept pace with their success.

If you can't get any referrals, go to the Yellow Pages. You don't need the heavy artillery of a national accounting firm unless you have multistate residence or a particularly complicated situation, so I would pass over the really big ones. Concentrate on small and mid-sized firms with two to five partners. They are big enough to help and small enough to offer personalized service for the individual. (Big firms offer the same services, but their focus tends more toward very affluent individuals and corporate work—those who can afford their higher fee schedules.)

Armed with three or four names, call each firm and ask for the managing partner. Tell him that you are searching for a CPA and would like an interview with his firm. He will want to know, in general terms, what your needs are, and you should tell him. Don't be shy about revealing how much you earn and how much in assets you have. He will keep it in confidence, but that information is necessary to assess whether his services will fit and with whom you should work.

Ask to meet with someone younger. It is disheartening to reach age 65 and then go to your accountant's retirement party. If you start with someone your junior, you shouldn't have to make a new choice down the road. If the firm offers you a contemporary, ask whether there are other people who will pick up your work later on. Some firms fossilize—there are three or four good partners who established their business together but who have been unable to attract new blood.

Set up your interviews. You should go with your spouse. After all, he or she will need to work with these people at some point. So make that introduction right from the start.

Questions to Ask

At the interview, you want to be satisfied on several points:

1. *Fees.* How much, how often, and how computed. Typically, your accountant will bill you after completing your tax return. When you call by telephone for a piece of information, what does she charge? Does a telephone call automatically result in a minimum billing of 15 minutes? Your accountant sells her time. Find out how much is charged for the product. Practices vary, so you have to ask. The accountant should be able to give you a rough fee estimate. Bring a copy of your last two years' tax returns and a financial statement listing all your assets and liabilities. Be forthcoming. It is the only way your accountant can get an accurate reading.

2. *The work.* Will this accountant be doing your returns, or will the work be delegated to others and merely reviewed by the one you hire? This is an important point. You want to know exactly who does the hands-on work. It helps to avoid later misunderstandings. Most CPAs delegate their basic tax return "crunching" to staff, and they review the final product. This shouldn't bother you if it keeps your bill down by

using less expensive help for the easy work and using the CPA where expertise counts.

TIP It is helpful to know that your accountant can be held responsible for flagrant violations of the tax law and can even lose his license to practice. Don't ask him to file a fraudulent tax return for you. Don't ask him to cheat for you.

3. *Knowledge of the IRA area.* Since one of your primary needs is advice about your IRA and the tax treatment of the money going in and coming out, you need to be sure of that expertise. While all tax accountants are knowledgeable about basic items, you want to be confident that more complex questions won't result in several hundred dollars in research billings. Does the accountant have other clients with IRA rollovers like yours? Are clients being advised about "minimum distributions" and "excess accumulations"?

If the CPA doesn't recognize these terms and understand their implications, move on to the next one. To see what the CPA knows about investments, ask some of the same questions you would ask your financial consultant. A knowledgeable CPA will understand the investment world; a "number cruncher" won't.

Other Considerations

Aside from these issues, you want to take a look around you. Are the offices well kept? It's not necessary that they be new but they shouldn't look like a paper-work junkyard either. Large stacks of paper piled on a desk, journals piled in the corner, file cabinets open and stuffed all point to a disorganized individual who, while perfectly competent, may not be able to find your files. Your chances of getting a return filed by April 15 are pretty small with an accountant like that.

Finally, ask for three references of people in similar circumstances to yours. You want to speak with clients who are as similar to you as possible. Then, check those references. Are they generally satisfied? Is the billing fair? Is the work good? Are their returns completed on time? And just to probe a bit, ask them what the accountant doesn't do well. After all, none of us is perfect.

Go through the same routine with each candidate/firm. After you have gathered all your information, ask your spouse which one he or she prefers. Make sure your spouse is comfortable with whoever you choose. Don't pick strictly on price. Unless fees are clearly out of line, don't worry about paying an extra $100 or $200 when you're trying to protect $500,000 from premature tax or tax penalty. And don't get hung up on hourly rates. It's better to pay $150 an hour to someone who is knowledgeable than $50 an hour to one who may not even recognize the question.

> **TIP**   Even though most CPAs are competent in tax matters, don't take that for granted. There is considerable variation in the delivery of services and specializations among accountants and their firms.

THE FINANCIAL CONSULTANT

Good brokers are as prevalent as good doctors, good lawyers, or good accountants; no more, no less. As a matter of fact, if you can find yourself a good doctor, good lawyer, good accountant, and good broker, you've got a shot at solving most of the problems money and health will throw at you. A good doctor can't keep you healthy if you smoke, for instance, but she will get you on your feet quicker than a bad doctor will.

So it is with a good broker. A good broker won't make you wealthy if you don't know how to save money, but he will probably get you a greater increase in your net worth than a poor one, who may lose all your money.

At my firm we are called financial consultants. I prefer this name to broker or stockbroker, because it is more descriptive of the work we do. Clients consult with us about their money. They may ask for advice about a mortgage, credit, or how to find a good lawyer. And they come for investment advice. The days of simply selling and buying stocks are deep in the past. Good financial consultants take the role of family and company advisor to millions of Americans.

This brings out the first point in starting your search for a good financial consultant—knowing what you need. You should recognize that your financial consultant will, if she's good at what she does, provide advice far beyond simply buying and selling investments. You will rely on her counsel for a whole series of life's financial problems: caring for parents, college expenses, buying a home, estate planning, changing jobs.

This used to puzzle me. Why would a client seek my advice about a change in careers or jobs? It became evident that I was one of the few people with whom he or she could discuss a problem without baring his soul to family, friends, or co-workers. And I was someone who could understand the language of headhunters, up-front bonus, and restricted stock options.

You should view your financial consultant in a broad context. Good financial consultants will wear many hats for you, so it is important that you view the person in the whole. It is not necessary to particularly like, on a personal basis, the professional money manager that your financial consultant hired for you, but it is important that you feel good about your financial consultant. The relationship with your financial consultant is much more intimate than is that with other professionals. You may speak with your attorney once every two or three years and, then, only on a specific problem. You see your doctor once a year, and meet with your accountant at tax time.

Your financial consultant is another matter. If you are actively involved in your investments and active in your strategy, you may meet with your financial consultant several times each year. You'll interact continuously with her in the pursuit of your investment and financial goals. If you don't like her as a person, the relationship may not survive the stress of the investment battle. Your financial consultant should be someone with whom you'd like to build a close friendship, without actually doing so.

In selecting a financial consultant, beware of hidebound thinking. The placement of funds in the equity or bond markets is a constantly shifting thing. Financial consultants who cling to particular points of view, without flexibility, are heading for trouble, as are their clients.

The financial consultant who buys XYZ, utterly convinced of its great potential, will ride that position to disaster if she doesn't sell when actual earnings and sales prove her wrong. A good financial consultant recognizes when she is wrong and is able to shift gears and get back in sync with events as they unfold.

Inflexible financial consultants are not hard to spot: They generally have a pet theory or point of view at which they expound at some length, in a generally negative manner. If their pet peeve is the federal deficit, they will go on and on about how the deficit will be the ruin of us all. (The deficit may just do that, but it is only one of many relevant issues.) They also may have a general tendency to feel that everyone else is on a lower intellectual level.

Those with fixed opinions on the market are incapable of changing their points of view, until the market has shoved a multihundred-point loss against them. Only then, and belatedly so, do they admit to a mistake, not because they were wrong but because everyone else was so stupid!

Good financial consultants do a lot of listening. They listen to the markets, to the news, to commentary, speeches, their critics, their supporters. Most of all, they listen to their clients. If a financial consultant spends most of the time talking about herself and her work she gathers a correspondingly smaller amount of information about you.

Eventually, the client will say, "But that's not what I wanted." He says this because the financial consultant didn't listen to what he had to say, and so applied the wrong solution to the problem.

The financial consultant must be able to translate complex financial concepts into plain English.

EXAMPLE   "Since your tax situation is so heavily affected by the high level of W-2 income, we find shelter particularly difficult to find, but it is possible to defer and realize the taxable event in out years."

Translation: Since you earn so much, it's hard to avoid paying taxes. But if you put some of your money in your company's savings plan, it won't be taxed until you pull it out when you retire.

EXAMPLE   "We believe a major commitment to equities is warranted, given our view that a lower interest-rate environment will produce correspondingly higher P/E ratios in quality issues."

Translation: Since interest rates are going down, stocks will go up. Let's buy a bunch now.

If the financial consultant can't translate the strategy into plain English, the client is left with anxiety over investments he doesn't understand. This situation does not have a high probability of success over time.

The good financial consultant is a student of human nature and the human-condition. Investing is really about interacting with people. Whenever you buy or sell something, there is a person on the other side of the transaction. Understanding what that person may be thinking (his reason for selling) is crucial in successful investing. Your financial consultant needs to understand what makes people tick if she is to serve you well. Issues such as fear, anxiety, success, ego, assertiveness, and the entire range of emotion and psychology are integral parts of the daily work. Since markets and people swing back and forth between greed and fear, it helps to understand those emotions and their genesis.

Everyone will have poor investments now and then. Good consultants have poor investments as well. The big difference is that they tend to have fewer of them than other people do. They believe in investing for the long haul. They look for quality. They don't strike out too often because they're not swinging at the fences. This is the most difficult attribute to discern. After all, published track records of financial consultants are not available, and probably never will be. How can you tell if a financial consultant is a smart investor? The answer can be found, and it lies in the way you go about finding one.

FINDING THE BEST FINANCIAL CONSULTANT FOR YOU

We've identified the person we want. Our financial consultant should be smart, flexible, hard working, one who applies good listening skills with sympathy for his client.

How do we find him? The process shouldn't be difficult. I will give you methods you can use, but they're not worth a nickel if you don't apply them. If you do, you should end up with a successful relationship.

Get Referrals from Friends

This is a surprisingly effective way to find a good financial consultant. A friend often shares a common lifestyle, viewpoint, and economic success. Chances are, a financial consultant who satisfies a good friend has a pretty good chance of satisfying you.

You need to ask the right questions, however. Even though your golf partner is happy, he may have different investment needs. It is necessary to probe a bit. What does your financial consultant do for you? What kind of investments does she buy? How long have you had a relationship with her?

Too many investors make the mistake of stopping with a recommendation from a friend. You need to frame the circumstances to see if you fit. The financial consultant may be a specialist in bonds and be perfectly satisfying to your bond-buying friend. As an equity investor, you would be less than satisfied.

Ask questions. Show you're serious about the issue and you'll get a more thoughtful and serious response.

Get Referrals from Other Professionals

If you already have a trusted accountant or attorney, they can be excellent referral sources. Since they spend so much time in the business of serving people, they get to know who carries a good reputation. In addition, they have other clients whose tax returns, for instance, show the history of a client's successes and failures in investing.

While many are reluctant to make a blanket referral to you (they worry about a bad referral costing them your business) they will often be able to direct you to two or three names, helping you to cut down on the search.

Look on Your Own

If you don't have friends or other professionals who can steer you to a couple of candidates, open the Yellow Pages and look under Investments. You'll find listings for all the companies in your area who offer investment services. You'll see many names you recognize and many that may be new to you.

If in doubt, stick with a nationally known firm. This is much like buying a brand name such as Goodyear or Goodrich—there may be better tires at a better price, but you get a good product with the brand name. In addition, big national firms have a wide variety of products and services to meet nearly any investor's need. One-stop shopping has a benefit in convenience and variety.

Don't eliminate a firm simply because it is small or regional, however. Some of the country's best people work in those firms, and they're worth a serious look. In addition, a regional firm, because it must rely on a smaller marketing area, can be more attuned to the regional quirks of the people it serves. It is much more important to focus on the individual and not on the firm. Keep an open mind.

Just because you've decided on a good firm doesn't mean that the financial consultant you have will be more competent than will another. Nor will a relationship with a big firm guarantee it; don't take the name on the door as a pledge against investment failure. The quality of financial consultants in any company can vary all over the lot, from poor to outstanding.

Once you've picked a couple of firms that appeal to you, call the local office and ask to speak with the branch manager, the individual in charge of that particular office. He's the one who hires and fires, helps settle client disputes, and is responsible for the proper functioning of the office. As part of his duties, he must continually train and retrain the financial consultants in his office. So a good manager will have an understanding of each financial consultant in his office, what they are like as personalities, the investment areas of strength, the quality of their work. He becomes your best source in finding the right financial consultant in his office.

Once you've arranged to meet with him, you want to outline the types of investments you seek and the degree of risk you're willing to assume, along with the amount of money you have to invest. Impress upon him your desire to formulate a long-term plan, develop a long-term relationship, and let him know you're considering another firm. Then ask him if he could suggest one or two financial consultants in his office who would fit your investment profile. Ask to be introduced to them and schedule an appointment to discuss the situation in more detail.

At that appointment, you want to closely observe the financial consultant. Preferably, meet with her in her office. Seeing where she spends her days gives you an excellent feel for how she works. Observe the office. Neat? Messy? A power office with leather and dark wood, or a functional working office? What pictures are on the wall? This will tell you much about what is important to her. A messy office can indicate a lack of organization, which can be a problem in organizing your investment life. If she can't organize a 10- by 10-foot space, how can she organize her clients' investment portfolios and keep them that way?

If the office is squeaky clean, you have to wonder if the person works very hard or at all. Some clutter is understandable in any working environment. Observe the way she dresses. The look should be businesslike. While short-sleeved and open collar shirts may be fashionable in certain parts of the country, most financial offices tend to be old-fashioned in that respect: business suit, business blouse or shirt, and so on.

Keep in mind that you're looking for evidence of a good financial consultant. Is she listening? Does she exhibit intelligence and empathy? Can she discuss her investment philosophy in a way that you can easily understand? Above all, do you feel comfortable with her? If you can't establish a feeling of comfort during the interview, it will be difficult to sustain a relationship once money is put at risk.

After you have outlined your situation, listen carefully to her response. Does she fumble for words and concepts? Does it sound as if she's winging it as she goes along?

Another way to handle the interview is to ask her what kind of business she does and what her strong and weak suits are. Good financial consultants can speak clearly about what they do, with what account size they expect to work, and what they tend not to do very well, or at all.

You want to get some idea of whether this person is going to be a good fit with your personality, and to understand the level of experience of the consultant. You need to close the loop by asking for client references. Say you want the names and telephone numbers of five of her clients who are in a similar situation to yours. And, you want only people who have been clients for at least three years. This list will enable you to check with others to verify her representation to you. She should be delighted to provide references.

If she can't provide references, regardless of reason, you have no way of independently verifying what she is saying to you. You can't take the chance on a gut reaction. If you are unable to check references, you are relying on the word of her boss, and on hers as well. I am unaware of any quality financial consultant of my acquaintance who couldn't provide 10 or 20 or 30 references if asked. She may not be able to provide them on the spot. So few people actually ask for references that she may not have been asked in some time. If she doesn't have a list, ask her to send you one in a couple of days. This will give her time to call some people and get their permission to use their name.

Asking for references is really a substitute for getting a referral from a friend. These references are the friends you don't have, that do business with this financial consultant. Once you get the list, use it. Call three or four names from the list (you don't really need to call all five). They'll know why you're calling. Tell them what you intend to do, what your general needs are (bonds, stocks, aggressive investing, and so forth.) and ask them if they believe their financial consultant can fit the bill.

They want to say nice things about their financial consultant. After all, they do business with her. But you want to probe a bit below the surface. For instance, if they say they've had excellent results in the market, ask them how they were generally achieved. Did she pick individual stocks or retain a professional money manager? Did the client pick the stocks and the financial consultant merely execute? Try to get the detail behind the results. Ask if she has any weaknesses—most people do and the reference will probably tell you what they are.

Don't worry too much about a stranger finding out that you have a pension lump sum to invest. People really don't care about that and will forget it in a few days. And, if you've got a million to invest and you're talking to the president of a local company, you can assume that you're talking with an investment peer. If the financial consultant was foolish enough to give you references with little in common with your situation, she wasn't a very good listener and so should not be hired.

After you've spoken with the references, you should also ask your accountant if he's heard the consultant's name and knows her reputation.

You've now done more than 99 percent of what people do when they hire a financial consultant. Most rely on a single word of mouth or pick people they like, without systematically going through a selection process, Don't be hesitant about being so methodical. The quality of your life and the well-being of your family may depend on the advice offered by your financial consultant. Few decisions in life can be as crucial. The more money involved, the more thorough the process of selection should be.

Once you have made your decision, call each of the unsuccessful candidates and explain that you've made another choice. You need not be specific about the choice you made. Always keep the door open. If your choice doesn't work out, you have other people who are already potential alternatives.

HOW TO WORK WITH YOUR FINANCIAL CONSULTANT

Once you have selected a financial consultant, it is important to understand exactly what you should and should not expect her to do for you

What You Should Expect

- You should expect your advisor's advice to be based on your best interest. Every good advisor gives advice to clients that runs counter to the advisor's own near-term needs. For instance, you may call and ask whether to purchase a particular stock. If an advisor believes the investment to be a poor one, he should say so. A broker will earn a commission and fatten his paycheck by advising a purchase. By advising you truthfully and not executing a trade, he's taken a pay cut on your behalf.

A good advisor realizes, however, that if he gives good advice you will earn more over the long haul, and so will he. This is behavior you should expect and what your broker should provide. Be skeptical of any situation in which your broker always agrees to a commission-generating transaction. There are simply too many situations where the correct course of action is to do nothing.

- You should expect to receive prompt solutions to your problems. When you call with a problem, whether it's a dividend you think is missing or an investment question, you should expect quick action.

  Of course, if you're missing a dividend, it may take a couple of days to research the date of the dividend payment, examine statements, and call the appropriate department. Nevertheless, it should be rectified within the week. If you didn't get your current month's statement, a copy is usually available in your broker's office, or one can be ordered within the week. Other problems may take more time, especially those from several months ago. The longer the elapsed time, the longer it will take to solve, since old statements must be ordered and time must be taken to get reacquainted with what exactly happened.

- You should expect to receive timely and intelligent investment advice. The whole purpose of the relationship is to invest your money profitably. A lot of things can be sacrificed: quick problem-solving, pleasant conversation, an occasional lunch. But if you are looking for investment research or a recommendation, you can expect a prompt reply, usually the same day. If your goal is a high degree of safety in municipal bonds, you should expect to receive specific bonds to buy that meet high credit quality with best available yield. Your broker should offer advice about the overall structure of your portfolio's maturities and how interest-rate movements would affect the current market value. Whenever cash builds in your account, she should initiate the call to suggest reinvestment. By taking the initiative, she is showing her interest in your account and monitoring its progress. She is fulfilling her role of advisor and strategist.

  Recommendations to invest should be accompanied by well-reasoned explanations of why the investment makes sense, along with a description of the risks involved. The reasons for the investment need not be complicated. Sometimes the best ideas are elegant in their simplicity. What you are looking for is thought behind the action. You should expect that your money won't be put at risk on a whim.

- You should get an appointment with your broker when you want one, and you should expect her to encourage face-to-face meetings. The good broker enjoys personal contact with her clients. She feels it is a valuable way to continually renew the relationship. A friendly attitude is often the only thread that hangs it all together during difficult markets. Your broker should suggest personal reviews of your portfolio on a regular basis.

What You Should Not Expect

- You shouldn't expect perfection. Your advisor is human. He's going to make mistakes. Good advisors are distinguished not by absence of error, but by minimization of error. They simply make fewer mistakes than others do. In many cases he must work with other people over whom he has no control. The press of business may stop him from being able to meet with you exactly when you want to. This doesn't mean he doesn't value your business.

- You shouldn't expect your advisor to do the work of others. It may be less expensive to have your broker figure out tax questions for you since he doesn't bill for it. But it isn't right. Your tax items generally lie in the province of your accountant and should be directed to her. Ditto for legal issues and your attorney. If you need to know the drawbacks of a living trust, you should pay for a consultation with your attorney.

- You should have reasonable expectations. If you impress upon your advisor your fear of risk and your desire for very safe investments, you can't fault her if the stock market rises 25 percent and you're not invested in it. The flip side of avoiding risk is more modest investment return. Your reaction to your results should be consistent with your instructions.

What Should It Cost?

Few people have a good notion about how much they should be charged for their investment services. After all, if you're earning 25 percent per year, a 5 percent annual expense is probably bearable. But if you're losing 3 percent per year, any expense is too much.

Overall, you should pay about 0.7 percent to 2.5 percent per year in fees and commissions for an IRA focused on long-term growth and investment (note that this can vary in different parts of the country, depending on the general cost of doing business).

Bond accounts tend to generate lower levels of fees and commissions compared to stock accounts—usually less than 1 percent per year. This can be lower than many no-load mutual funds. Common-stock accounts can generate significantly more in commissions, depending on the trading activity. There has also been a general trend for the fees in equity mutual funds, even no-loads, to climb, and today fees of 1.5 percent to 2 percent per year are fairly common.

So in applying a band to these numbers, I would suggest the following as reasonable annual expenses for your IRA account:

Bond accounts	0.2 percent to 1.0 percent
Stock accounts	1.0 percent to 2.75 percent
Balanced accounts	0.7 percent to 2.0 percent

Active stock traders would tend toward 4 percent or even higher, while more passive accounts would tend toward the lower end of these ranges.

Remember that the more active your account, the higher the expense. Not only do you have higher commission expense, but you have the normal transaction costs of buying at the offering, or higher side of the market, and selling at the bid, or lower side of the market. This isn't a problem if you're making enough to cover these costs, but IRA accounts generally are not actively traded for speculation by most people.

A more recent innovation has been the advent of the flat-fee commission account. In lieu of commission charges on each trade, the broker offers a flat annual fee with a maximum number of trades per year. These can often be money-savers depending on your level of activity. The problem, of course, is that you often can't be sure how much you'll be trading. However, most people have a pretty good idea of their activity level, and so this can be explored as an alternative.

Don't fret too much about expense. Fret a lot about net performance. After expenses, what is the performance of the account? A top-performing no-load equity fund is a real bargain. So is a top-performing money manager charging more. By contrast a poorly performing no-load fund or manager isn't. Net performance—that is the bottom line you should consider.

THE FINANCIAL PLANNER

A financial planner acts as an independent advisor on tax, investment, and estate-planning issues for a fee. The basic professional credential is the certified financial planner. To become a CFP, the candidate must complete a rigorous, two-year course in all aspects of financial planning for individuals. Upon passing her final examinations, she is granted the CFP designation and can use it on her stationery and business cards.

A pure planner works on a fee arrangement. She is not selling anything but her professional advice. If you are going to retain a planner, a fee-based planner is your best choice.

Often, a planner will offer you the option of paying for your planning fees with investment commissions. This is where the distinctions blur and it is harder to judge. If the planner makes a recommendation, can you be absolutely sure that the advice is impartial? This must be explored in detail.

A good, fee-based financial planner can quarterback your team for you, helping out with taxes, finding a money manager, setting up your estate (but not drafting your will), and numerous other tasks.

Financial planners are not as numerous as brokers or accountants, so the Yellow Pages are your best hunting ground if you can't get names referred to you. Go through the same interviewing regimen that you would for any other financial professional and, as always, check client references. Be clear on how the planner is paid and how the fees are computed.

THE ATTORNEY

Of the three advisors you'll need, your attorney will be the one you use the least. Your financial consultant is a constant companion, your accountant an annual affair. Your attorney will draft an estate plan for you, and you may not need her advice ever again.

Nevertheless, you shouldn't be lax in your selection process; just as in any other profession, there are good and bad lawyers. There are those who are indeed estate-planning specialists and those who pretend to be.

Once you have an accountant and financial consultant on board, finding a competent attorney shouldn't be any more difficult than asking for a referral. The two of them should know many and will be able to tell you whom you can turn to for specialized estate work.

And if your attorney knows and has worked with your other advisors, they'll all be able to function together as an effective team. The receipt of a lump sum often moves the average estate deep into taxable territory. A will that was adequate when you were worth more dead than alive through your company life insurance is now hopelessly out of date. You need to think about trust arrangements and how to minimize estate taxes. This requires a good estate plan, and the drafting of the related documents: the will, trust agreements, powers of attorney, and so forth.

The attorney's job will go far beyond that. Once she has drafted your will, it will, as they say, wind up in her safe. When you die, she will expect to handle your estate for your family. So at that most sensitive of times she will pop up as a family advisor. Your family doesn't have to use her but probably will.

So once you have the referral, meet her with a critical eye. Apply the same standards you applied to your search for your accountant and your financial consultant. Odds are that if you are satisfied with your other advisors, their choice of attorney for you will be a good fit.

The key in this process is that the attorney be an estate-planning specialist. Any attorney can draft a will. But the specialized knowledge needed to protect complicated estates is the province of the trusts-and-estates professional. Just because good old Bob handled your house closing doesn't mean he knows enough to handle your estate planning. Make the distinction. Estate planning is a financially dangerous and complex area and requires specialized work. Remember, if your will is drafted in error, you won't be around to fix it.

THE IRA CUSTODIAN

An Individual Retirement Account is a trust. As such, there must be a custodian who is responsible for holding the assets, reporting account activity, and making sure that the basic rules are followed. In order to regulate activity, the government licenses IRA custodians. You can't simply open an account at a bank and call it your IRA. You must open it under the bank's approved IRA documentation.

The IRA custodian is not responsible for steering you away from income tax penalties or incorrect distributions. It is your responsibility to know the income tax rules and how they apply in your situation. Simply because your custodian allows you to take money out of the account doesn't mean that a tax penalty will not be charged to you.

IRA custodians are companies that have applied for the position. Four types of companies qualify as IRA custodians: brokerage houses, mutual-fund companies, insurance companies, and banks. The term "bank" also includes entities like trust companies. Depending on the type of IRA you wish to have, you will find one type more advantageous than another. Let's took at each in turn along with their strengths and weaknesses.

Brokerage Houses

Brokerage houses offer IRA accounts with the broadest range of investment and distribution options. When you open an IRA with a broker, you are opening an investment account under the IRA umbrella.

If it is a full-service firm, the house will assign a broker to you if you don't already have one of your own. He will be able to give you investment advice on the account. If he is a discount broker, he will execute trades for you, but you'll pretty much be left on your own in selecting your investments.

While brokerage houses offer just about any investment imaginable, you will find that as a practical matter they will frown upon highly speculative investments for IRA accounts. IRA custodians do have certain responsibilities to their clients, and while there is no specific requirement against speculation in IRAs, it is generally not encouraged.

Your account is protected through a government agency called SIPC (Securities Investors Protection Corporation); brokerage accounts are insured against losses caused by your broker's insolvency. The insurance amounts to $500,000 in total, including up to $100,000 in cash. This agency is funded by insurance premiums paid by brokerage houses. Since many accounts now exceed $500,000, many brokers carry excess insurance through private insurance companies. This coverage often runs into the millions of dollars per account.

When you invest with a broker, your assets and funds should not be commingled with the funds used in the broker's daily business operations. And, as a general rule, your assets are held at an independent trust depository, not in your broker's vault. Loss through your broker's insolvency shouldn't be a major concern on your part. When you interview your broker, it is perfectly acceptable to question him about his insurance coverage, and you want to hone in on his private insurance if your account will exceed $500,000.

Finally, remember that the insurance is designed to replace assets lost, not to guarantee your account against investment loss. Whatever the insurance limits, you are still at investment risk.

Mutual Funds

Mutual funds, especially the larger mutual-fund families, offer IRA-custodian services. Unlike brokerage houses, your investments are limited to the funds available from that company, so the investment flexibility isn't as great as with an individually managed brokerage account. However, a fund family can offer all the choices you are likely to need, so diversifying your IRA is quite easy.

Some mutual-fund organizations are now branching out into brokerage services, so the lines between traditional brokers and mutual-fund companies are blurring. How can you tell if you're dealing with a broker? Look for the logo, "Member SIPC." Just as with a discount broker, you'll be on your own in investing with a mutual fund. If the fund company offers several different funds, you'll have to make decisions as to which funds to invest in, how much to place, and when to switch.

Given the number of people investing in mutual funds, it isn't surprising to learn that a whole industry of newsletters and advice has sprung up around these funds. A fund newsletter or a switch letter (makes recommendations about switching from fund to fund) can help you manage the allocations you have between funds.

If the fund group is a no-load fund, you will pay no commissions to purchase the funds, but you might pay a modest annual IRA custodial fee. Each fund, whether load or not, levies a management fee and passes along trading expenses as well. Expect to pay on average .5 percent to 1.5 percent per year in management fees, sometimes more, sometimes less.

Banks

Your bank will be happy to open an IRA account for you. Your investments will be limited to certificates of deposit or other insured savings accounts with that bank. From that standpoint a bank IRA has very little investment diversity to offer, and you'll earn only what the bank declares as a rate of interest on your IRA deposit.

A bank IRA usually makes sense only for smaller lump-sum distributions. The bank IRA's greatest strength is simplicity and safety. Your deposit is insured by the U.S. government, you can earn a reasonable rate of interest, and you can certainly sleep at night.

Many banks, eager to keep deposits at the bank at a time when CDs aren't particularly compelling, offer brokerage services through subsidiaries. These accounts are not FDIC insured and should be judged on the basis of a brokerage account, not a bank account. If your banker introduces you to an "investment representative" or some other person selling investments, you should not confuse that relationship with having an FDIC-insured savings account.

Bank trust departments generally offer IRA accounts. An IRA held by the trust department will generally be billed on a percentage management, and custodian fees will be based on the size of the account. In addition, your account will be billed for any commissions generated by the account, or you will be invested in mutual funds, some with a load.

As with any other investment relationship, you want to question the bank about investment options and performance. Ask for client references and obtain assurances to verify that you will indeed have a personal representative working for you.

A bank does have merit in a situation where you intend to have the bank handle your family's affairs once you are gone. By establishing your IRA at the bank, this institution will have ongoing knowledge of the progress of the account. Indeed, they may be primarily responsible for its success or failure.

While bank trust departments are often criticized for pedestrian investment returns, this has begun to change in today's increasingly competitive environment. And, you generally won't experience disasters either. Also, the comfort you may feel with a caring and knowledgeable trust officer can be very important to you and your family.

Insurance Companies

Insurance companies act as IRA custodians. Typically, they offer an IRA through tax-deferred annuity vehicles or through variable annuities. A tax-deferred annuity typically pays a stated rate of interest for a specific period of time. A variable annuity will have a group of mutual funds under the IRA/Annuity umbrella. Your return will be only as good or as bad as the performance of the funds in the contract.

Because insurance annuity contracts are guaranteed by the company that issues them, you need to check into the quality of the firm. Many states also have provisions that require other companies to assist in the case of insolvency of an insurance company. If your company goes out of business, you could lose your money. Yet, this is not a likely occurrence and shouldn't be a major concern on your part. Bankruptcies in the industry several years ago made regulators extra vigilant. Check with your state insurance department to learn more about how insurance annuity contracts are protected in your state.

Insurance company IRAs can be attractive or not, depending on fees and liquidity. A mutual-fund family can offer the same investment alternatives without the penalties that often accompany annuity contracts. And since a lump sum is taken precisely to avoid a check-a-month pension for life, it makes no sense to take a lump sum and then buy a lifetime annuity from an insurance company. Your employer could probably do a better job of it than you. So if you intend to buy an annuity, you might as well take the pension from your employer. This way, you let him shop for the annuity.

If an agent wants to sell you an IRA contract through her insurance company, question her on her investment expertise. In many cases his primary focus is on insurance, but she does have an IRA in her quiver of arrows.

> **TIP**   A clear and unmistakable trend in financial services has been a blurring of the lines in investment services. More and more companies, whether a traditional insurance company or a bank, are offering a more diverse menu of financial services. Therefore, if you have a current relationship with a financial-services institution and are pleased with it, explore other services available. You may find that you can continue the same relationship and get the services you need.

HOW TO CHOOSE A CUSTODIAN

Given all the choices available (see Table 4.2) this can seem like an impossible task. However, you can simplify the decision-making process if you focus on a couple of basic questions.

If you need investment advice, go to a full-service broker or consider a bank trust department. These organizations offer specialized help, and you'll have a broad range of investment alternatives.

Table 4.2 Summary of the Various Custodians and the Features They Offer

	Full Service Broker	Discount Broker	Bank Trust Department	Mutual Fund Family	Insurance Company
Custodian Fees	None-Low	None-Low	Low-High	None-Low	Low
Commissions	Medium-High	Low	Low-Medium	None-High	Medium-High
Personal Service	High	Low	Medium-High	None-Low	Low-High
Investment Choices	High	Medium-High	High	Low-Medium	Low-Medium
Ability to Transfer Out	High	High	Medium-High	High	None-High
Fee to Transfer Out	None-Low	None-Low	Low-Medium	None-Low	None-High
Reporting	Monthly	Monthly	Monthly-Quarterly	Quarterly	Quarterly-Annually

If you want to go it alone, then a discount broker or mutual-fund company may be the best choice. Here you can separate the choices by the investment alternatives they offer. For instance, if you have a small IRA that you would like to diversify, use a mutual-fund family.

If, however, you simply want a fixed-rate deposit, you may want to go to your bank.

I can't emphasize enough the importance of shopping for the custodian that best fits your needs. If you seek out an investment advisor or broker, you will tend to place the custodian's role in a secondary position. After all, you are much more interested in the person or people actually advising you.

If there are two issues that bring an individual to grief with his or her custodian, it is performance and fees. Thoroughly explore all the costs in advance before you sign aboard.

And remember: If the investment advice is poor, any cost is too high. If the advice is good, the price is usually a bargain.

THE PROFESSIONAL MONEY MANAGER

I believe in the benefits of retaining professional money managers. Many Americans seem to agree? When you invest in a mutual fund you are hiring a money manager to handle a portion of your assets for you.

However, when I use the phrase "money manager," I am referring to managers who work with individual portfolios. Unlike someone managing a mutual fund, a money manager will construct separate portfolios for each client. They are not all bundled together in one account. He may manage each one the same way, but the assets are still segregated and identified by each individual investor.

A money manager, also known as a portfolio manager, is paid a fee to manage a portfolio of stocks, bonds, or cash. One manager will specialize in portfolios containing all three classes of assets. Another will invest only in stocks, ignoring cash and bonds. The manager has complete discretion; he selects what to buy, when to buy it, and how much to buy. You are not consulted on any buy-or-sell decision.

The manager is paid a fee for his work, typically a small percentage of the account value, billed quarterly. In addition, you must pay for all commission expense. If you wish performance to be monitored, a consulting fee will be paid for that. You can sometimes obtain all these services in one bundled package called a "wrap fee." Many brokerage houses offer them.

You must trust the manager. Since he is paid on a fee basis, he has every incentive to make your account grow. Only by increasing the value can the manager increase his fee.

There are thousands of money managers available today. They range in size from the lone practitioner to large organizations with hundreds of employees. While size is no determinant of performance results, I prefer to retain managers with depth in both people and systems. These managers can be found in most of the large- and medium-sized cities in this country, and in some areas, such as New York or Boston, you can find dozens of money-management organizations.

These organizations are typically broken up into three areas of responsibility: portfolio management, operations, and sales and marketing.

The portfolio managers are those responsible for doing all the investing. They analyze the markets, the economy, industries, and companies to decide what and how much to buy. They usually spend part of their time visiting companies in which they are interested and a lot of time reading research from many different securities firms and research organizations.

If you ask to meet your individual portfolio manager, don't be upset if that can't be arranged. Many money managers try to keep their portfolio managers away from clients, feeling that they should be insulated from the emotional give and take that can occur when losses (or gains) accrue.

Yet there are sales-and-marketing representatives available to meet with you. The larger your account, however, the more likely the manager is to comply with your request. And if your account is really large, they'll even fly a portfolio manager out to see you.

Operations cover all the account maintenance, including client reports and billing. If the manager maintains a trading desk, it will be part of the operations function. All trades will be handled in this area and customer service will originate from here.

Finally, the sales and marketing staff will be responsible for bringing in new business and keeping current clients happy and informed. In smaller shops individuals wear several hats at once, and it is not unusual to find a portfolio manager also going out on sales calls and making presentations to prospective clients.

WHY EMPLOY A MONEY MANAGER?

Most people would panic if asked to perform surgery or argue a case in court, yet they don't hesitate to risk significant amounts of their savings on their own investment skills.

A money-management organization will be staffed by several graduates of good universities, many with advanced degrees in business, statistics, finance, and analysis. As a group, they carry a fairly high degree of intelligence and work hard at what they do.

They are backed by relationships with many analysts on Wall Street and have access to the management of the companies in which they invest. Their computer systems are sophisticated, and their experience in the markets is measured, collectively, in hundreds of years.

Beyond the brain power and sheer effort, a professional manager brings continuity of effort. This is not to be underestimated. Even when an individual is talented, his or her investment performance may be affected by personal circumstances. Whether it's the flu, a family vacation, or a job change, life has its way of altering the best of investment plans.

While management organizations can suffer from interruptions due to changes in ownership or personnel, the effort does have a continuity that the individual can't duplicate.

Using a money manager is cost effective. For a modest annual fee, all the work is done for you. All the anxiety of what to buy and when to buy it is removed.

Why, then, don't more people use professional managers? Many assume, erroneously, that by hiring a manager they lose control over their portfolio. Somehow they feel better deciding themselves whether to purchase IBM. The truth is that once the proper manager is hired you get a greater, not lesser, degree of control. The reason for this is simple. If you hire a good money manager who adheres to a specific investment discipline, you can be sure that she will buy only those investments that meet that discipline. If the discipline is one you embrace, you now have complete control that the strategy you want will be delivered.

Yet there is a definite language and body of knowledge that must be mastered before a manager can be hired, and most people don't speak the language. Even if a manager can be found, the experience of interviewing one can be daunting. So many don't make the effort.

MANAGEMENT STYLES

Management styles are important. The style your manager follows will dictate her risk profile and over time her investment returns.

Fully Invested

These managers always have their clients' funds fully invested in the market with a minimum amount of cash. They believe it is not possible to time the rise and fall of the market with any consistent accuracy over time, and so they prefer to beat the market with superior stock selection. In a severe down market you cannot expect to sidestep a lot of the damage that a bear market can cause. If the market drops 15 percent, a superior manager in this style might be down 9 or 10 percent, but down nevertheless. Of course, the flip side is that this manager should give excellent performance in an up market, and you should expect to enjoy significant gains.

Fully or Partially Invested

This manager will raise cash if he doesn't feel the market offers opportunity. While he will rarely leave the stock market entirely, it is not unusual to see this manager in 25 to 40 percent cash, depending on market conditions. You should expect a more defensive approach here, with the occasional pleasant surprise of missing most of a bad market by sitting on cash. However, this manager can at times miss a call, and you can find cash burning a hole in your portfolio while the market races ahead.

For downside protection, you give up some upside potential.

Asset Allocator

This manager looks at the relative attractiveness of stocks versus bonds versus cash and decides where to place assets to take advantage of these superior returns. You might find him fully invested in bonds, and then, suddenly, half in stocks and half in cash. The moves in portfolio composition can be both large and swift. Often this manager will take a contrary point of view, and that can be uncomfortable. Who wants to be in cash in a roaring bull market? Yet a good asset allocator will add value for you over longer periods of time. There are a few around to dispel the argument that the market can't be timed.

Warning! You need a strong constitution and sense of discipline to stay the course with an asset allocator!

Contrarian

As the name implies, the contrarian attempts to take an independent point of view, seeking to buy out-of-favor securities and selling popular ones. It is the modern version of buying a straw hat in January.

The contrarian loves to buy when prices are cheap. You may not appreciate owning auto stocks when the press is full of bad ink about the auto industry. Would you want to own computer stocks when a major high-tech bankruptcy is making news? If the answer is no, then a contrarian may not be for you. His stock selections can sometimes keep you awake at night.

However, a good contrarian offers excellent portfolio management because he buys when prices are low. This means greater safety over time. Many managers profess to be contrarians, but in my experience few genuine contrarian investors exist. Examining stock selection is often the only way to ascertain just how contrary the manager is.

Two-Way Versus Three-Way

A two-way manager invests in stocks and cash. A three-way manager, often called a balanced manager, invests in stocks, bonds, and cash. If you have only one portfolio and one manager, a balanced or three-way manager is probably the best choice. However, you must remember that you will be paying annual management fees for the bond portion of the portfolio. This will cut into your investment income.

Value Versus Growth

The final distinction to make is whether the manager likes to buy growth stocks or value stocks. Growth stocks, as the name implies, are companies whose sales and earning are on a high growth curve. These stocks can be very pricey, with the attendant higher risk. They occasionally crash and burn from spectacularly high levels, but the returns can be equally high.

A value manager, by contrast, tends to invest in companies that may not be high growth in nature, but are selling at reasonable levels given dividends, earnings, book values, and so on. The manager is more concerned with the basic value of the company and its assets as opposed to a high rate of growth. Value portfolios tend to be less volatile than growth portfolios and are generally (though not always) suited to more conservative investors.

You should prefer a manager who says; "This is what we do. It's not for everybody, but if it's what you're looking for, we do a pretty good job at it." That's much preferable to one who says, "Tell me what you want and we'll do it." A manager can't master several different styles and do a good job with all.

HIRING A MANAGER

Several factors must be considered before you hire a manager.

1. You need to decide on your asset allocation: how much to have in the stock market.
2. Then decide whether you want a manager who will remain fully invested or one who will raise some cash when he doesn't like the market.
3. Next decide whether you want a growth style or value style of stock selection.

You can adjust the amount of money under management depending on the style: $100,000 with a fully invested style, $150,000 with a manager who may average 30 percent cash over time. The reason for this mix is that you may want more potential exposure with your larger account.

You've now made the two most important determinations.

1. Fully invested versus partially invested
2. Growth versus value

If you're going to hire only one manager for your stock portfolio, hire a value manager. He will tend to have fewer gut-wrenching moves in the market. While his potential returns in a good market are generally less than that of a growth manager, his downside in a bad market is less. For a retiree, value tends to work better than growth. You can sleep better at night.

If you can afford two managers, then by all means consider a growth manager as well, with your capital skewed slightly toward the value manager. Growth and value tend to come in and out of favor at different times, so having both can boost your returns more consistently than simply having one or the other.

If you worry a lot about being in the stock market and having major losses, consider an asset allocator. An asset allocator can take you all the way out of the market at times. Examine closely her record in various markets to get a feel for her style. Keep in mind, however, that the price you may pay is to miss part of a good bull move.

Hiring Multiple Managers

If you hire more than one manager, put the performance of the managers together to see how they would have performed, as a group, over the past five and seven years. Look at the worst quarter you would have had, and the best. Make sure those results are within your risk tolerance.

Sometimes, the combination of two managers can dampen bad performance as well as good performance. And sometimes the combination can exaggerate good and bad performance. Look for unintended consequences in the combination. This is very important.

Don't view each manager separately. They both form portions of your portfolio and should be viewed as one to make sure the combination will work for you.

Don't try to be too analytical about analyzing track records. They are merely the result of past actions in past markets. They give you clues as to how you would expect, in a general way, to see your manager perform in various markets.

Don't hire one manager because his record is 2 percent better per year than another. You hire him because you expect he will give you what you want in the future. That means that a manager with strong personnel and staying power would be preferable to a slightly better-performing manager with high personnel turnover.

Finally, don't drive entirely in the rear-view mirror. Check out some managers whose performance has been subpar during the past three years. Try to examine why and whether this subpar performance is a temporary thing having to do more with the nature of the markets than the manager. The real successes come from hiring managers who will come back into favor, not the ones just beginning to go out of favor.

Given these problems, what do you look for? First, look for a five-year track record. This allows you to see the performance of the manager and his system over several different types of markets, both good and bad.

Of course, if everyone waited for a five-year record, managers would all starve and go out of business long before a record were established. You can't always keep this as a hard-and-fast rule. Even measuring performance has its pitfalls. You can't believe every manager's numbers as she presents them to you. Let me give you a simple example:

We looked at a money manager who reported that his accounts were up 15.7 percent for the trailing 12 months. This number included all accounts, both old and new. As such, it was a fair representation of how a typical client with that manager had done for that year.

Yet, consider these other perfectly acceptable ways of reporting:

Clients who had been with him longer than five months: +16.4 percent

Clients who had opened their accounts more recently: +3.4 percent

Clients who had opened their accounts with cash: +16.6 percent

Clients who had opened their accounts with cash and securities that had to be sold: +13.2 percent

He could report any of those numbers. In addition, he could have reported the figures before fees to further increase the apparent returns. He chose to use the broadest measure of 16.4 percent as the best representation overall, but he could have made a very strong argument for reporting 16.6 percent (cash only to start) on the basis that liquidating securities put into the account hampered his performance and shouldn't be counted.

By including all his accounts, both old and new, he was reporting the most comprehensive measure of his performance. He wasn't cherry picking his best accounts for performance reporting. Besides, a good manager will have consistent performance from account to account, so a complete record of performance will be an accurate representation. We hired him.

When a manager shows you his record, your first questions should relate to the basis of those numbers. Exactly what do they represent? How much variation from account to account? (There should be very little.) Do the results include fees? Are you looking at performance from pension accounts only? It is fair to say that since so many games are played with reporting of returns, you need a strong base of knowledge to cut through it.

Performance isn't accomplished in a vacuum, so a return is only as impressive as the markets in which it was earned. If the Dow Jones Industrial Average rises 21 percent, a manager who earned 17 percent might not be cutting it. You want to measure the manager against an appropriate index to place the return he earned in context. You also want to look at some comparable numbers for other managers. There are many indexes and comparisons that can be run, but the effect is the same: Given the markets that existed, how did the manager do?

No decision can be based solely on raw returns. If the manager's market segment has been performing poorly, you can't expect outstanding absolute performance. If you are interested in having a manager handle international stocks for you, you need to look at a representative index, such as the EAFE (Europe, Australia, Far East), to measure his performance. Perhaps the manager has only earned 8 percent per year for the last three years. But, placed in the context of an EAFE Index up only 3 percent per year, you would have a manager with outstanding performance. Look at the manager's placement on a risk/reward chart. By viewing his returns two-dimensionally, you can observe the risk he ran for the returns he earned.

Beyond performance, you want to hear a coherent and simple statement of the manager's investment discipline. Ideally, the manager should be able to state his discipline in two or three sentences. No matter how complex in practice, it should be easily summarized. If he cannot, how can you hope to have a clear understanding of what he is buying and how your portfolio will be run?

You need assurance that the organization is a stable one. Who are the principals? Who makes the investment decisions? How long have they been with the firm? What was the personnel turnover last year? The only product a manager sells is the skill of the people in the organization. What good is the track record if the people who created it are no longer there?

Finally, you want to know exactly who is going to be managing the account. Often, if the manager has a particular "star" on the staff, the impression may be left that the star will be handling the portfolio when the truth is that if the account is fairly small, a junior partner will be assigned to it. If so, you need assurance that your performance will mirror the overall performance of the management organization.

Once you've hired your manager, you will want to see quarterly performance reporting. You are measuring your own account performance against appropriate market indices in context. What you'll do now is net out the fees you pay before arriving at performance. You don't mind paying fees if the manager is earning them. But it is not fair to report returns before fees are deducted. The net return after expense is the measuring stick.

Often, if you have had a particularly good quarter and the manager's performance is within the bounds of his stated discipline, no conference with him is really necessary. But, in any case, you want to

meet with him at least annually. Do so even if you had a great year
and don't feel the need to meet. You want to review his investment
philosophy and his situation. Are the people still in place? Has he
been adhering to his philosophy? And, does that philosophy maintain
relevance?

Your manager can't control the market. He can only succeed or
fail in the context of the market's overall performance. If the market
offers profit opportunity, he will capture profits for you. A good manager can reduce losses in a poor market but can rarely generate
returns when the market is in decline.

You can help improve your manager's performance by avoiding
one common pitfall—micromanagement. Don't question each and
every trade. Why did you buy this? Why didn't you sell that? Observe
his performance diligently each quarter by looking at the numbers
and meet with him each year to review. That's plenty. Too many meetings are another form of micromanagement. It takes a long time for
the picture to emerge.

FIRING A MANAGER

Letting a manager go is usually a very difficult thing to do. Since I'm
not particularly well suited to giving people the heave-ho, I make a
point of not getting to know a manager too well on a personal basis. I
keep it strictly business,

I believe too many managers are fired without proper cause. The
single biggest reason by far is poor performance. Having said that, I
should also say that I'm not convinced most people really understand
how to measure performance. If you hire a manager whose style is to
be fully invested in the market at all times, you should not be surprised to be down 18 percent when the market takes a 20 percent hit.
Yet managers are fired for similar performances despite the fact it
should have been anticipated.

Beyond the performance is the lack of patience many people
exhibit with their manager. If you have worked hard to find a good
manager with a good track record, and if her discipline is in keeping
with the way you want your money managed, a three- to five-year time

frame is the appropriate period to judge performance. This gives you time to watch her through both good and bad markets. Only then can you get a fair picture of her capabilities. Jumping from manager to manager is as futile as jumping from stock to stock.

When do you fire a manager? I believe there are only three reasons for doing so:

1. *The manager has strayed from her discipline.* You have every right to expect that your manager is going to do exactly what she said she would do. If she deviates from it, she should be fired and fired immediately. Hiring a growth manager who then invests in value means that the manager has either misrepresented herself or has lost confidence in her work.

2. *The people have changed.* When you examine a track record, you are looking at the accomplishments of that organization. If half the employees leave to form their own firm (not at all unusual these days), not only have you lost many of the people responsible for the track record, but you can anticipate a certain amount of turmoil at that firm. New people need to be hired, educated in the culture of the firm, and so forth. It is often grounds for an immediate dismissal.

3. *Your objectives change.* You may have an excellent growth manager, but with your retirement you feel you need to pull in your horns a bit and switch perhaps to a balanced manager, or a value manager. The manager you have no longer meets your needs since your risk tolerance has changed. A change in manager is warranted.

There are other reasons you could pose for firing a manager; you might be concerned that the discipline he uses is obsolete. The fact is that basic investment disciplines go in and out of favor, but rarely become obsolete. Just as you've convinced yourself that value investing has become passé and you fire your value manager, value comes roaring back to lead the pack.

Your manager's performance might have been lousy last year. Any manager will have good and bad years. If he adheres to his discipline, the odds are actually quite good that a good year is about to unfold for him.

These are not adequate reasons for firing a manager.

INDEXING: THE RANDOM WALK

Much ink has been spilled over the theory that the market engages in a random walk. That is, stock prices can't be accurately predicted, and so one is better off simply indexing a stock portfolio and not bothering with managers, stock selection, or mutual funds. By indexing, you buy a fund that attempts to match the performance of a broad market index, like the S&P 500. The theory is that your performance will mirror the market that, in turn, will be better than the majority of investors, managers, or funds.

This logic has a seductive appeal to it. It seems to make sense and in many cases would improve the investor's performance. Many people are terrible managers of their portfolios, and indexing would certainly help their performance. If you have no access to professional managers or good investment advice, taking a portion of your portfolio and simply indexing it would be a better choice than trying to pick stocks on your own. You simply decide how much of your portfolio should be allocated to common stocks, and you index it in an S&P 500 index fund. If you do have access to professional management or good investment advice, however, indexing doesn't make a lot of sense.

The major drawback to indexing is the large losses that can accrue. When you index, your portfolio is on auto-pilot. Your performance will indeed mirror the movement of the broad stock market. If an investor had indexed in 1929, he would have experienced a 90 percent loss on his capital in the ensuing years. You could argue that if the investor had merely maintained his position, eventual profits would have more than compensated for his losses. But individuals aren't institutions. An institution can wait 10 or 20 years for things to work out. A 62-year-old doesn't have that time.

There are superior alternatives. There are many money managers and mutual funds that have outperformed the indexes over time. In addition, the index itself can fall out of favor. During the 1980s, the S&P 500 grew in popularity as its overall return exceeded most other indexes. Certainly the number of takeovers and buyouts in the 500 ranks helped this process. But indexes ebb and flow in popularity. You may wind up chaining yourself to a poorly performing index.

Indexing originally became popular with corporations and other institutions who experienced subpar performance from many money managers during the 1980s as most stocks failed to keep pace with the bigger issues represented in the S&P 500. But this period was unusual. Small-company stocks have outperformed most other major classifications over time.

An institution willing to put $25 million in the S&P 500 on a continuous, multidecade program for its pension fund is far different from the individual with $400,000 to invest in an IRA and a need for income.

BOND MANAGERS

I am less inclined to use a bond manager. A passively laddered bond portfolio should pick up enough return over time to justify forgoing the use of a professional manager. Fees in bond accounts tend to be higher relative to the potential return. After all, a portfolio earning just 7 percent in interest gets hit relatively hard by a 1 percent annual fee. (That amounts to 15 percent of the total income of the account.)

Nevertheless, there are managers who are able to overcome the fee and generate additional returns through active portfolio switching, buying when rates are high and selling for gains when rates fall. Using a bond manager makes sense when you have a fairly large account and can use some active management as a counterpoint to a large, passive portfolio.

Bond managers have a more difficult time when rates are rising, because bond prices are falling. It is impossible to earn capital gains in that environment. However, by switching your bond funds to short maturities, they can certainly add value by avoiding losses in long-term bonds.

Bond investing can be a very difficult area to negotiate, given the many credit downgrades and defaults that can occur, as well as the difficulty inherent in analyzing the direction of interest rates. In addition, many new forms of debt have come onto the market, so analysis of the terms of a bond has become much more specialized. For the investor unwilling to navigate these difficulties, a professional bond manager can be a big plus.

Most managers use U.S. Treasury securities for portfolios because of the active and liquid nature of the Treasury market. Corporate bond managers exist, although not readily for smaller (less than $1 million) accounts. Municipal bond managers are generally available at the $500,000 level and offer value compared to the abilities of most investors to select and purchase municipal bonds.

Generally, you use a bond manager when you find it difficult to create your own bond ladders or when you feel that the volatility of the bond market in the future will make active management a must. However, you'll often be better off hiring a common stock manager and buying the bonds yourself. Pay the fees where the risk is greatest.

HIRING A MANAGEMENT CONSULTANT

If you feel that the benefits of professional money management make sense but you're unwilling to do the work on your own, help is available. A management consultant is one who helps you find, hire, monitor, and evaluate money managers. Your broker may be able to fill that role; others are available, for a fee, as full-time consultants in hiring money managers.

The overwhelming choice among lump-sum recipients hiring a manager is to use one of the various "wrap-service" or "wrap-fee" programs offered by their brokers. An IRA can be invested with a money manager. And since multiple IRAs are permitted, you can have as many managers as you want. Multiple IRAs become necessary because your broker will want to monitor each manager separately. So, if you have a $400,000 IRA rollover, you may have three IRA accounts: one each for your two managers and a third for your IRA bond account. Your broker acts as your IRA custodian, with investment discretion over the account passed to the manager.

Many brokerage houses offer "wrap-fee" programs that bundle the entire money-management process into one basic cost. Minimum account sizes are usually in the $50,000 to $100,000 area. Fees for this type of program begin at 3 percent per year of the assets under management, declining as the amount of money under management increases or as you negotiate a discount on the fee. Of course, if your custodian charges any IRA maintenance fees, those may be separate.

For this flat fee, brokerage houses maintain short lists of preferred, independent money managers who have passed through a rigorous search process to weed out weaker organizations. Your account can be placed with any of the managers on his list, and your account is carried at the brokerage firm.

You should receive confirmations of purchase and sale, monthly statements, and quarterly performance reports. And your broker should advise you when problems have surfaced with that manager. All your commissions should be part of that wrap fee. Indeed, there should be no other costs associated with the program. Your IRA pays the fee, and you can't reimburse it for the expense, nor can you deduct it on your tax return. Since your broker receives part of the fee you pay, his compensation is tied directly to the success of your account. If the account grows in a satisfactory way, he'll keep your business and his fee income will increase.

This eliminates the inherent (and often much overstated) conflict between you and your broker when she is compensated on a commission basis for executing a trade. However, you should be alert to signs that your broker merely placed your money with a manager and then forgot about it.

Does your broker communicate with you regularly about your accounts? Does she review your investment goals and risk tolerance on a regular basis to ensure that you continue to have the proper manager? Is she knowledgeable about the manager when you have questions? If the answer is no to these questions, you may not be getting full value for the fees you are paying.

Wrap-fee accounts have their critics. Some say that the fees are too high to ensure market-beating performance. Others feel that they are merely mutual funds in disguise, offering a snobbish cachet at an expensive price. Managers would argue that an individually managed account offers an insulation from other investors.

Second, I don't think people are impressed by the notion of having a money manager. They are much more sophisticated and hard-nosed about such things. They want a money manager because they like the idea of a specific group with a good track record handling their money for them. The flat-fee arrangement allows them to select on a level playing field: Portfolio turnover isn't a cost consideration. Compared to the commissions most investors pay to manage their own stock portfolios, even using discount brokers, a wrap fee can be a bargain.

The tremendous popularity of wrap-fee programs is a testament to the value they offer. The flaw can lie in the expertise of the broker or consultant recommending the manager. If he isn't sensitive to the proper matching of you and your manager, if he overstates the possibilities and understates the risk, a managed account can be as difficult an experience as an investor can have. You can lose money and pay a fee to do it.

Finally, hiring a money manager engages you and your advisors in the right kinds of discussion; how much risk to run, how to run it, and with how much money. You discuss overall philosophy and strategy. You don't get bogged down in analyzing specific stocks or short-term considerations. The process keeps you focused on the long-term goals you have set. You more closely control your risk by the type of manager you hire.

And you have a much better opportunity to realize your goals through his market performance than through your own. An IRA account needs strong investment talent to help ensure good long-term returns. It is often deceptively easy (and dangerous!) to engage in clumsy speculation with an IRA, especially if the funds aren't needed for many years. A good money manager avoids that kind of behavior and helps focus you on long-term results.

SUMMARY

Finding good professionals to assist you gives you an advantage that will eventually be measured in more money for you and your family. The proper handling of a lump sum requires a careful navigation of a myriad of tax, investment, and planning issues. Missteps can be costly and, if repeated, will affect your income and the happiness of your retirement.

An accountant can be indispensable in helping you to minimize your tax obligations. Working with a good financial planner, investment manager, or financial consultant, your accountant and investment advisor form your basic advisory team, working together each year in a coordinated way to minimize tax and maximize the return you earn for the risk you're willing to take.

A good estate-planning attorney will help fashion the proper mix of trusts, wills, and estate tax strategies that should result in greater inheritance for your children and other beneficiaries.

These professionals can also assist in finding the right IRA custodian (there are differences) as well as whether or not additional professionals, such as independent money management, should be brought to bear on your behalf.

A great deal of competition exists today among professionals offering these kinds of advisory services, and so fees have moved inevitably down. Given the heavy burden of taxation and the potential for mismanagement in the investment arena, the cost to retain professionals is certainly one that can be justified by the potential for increased return and lower tax burden.

Finally, the creation of a personal financial team can give great comfort to you and your family, when illness may prevent your full concentration, or your demise leaves a large gap for your spouse to fill.

CHAPTER FIVE

Taking Income from an IRA

There are many tax rules for taking income from the IRA account, and they are complicated. Remember that we divide IRAs into two types—Traditional IRAs and the new Roth IRAs. (Traditional IRAs include Rollover IRAs and tax-deductible, contributory IRAs). To help you sort through them, we need to divide income recipients into four groups, sorted by age at the time the distribution is taken and by the status of the recipient:

1. IRA owners under age 59-1/2
2. IRA owners between age 59-1/2 and 70-1/2
3. IRA owners over age 70-1/2
4. Beneficiaries of a deceased IRA account owner

Regardless of age there are a few basics that affect everyone.

We have already learned that income from a Roth IRA is exempt from tax under certain circumstances. Since the funds were taxed before being placed in the Roth, and since the Roth allows for tax-free withdrawal if the funds have been in the account for more than five years, the following discussion on tax treatment refers to Traditional, not Roth IRA's. Remember, that in a Traditional IRA, money going in is not taxed and the earnings grow tax-deferred. However, upon distribution, the funds are taxed.

Any distribution taken from a Traditional IRA and not rolled over to another Traditional IRA or qualified employer plan is taxable income. If you take out cash, the amount of the cash is the taxable amount. If you take out securities, the fair-market value of the securities on the date of distribution is the taxable amount.

EXAMPLE   You take 100 shares of stock out of your Traditional IRA as a distribution. Your IRA paid $10 per share. The stock is worth $15 per share on the day you take it out. Your taxable income is $1,500, not $1,000. (Your new cost on the stock for tax purposes is now $15.)

The income you take must be reported on your tax return for the year in which you took it. If you file quarterly income tax estimates, your Traditional IRA distributions might affect your quarterly estimates.

I can't emphasize enough that you can't beat this income tax bill. No matter what you do, the simple fact is that by taking the money out of your Traditional IRA, you have to pay income tax on it.

TIP   In discussing age when dealing with IRA accounts, the measure is the day on which you turn that age: You are 59 years old on June 15. Since you will turn 59-1/2 years old on December 15, that is the date on which you are age 59-1/2 for IRA purposes.

A TRADITIONAL IRA IS A TAX-DEFERRED ACCOUNT

It is important to remember that a Traditional IRA is a tax-deferred account. You do not have to pay current income tax as a result of any activity within the IRA.

EXAMPLES   You earn $2,000 interest in your Traditional IRA. No income tax is due. You sell 200 shares of stock for a $1,000 profit in your Traditional IRA. No income tax is due.

Your Traditional IRA receives a $50 stock dividend. No income tax is due.

The only time you do pay income tax on a Traditional IRA is when you withdraw money from it:

> **EXAMPLE**   Your Traditional IRA earns $12,000 in interest and capital gains. You withdraw $1,500. You owe income tax only on the $1,500.

By the same token, you can't deduct a loss if it occurs in your Traditional IRA. Nor can you claim a credit for any foreign tax withheld on foreign stock dividends.

> **TIP**   If you are considering buying a foreign stock in your IRA, you can generally assume that a 15 percent foreign withholding tax will be paid before you get the dividend. So reduce the dividend by 15 percent to find your net yield, For instance, if a stock pays a 5 percent dividend, you can expect to receive 4.25 percent net (5 percent less 15 percent withholding). Check with your broker if you are unsure about a particular investment.

Buying tax-free bonds in your IRA will not circumvent these rules. No matter what the source of the funds in the IRA, it is all taxable when it comes out.

If You Are Between Ages 59-1/2 and 70-1/2

If your age falls in this range, you can pretty much do what you want with Traditional IRA distributions. You can take as much or as little as you desire from the account. You have no requirements to meet about taking income, so do as you please. (However, see the five-year rule if you begin distributions prior to age 59-1/2 under one of the premature-distribution exceptions.)

Generally, people take distributions based on how much money they actually need to spend, with one eye kept on their overall tax bite. A little bit of planning goes a long way. Things like taxation of Social Security benefits and other income sources should be taken into consideration before taking IRA income. Remember, IRA income is added in to compute whether your Social Security benefits are taxable.

TIP   Some states allow tax exclusions from state income tax on IRA distributions. Regulations vary from state to state, so check carefully. You may not have to pay state income tax on some or all of your IRA distributions.

Some people take monthly income from the IRA, and some take an occasional distribution to pay for a special vacation or a new car. It is entirely up to you.

If You Are Over Age 70-1/2

While the government will allow you to defer taxes on your Traditional IRA to help you build a secure retirement nest egg, they won't let you defer the tax forever. After all, if this really is retirement money, you should be spending some of it.

The way they force you to recognize the income tax you have deferred is by requiring you to begin distributions once you reach age 70-1/2. At that point, you must begin withdrawals according to a specific schedule. One way this is calculated is by dividing your life expectancy into the value of all your Traditional IRA accounts on December 31 of the prior year. You can also use a joint life expectancy of your age and the age of your Traditional IRA beneficiary to compute the minimum required distribution.

There are a couple of definitions you need here to proceed. First, the required beginning date (RBD) is April 1 of the year following the year in which you turn 70-1/2 years old.

EXAMPLE   You turn age 70-1/2 in December 1998. Your required beginning date is April 1, 1999.

There are two methods you can use to compute your minimum annual distribution; the term-certain method and the annual-recalculation method (see Table 5.1). In the term-certain method, you compute your life expectancy from the IRS tables and subtract one from that number each year to arrive at the number you will divide into your account value at the end of the preceding year:

TABLE 5.1 Computation of Minimum Annual Distribution

Age	Term Certain	Annual Recalculation
70	16	16
71	15	15.3
72	14	14.6
73	13	13.9

EXAMPLE   You turn 70-1/2 years old. According to the tables, your life expectancy is 16 years. You need to withdraw 1/16 of your Traditional IRA the first year, then 1/15 the following year, and so forth.

If you use the annual-recalculation method, you go to the tables each year to figure your life expectancy.

EXAMPLE   The first year, you must withdraw 1/16 of the account, given your life expectancy of 16 years, The second year, the tables give your life expectancy as 15.3 years. You divide 15.3 into the value of the account at the end of year one.

In either case you divide your life expectancy into the account value, but depending on the method you get a different life expectancy.

You will see later on that the term-certain method will be our preferred method to use, and that there is a big difference in the results achieved between the two.

Once you select a method, you cannot change it later on to slow down the minimum requirement. It is an irrevocable election. Finally, keep in mind that all these calculations refer to the minimum amount you must withdraw; you can always take out more than the minimum.

ROTH RULES

Unlike a Traditional IRA, funds withdrawn from a Roth IRA are not taxable, if certain rules have been met.

If You Are Over Age 59-1/2

The rules are quite simple if you are over 59-1/2. The distribution will not be subject to income tax if you have held the account for five years.

If you haven't held the account for five years, but are over 59-1/2, any distributions in excess of your contributions to the Roth IRA will be subject to ordinary income tax, just as a Traditional IRA is. "Held the account" is counted from the year of the contribution—a contribution made in 1998 must be held until 2003 in order for the earnings to be withdrawn without tax.

If You Are Under Age 59-1/2

If you are under 59-1/2, and have held your Roth IRA for five years or more, your withdrawal will not be subject to a 10 percent penalty if you become disabled or die.

If you are under 59-1/2 and have held your Roth IRA for five years or more, withdrawals for college expenses are not subject to the 10 percent premature withdrawal penalty for you, your spouse, your child, or even your grandchild; but they are subject to ordinary income taxes. Be careful! This benefit can be reduced or eliminated if tax-free scholarships are available to the recipient.

Otherwise, if you are under 59-1/2, the withdrawal in excess of your contribution is taxable and the 10 percent penalty for early withdrawal applies.

The 10 percent penalty does not apply if you are using one of the annuitizing income formulas that I discuss later in this chapter.

Finally, you can withdraw up to $10,000 for the purchase of a first-time principal residence. You're a first-time homeowner for this purpose if you haven't owned an interest in a principal residence for the past two years.

There are a couple of other medical exceptions to the 10 percent penalty if you are under 59-1/2. For instance, the penalty is waived if the distribution is used for medical expenses that exceed 7-1/2 percent of your adjusted gross income. Similarly, distributions for purchase of medical insurance, once you have passed 12 weeks of unemployment compensation, are also exempt from the penalty. However, ordinary income tax applies in both situations.

Remember, however, that distributions are always tax-free up to the amount of your contributions, then taxed.

> **EXAMPLE**   Mary, age 52, contributes a lump sum of $120,000 to her Roth IRA. Four years later, the Roth IRA has grown to $170,000. She then withdraws $130,000 from the account. Her taxable income is $10,000. The following year, any money she withdraws will be taxable because she has used up her original $120,000 after-tax contribution.

If You Are Over Age 70-1/2

Once you are over 70-1/2, the old minimum distribution requirements do not apply to a Roth IRA, but they remain in force for Traditional IRAs.

MULTIPLE IRAS WITH DIFFERENT BENEFICIARIES

If you have more than one Traditional IRA and the beneficiaries are different, you need to use different life expectancies for each Traditional IRA. Remember that the calculation for each Traditional IRA is done separately, even though all the money may be taken out of one account.

> **EXAMPLE**   You are 70-1/2 years old and have two Traditional IRAs. IRA X was worth $100,000 on December 31 of the prior year, and your son, age 45, is the beneficiary of the account. IRA Y was worth $200,000, and the beneficiary is your wife, age 68. There are several ways you could compute your minimum required distribution, (Use the life expectancy tables found in IRS Publication 939.)
>
> Your life expectancy: 16.0 years
>
> You and your son: 26.2 years (if your beneficiary is more than 10 years younger, you must use an age no more than 10 years less

than yours. In this case, we had to use an assumption of age 60 for the son.)

You and your wife: 21.5 years

Required from IRA X:

Using your life expectancy: $6,250 ($100,000 / 16 = $6,250)

Joint with your son: $3,816 ($100,000 / 26.2 = $3,816)

Required from IRA Y:

Using your life expectancy: $12,500 ($200,000 / 16.0 = $12,500)

Joint with your wife: $9,302 ($200,000 /21.5 = $9,302)

Required total:

IRA X: $ 3,816 or $ 6,250

IRA Y: $9,302 or $12,500

Total: $13,118 or $18,750

Since this is a minimum required distribution, you should compute the distribution requirement using joint life expectancies. This establishes a lower minimum requirement. You are still free to withdraw more than the minimum. Whatever the amount, it can be taken from both accounts or from one account. Also note that in doing the computation it is your age on your birthday in the year in which you turn 70-1/2 years old that is important.

EXAMPLE   You turn 70-1/2 years old in May 1998. You will turn 71 In November. You use age 71 in computing your life expectancy,

You must make the first year's distribution by April 1 of the following year. Thereafter, it must be completed before the end of the calendar year.

EXAMPLE   You are age 70-1/2 in December 1998. You must make your required 1998 Traditional IRA distribution by April 1, 1999. You must also make 1999's distribution by December 31, 1999. So in the first year you may have to make two years' worth of distributions if you delay the first one beyond the end of the year. Both distributions, if taken in 1999, are entered on your 1999 tax return. The income tax is due by April 15, 2000, or perhaps earlier if you are on quarterly estimated payments.

If you delay your first year's distribution into the next year, this reduces the amount that you take into account in computing the next year's distribution.

EXAMPLE You withdraw $2,325.58 by April 1, 1999. The value of the account at year end 1998 is $50,000. The account value to use for the required 1999 distribution is the December 31, 1998, value of $50,000 minus the $2,325.58 taken out as the 1998 distribution, or $47,674.42.

You are allowed to recalculate your life expectancies each year when using a joint life expectancy with your spouse. This has the effect of keeping the required distribution lower than if you simply subtract one year from the first year you began distributions.

In the preceding example, you take $2,325.58 from the account. The following year you recompute your life expectancy for a 71 year old with a 69-year-old beneficiary. The new life expectancy is 20.7 years (using the annual recalculation method). Alternatively, you could have subtracted one year from your original life expectancy of 21.5 years to arrive at 20.5 years (the term-certain method). Assuming the account is still at $50,000:

20.7 years divided into $50,000 equals a requirement of $2,415.46.

20.5 years divided into $50,000 equals a requirement of $2,439.02.

However, the annual recalculation method can have devastating tax consequences on your heirs. You should read the section later in this chapter having to do with the treatment of Traditional IRA distributions by heirs if the account holder passed away after age 70-1/2. You will find that the term-certain method, while increasing the minimum distribution amount each year, will also allow your heirs to postpone receiving the entire IRA account and paying a heavy tax bill. If your beneficiary is not your spouse, further rules apply:

1. You must subtract one year from the first life expectancy computed, then look up what age approximates that life expectancy, then use that age to compute a new joint life expectancy. (Who ever said life was easy?)

    EXAMPLE   Same facts as above, but the beneficiary is your 68-year-old brother instead of your spouse. The second year you would look at the original, single life expectancy for a 68 year old, which according to the tables is 17.6 years. Since one year has passed, you would reduce this to 16.6 years. Now look at the unisex IRS life-expectancy table and you can see that the closest age to a life expectancy of 16.6 years is age 69. You would then use your age of 71 and your beneficiary's age of 69 to recompute the new joint life expectancy.

2. Let's say you're thinking about naming your 12-year-old grandson as your beneficiary, since your joint life expectancy is decades long. That won't work. No matter how young your beneficiary, the IRS will not allow you to use an age more than ten years younger.

    EXAMPLE   Your sister, who is 57 years old, is your beneficiary when you turn 70-1/2 years old. In computing joint life expectancy, you must assume her age as 60, since she is more than ten years your junior.

3. What if you have more than one Traditional IRA account? You must do the calculations separately for each account, using the respective beneficiaries for each account and computing separate life expectancies. Your required distribution is the sum of all the separate IRA calculations. Even though you need to compute the distribution separately for each account, you have no restrictions or requirements on selecting the account or accounts from which the money must be taken.

    Will you ever outlive these accounts if you distribute according to the minimum distribution rules? Not likely. Following the rules and recomputing life expectancies each year will not deplete the accounts until after age 100. You can expect, however, that if your beneficiary is roughly the same age, you will begin to dip into the principal as well as taking all the income by age 77 or 78.

TERM CERTAIN VERSUS ANNUAL RECALCULATION

In computing the life expectancy factor that can be divided into the account balance, there are two methods that can be used, term certain and annual recalculation. In addition, a more complex version, called the hybrid method, combines the two.

In the term-certain calculation, you reduce the life expectancy factor by one each year, and in the annual recalculation method, you take a new life expectancy each year from the tables. In the hybrid method, you elect annual recalculation for yourself and term certain for your spouse. Table 5.2 shows what the differences look like for a 71-year-old account owner and his 64-year-old spouse with a $100,000 account earning 7 percent per year. Assume that the first distribution is made on April 1 of the second year. Each subsequent distribution is on December 31 of that year.

Remember, you can use either the term-certain or the annual-recalculation method if the beneficiary is your spouse, but you should use only the term-certain method if your beneficiary is not your spouse.

> **TIP**   Elect the term-certain method in writing to your IRA custodian prior to beginning distributions and save a copy of the letter. Should you die before making the second year's distributions, there will be proof that you intended the term-certain method.

THE HYBRID METHOD

The hybrid method can work in a few situations. If your spouse-beneficiary is in poor health and you are concerned that you will be the survivor and you have children or other heirs that would benefit from continued tax deferral, the hybrid method may work for you. Warning!

TABLE 5.2 Term Certain vs. Annual Recalculation

Ages	Term Certain Method Life Expectancy	Term Certain Required Distribution	Term Certain Remaining Account Value	Annual Recalculation Method Life Expectancy	Annual Recalculation Required Distribution	Annual Recalculation Remaining Account Value
71/64	23.4	$4,273	$ 95,727	23.4	$4,273	$ 95,727
72/65	22.4	$4,274	$ 98,153	22.5	$4,254	$ 98,173
73/66	21.4	$4,586	$ 100,437	21.6	$4,545	$100,500
74/67	20.4	$4,923	$ 102,544	20.8	$4,831	$102,704

The hybrid method is quite complex and so you should take the idea to a CPA or other tax specialist for evaluation in your particular situation.

In the hybrid method, you mix together the two different calculations for life expectancy. You use annual recalculation for yourself, and the term-certain method for your spouse beneficiary. Your annual distributions will look a lot like the term-certain method, but you pick up a new benefit—your payouts are not accelerated because of the death of your spouse. Using the term-certain method for your spouse accomplished this.

Upon your death, your heirs (typically your children, although they need not be) can continue to receive many years of payouts for the single, term-certain period of your spouse—an immediate distribution is not necessary.

> **EXAMPLE**   You are 70 and your wife, 65. You choose the hybrid method. Your joint life expectancy is 23.1. In subsequent years, her single life expectancy factor at age 65 (20.0) is reduced by one for each calendar year that has elapsed. The age, rounded if necessary to the higher age, is then located on the life-expectancy table, which corresponds to her applicable life-expectancy, and this adjusted age is used to determine the joint life-expectancy factor for purposes of calculating required minimum distributions. After five years, her life expectancy factor is 15.0 (20.0 - 5.0 years). If she dies after five years, the IRA can continue to pay benefits to the husband for 17.8 years (the hybrid factor). If the husband were to die after five years also, the IRA could continue to exist and pay benefits to children or other heirs for 15 years (her single term certain). The relevant numbers are summarized in Table 5.3. Note that "RMD" refers to required minimum distribution.

As you can see, the hybrid method is complex. Approach it with caution and thoroughly understand it before using it. Seek qualified help before deciding.

If You Are Under Age 59-1/2

If the rules for those over age 70-1/2 sound complicated, get ready. Distributions for those under age 59-1/2 can be even more complex.

TABLE 5.3 The Hybrid Method

His Age	Her Age	Her Single Term Certain	Her Adjusted Age	Hybrid Factor for RMD	Term Certain for RMD
70	65	20.0	65	23.1	23.1
71	66	19.0	67	21.7	22.1
72	67	18.0	68	20.8	21.1
73	68	17.0	69	20.0	20.1
74	69	16.0	70	19.1	19.1
75	70	15.0	72	17.8	18.1

A basic rule that governs our discussion here is that distributions taken before age 59-1/2 are subject not only to normal income tax, but to an additional 10 percent penalty as well.

> You are 48 years old and need $2,000 from your IRA account. You take $2,000 as a distribution. Not only do you have to pay federal and possibly state income taxes on the $2,000, but the federal government assesses an additional tax penalty of $200.

You are being penalized because, by taking the distribution at an early age, you are not treating this money as true retirement money. The government defines this by using your age at distribution. Distributions prior to age 59-1/2 are considered early distributions subject to tax penalty.

So far as this goes, the rules are quite simple: Wait until age 59-1/2 or face a tax penalty; however, exceptions to this rule exist, allowing you to take distributions prior to age 59-1/2 without tax penalty. The rules are complex, but considering the amount of tax penalty they can save they are well worth learning.

Before we get to those calculations, we need to examine whether or not you should convert your Traditional IRA to a Roth IRA.

CONVERTING TO A ROTH

Whether or not you decide to convert is a fairly straightforward, yet complicated calculation (as you can see in IRA mathematics, complications are the norm). Let's try to give you some basic advice to guide you in your calculations.

If you convert to a Roth IRA, you have to empty out your Traditional IRA (or you can partially convert a Traditional IRA) and place the assets in a Roth IRA. You are allowed to pay the tax from the Traditional IRA proceeds, without the 10 percent tax penalty, or you can dip into your other savings, to pay the tax, thereby converting the entire amount to a Roth IRA. The calculation as to whether or not you should convert, then, revolves around your ability to earn more, over the long haul, by not having further taxes, offset by the tax bill you pay today.

Now, it should be mentioned that if you can't replace the tax money you are paying to convert to a Roth, conversion makes no sense. You need to replace the tax money with other savings and then, and only then, is it worth doing. Generally speaking, the younger you are, the more compelling the case to convert to a Roth IRA. I have found in my work that individuals over 50 taking full income available from their IRA, generally should not convert to a Roth IRA and those under 50 can consider it. For instance, if you are 40 years old and have a Traditional IRA worth $200,000, you would pay about $80,000 in taxes on the Roth, leaving you with $120,000 to put into the Roth. By pulling that $80,000 from savings, you can roll $200,000 into the Roth. Eventually, when the account is worth, say, $1,000,000, you have avoided a $400,000 tax bill by converting to a Roth.

Now the conversion makes sense, because in a Roth IRA you can invest in normally taxable bonds and earn, say, 7 percent. Because the Roth grows tax-free, you have, in effect, created a tax-free bond at a 7 percent rate, when real municipals would be yielding only 5 percent if taxables were at 7 percent. So, you can pick up 2 percent per year in additional return.

It should also be mentioned that if you hit several years of negative or flat returns, however, the benefits of the Roth begin to diminish. Fortunately, most advisors and product purveyors have software that can compute Roth IRA calculations and give you some guidance on conversion. Again, if you are unsure, do not convert.

Similarly, you can avoid capital-gains taxes in a Roth IRA so instead of paying taxes outside the IRA on a capital gain, you eliminate them inside a Roth IRA.

If You Are Under Age 59-1/2 in a Traditional IRA

To avoid the pre-59-1/2 tax penalty for premature withdrawals, you need to take your distributions in a way that illustrates you are treating them as retirement income. You need to create an income stream that mimics a lifetime annuity, sometimes called periodic payments. When you create this stream, you must continue to take your distributions on a specific schedule for five years, or to age 59-1/2, whichever comes last.

> **EXAMPLES**　　You are 51 years old. You wish to avoid the 10 percent pre-59-1/2 tax penalty on IRA distributions. You must follow your computed amounts each year until you are 59-1/2 years old.
>
> Your brother is 57. He wishes to do the same thing, He must continue his distribution schedule until he is 62 years old, since five years comes after age 59-1/2.

If you vary this schedule anytime before you are scheduled to complete it, the 10 percent tax is applied retroactively to each year's distributions already taken.

> **EXAMPLE**　　You begin your pre-59-1/2 distribution schedule at age 51. At age 55, you stop all distributions, or you vary the schedule in some way. You are assessed a 10 percent tax penalty on each distribution since age 51.

Given the tax penalties involved, it is not practical to vary the stream once you begin, so think carefully before doing so.

THREE METHODS OF COMPUTING DISTRIBUTIONS

The IRS allows three different methods to compute your distributions. You might want to review the life-expectancy methods presented earlier in this chapter before proceeding.

The First Method: Minimum Distribution

The first calculation follows along the lines of the post-70-1/2 distribution calculations. You use your life expectancy, or your joint life expectancy with your beneficiary to compute the calculation.

EXAMPLE   You and your spouse-beneficiary are both 55. Your IRA is worth $125,000. You look up your joint life expectancy in IRS Table V and find that it is 34.4 years. You divide 34.4 into the value of your IRA as of the prior December 31 to compute your current year's required distribution ($125,000 ÷ 34.4 = $3,633.72). Alternatively, you could have used your life expectancy only. That would have the effect of reducing your life expectancy to 28.6 years ($125,000 ÷ 28.6 = $4,370,63).

Each year you recompute your life expectancy to find your new figure, dividing that into the IRA account value at the end of the prior year. You can see from the preceding example that you would have had to distribute roughly 3 percent of the account value at age 55.

The Second Method: Level Income Amortized

The IRS allows a second method to compute your distribution. You may apply not only your life expectancy factor, but also a "reasonable" rate of interest in doing the calculations.

Assuming a reasonable rate of return, how much must be withdrawn each year to deplete the account over the life expectancy of the account holder and his or her beneficiary? In order to do this calculation you must seek out annuity tables that build into them various investment rates of return. There is some latitude in this calculation because the operating definition is "reasonable" rate of return.

Annuity tables incorporating these calculations are readily available in any bookstore or library and can be calculated on some calculators or computers. Basically, you will find that they allow you to pull out all the interest you are earning and a little bit more.

> **EXAMPLE**   Same as preceding facts, but you incorporate a 7 percent interest rate since that is what you are currently earning on the account. Using this rate plus your joint life expectancy would produce a required distribution of $9,622, or about 7.7 percent. To do the calculation, you go to an annuity table, and using 34.4 years, the value of your account, and 7 percent, you compute your annual distribution. This amount remains the same, year after year.

How do you select a "reasonable" rate of return? If you have a bond-only account, you can use the actual interest rate you are currently earning. If your investment returns vary considerably from year to year, you can find out what the Pension Benefit Guaranty Corporation rate is and use that as your rate assumption. The key is "reasonable." If you're earning 6 percent on your account and you use 10 percent in the calculations, the burden of proof would be on you to show why 10 percent was reasonable.

So, if you need to live off all the income the account is generating, use this method. However, be warned! Whatever method you select, you must continue to use it. You can't start by using the life-expectancy-only method, then switch to the life-expectancy-plus-interest-rate method.

A variation to this is that you can use life-expectancy tables published by the insurance industry. Called the UP-1984 tables, they have the effect of slightly shortening your life-expectancy numbers.

The Third Method: Level Income Annuity

The third method entails dividing your account value by an annuity factor taken from any generally accepted mortality table. The annuity factor can be a monthly or an annual factor. It is a number that represents the net present value of an annuity commencing in that particular year as though computed over the account holder's life expectancy. This calculation, while slightly different from the second method, produces an annual distribution amount slightly more than the interest you are probably earning on the account. In the example we have been using, our 55-year-old couple with a $125,000 account would take out $11,120 per year.

In Table 5.4 the three distribution methods are placed side by side for easy comparison of the annual income provided.

The assumptions in Table 5.4 are an IRA account of $125,000, 7 percent interest rate, account holder and spouse age 55.

TABLE 5.4 Annual Required Minimum Distributions

Age	Life Expectancy	Minimum Distribution	Level Income (Amortized)	Level Income (Annuity)
55	34.4	$3,634	$9,622	$11,120
56	33.4	$3,933	$9,622	$11,120
57	32.4	$4,257	$9,622	$11,120
58	31.4	$4,609	$9,622	$11,120
59	30.4	$4,990	$9,622	$11,120
60	29.4	$5,403	$9,622	$11,120

The services of a qualified tax advisor are very important in doing these computations correctly.

WHICH IRAS HAVE TO BE INCLUDED IN YOUR CALCULATIONS?

Unlike the rules for those over age 70-1/2, you do not have to include each IRA in the calculations (IRAs Private Letter Ruling 8946045). But if you do include the IRA, you must make a withdrawal from that IRA. Each IRA is treated as a separate calculation.

EXAMPLE   You have three IRAs. A is worth $100,000, B, $25,000, and C, $50,000. You decide to include only B and C in your calculations. You must compute the distributions from the two

IRAs independently and make a distribution from each, You need not make a distribution from the $100,000 IRA.

If you are contemplating distributions to begin in the future, you should adjust the amount of money in your IRAs so that your distributions match your requirements. Set up one IRA as your "income" IRA where your distributions will originate. The other IRAs can be invested toward growth and left on the shelf to grow.

There you have it. The only other caution to offer is that periodic distributions make more sense than do sporadic ones within any given year. If you're going to take, say, $24,000 from your account, take a single distribution of $24,000, or $6,000 each quarter, or $2,000 each month. If you are claiming that this is retirement income, it should look like it. While there is no specific requirement that you do it this way, it certainly can't hurt your case and will help you plan your income and household budget on a regular basis.

You may have heard something about "excess accumulation" or "excess distribution" taxes from IRAs. These were both 15 percent tax penalties for accumulating too much in an IRA, or distributing inflation-adjusted amounts that exceeded $150,000 in any one year. Both of these taxes were repealed.

BENEFICIARIES OF A DECEASED IRA ACCOUNT OWNER

The rules for beneficiaries can also be quite complicated. Once again, your status (spouse or nonspouse) as well as the actions of the account owner before he or she passed away are important in determining what you can do.

As the spouse-beneficiary of the deceased IRA account owner you can enjoy the same tax privileges. As the beneficiary, you can either pay income tax on the IRA distribution or you can roll it over to your own IRA account and continue the tax deferral. You could, for instance, elect to take the funds out over the five-year period discussed later. Overwhelmingly, spouse-beneficiaries elect to roll over the IRA to their own and continue to enjoy the tax-shelter benefits of the IRA.

TIP   This doesn't happen automatically. You need to inform the IRA custodian that you wish to roll over the IRA to your own account. Then you must open a new IRA, name your beneficiaries, and establish the new account.

You can take income from the account or not, as you choose. As the new IRA account owner, all the regular tax rules that we have explained so far apply to you. There are, however, a couple of wrinkles that you need to know about. They have to do with your spouse's age, when he passed away, and what he was doing about income from the account.

What If You Don't Roll Over the Account?

If you do not wish to accept your spouse's IRA as a rollover into your own, you must begin taking distributions beginning in the year after her death and continue until the frozen IRA account is depleted. If your spouse was over 70-1/2 when she died and had begun her post-70-1/2 distribution schedule, you must withdraw the money at a rate at least as fast as she would have taken it. Basically, this means that you would follow her distribution schedule and compute it as though she were still alive, using her date of birth, and yours, if she elected a joint life-expectancy calculation.

If your spouse had not yet reached age 70-1/2, you have the option of withdrawing the money over your life expectancy, a calculation similar to the post-age 70-1/2 life-expectancy-only method. (Again, use the term certain method, subtracting one from your life expectancy each year.) You divide the value of the account at the prior year end by your life expectancy. That is your required distribution. Alternatively, you can elect to take the money out over five years and deplete the account entirely. The five-year clock begins ticking the year after your spouse's death.

If you choose to receive your distributions based on your life expectancy, you must begin by the December 31 of the year after your spouse's death.

It is the overwhelming choice of spouse-beneficiaries to roll over their IRA inheritance and continue tax deferral. The only reason(s) to elect one of the more rapid methods of distribution might be to take possession of the funds to gift them out of your estate.

If you are a nonspouse beneficiary, your options are more limited.

First, you cannot roll over your IRA inheritance to your own IRA. To do so would make the entire distribution immediately taxable. However, since you probably would want to continue the tax benefits of an IRA, you can have your distribution placed in a frozen, conduit IRA. The account is titled with reference to the deceased account owner.

> **EXAMPLE**   Your father, John Jones, passes away. As his daughter, you are the beneficiary of his IRA. You open a new IRA titled:
>
> Sally Jones IRA
>
> As Beneficiary of John Jones IRA, Deceased
>
> International Bank as IRA Custodian

The language will vary somewhat among different custodians, but the key point is that the account references the source of the funds, clearly identifying it as a frozen conduit account created as the result of the death of the account owner.

If the IRA Owner Died Prior to His Required Beginning Date

A nonspouse beneficiary can elect either the five-year rule or an exception to the five-year rule (term certain) if the account holder died prior to his required beginning date. Unlike a spousal beneficiary, you do not have the option of postponing distributions.

If the plan allows distributions over your life expectancy, you can apply your life expectancy each year to the account value at the end of the prior year and compute your required distribution by dividing your life expectancy into the value of the account at prior year end. You must continue to do so each year for the rest of your life or when the account is exhaused.

Each year you reduce your life expectancy by one year to compute your new minimum distribution amount.

> **EXAMPLE**   Your father dies on June 1, 1998. Your birthday in 1998 puts you at age 45. Since you must begin distributions by December 31, 1999, you use your age, 46. The IRS table shows a life expectancy of 36.8 years. So, in 1999, you divide the value of the account as of December 31, 1998, by 36.8. In 2000, you divide the value of the account as of December 31, 1999, by 35.8, and so on.

This is a minimum requirement. You can exceed the minimum in any one year, and you can do so from time to time without following any particular schedule. Just make sure you take out the minimum amount each year.

> **TIP**   If you are going to use the term-certain method, send a letter to your IRA custodian prior to beginning distributions, informing them that you are using this method. If you die without selecting the term-certain method, the IRA plan document would be consulted to establish distribution method to your beneficiaries.

The Five-Year Method

The other distribution method, the five-year option, requires you to take the entire account over a five-year period ending on December 31 of the fifth year following the year of death of the account owner. You must elect the method by December 31 of the year following the IRA owner's death.

You do not have to take equal amounts each year, but as a practical matter you will want to make each year's distributions relatively equal. This will avoid a particularly large income in one specific year that would throw your income into a higher tax bracket.

This also means that you could take nothing during the first four years, and then take everything in the fifth year. However, since a large distribution could have adverse tax consequences, it is important to consult with your accountant about when to take the distributions. The calculation will take into account your current and anticipated income levels, the value of tax-deferred growth in the IRA, and the effect of paying out tax payments if the money is taken immediately.

Remember that you do not need to take your distributions in cash. If you find some of the investments particularly attractive, you can take the asset as a distribution, applying the fair-market value on the date of distribution as the amount of the distribution.

> **TIP**   Be careful with the ticking clock. If you don't take all the money out by the end of the five-year period, a 50 percent tax penalty applies to the remaining money in the account. If you make a mistake, the IRS can grant a waiver if you can prove that a reasonable error took place and reasonable steps were taken to remedy the shortfall. Don't take that chance.

If an IRA Owner Dies After the Required Beginning Date

If the IRA owner died after April 1 of the year following the year in which she attained age 70-1/2, then the distribution schedule must take her life expectancy into consideration. This is the key difference from a death prior to this date. In addition, the distributions must be done at least as rapidly as the account holder would have taken them if she had lived.

The calculation method is similar to the others discussed in that you divide the account value by a life expectancy. However, the life expectancy used must be one of four:

1. The life expectancy of the IRA owner, had she lived, and a designated beneficiary

2. The life expectancy of the IRA owner, had she lived

3. The term-certain method using the IRA owner's life expectancy, had she lived

4. The term-certain method using the IRA owner's life expectancy, had she lived, and a designated beneficiary

Once you select the method to use, the choice is irrevocable and can't be changed in later years.

Keep in mind that if the IRA owner had already begun distributions using the term-certain method, you would have to continue that method. That includes the estate, if the IRA was passed into the estate.

> **EXAMPLE** Your father passes away at age 72. He had been taking his distributions using the term-certain method, beginning with 1/16 at age 70-1/2 and 1/15 of the account at age 71. You must now withdraw 1/14 as a minimum distribution, then 1/13, and so forth.

Again, this is the minimum required distribution. You can take more than the minimum amount each year.

> **TIP** The tax penalty for not distributing enough money is heavy: A penalty equal to 50 percent of the shortage is levied, in addition to ordinary income tax. Be careful!

Once you attain your required beginning date (April 1 of the year following your attaining age 70-1/2) the distribution of your IRA to your heirs is irrevocably linked to the same method of distribution and your life expectancy as if you had lived.

> **TIP** Always select the term-certain method for distribution from your IRA. This will preserve the right of your beneficiaries to continue distributions over a several-year span.

The key difference between a spouse beneficiary and a non-spouse beneficiary is that a spouse retains the right to roll over the IRA to his or her own IRA and continues to defer all taxes and delay distributions.

When There Are Multiple Beneficiaries

When there are multiple IRA beneficiaries, each beneficiary can elect his or her own treatment. If three children are the beneficiaries, each can roll his or her share into a frozen IRA. One may elect to take the money out over five years, while the other two may elect distributions over their lifetimes.

TIP   If you have multiple beneficiaries, including your spouse, set up separate IRA accounts—one for your spouse and one for your children. In this way you can tailor the more conservative investments for your wife's IRA and the more aggressive for your children's. On your death, your wife automatically inherits the conservative, income-producing account, while your children inherit the more aggressive, growth-oriented account. If all your IRA assets are in one account, the executor of your estate may require that equal portions of each investment be given to each beneficiary. This may necessitate a complete reworking of your wife's IRA to keep her invested more conservatively. You'll save your family expense by setting up the accounts to reflect the needs of the beneficiary on the account.

Trusts As Beneficiaries

A trust can be named as the beneficiary of an IRA.

The IRS has ruled that if an IRA is paid to a trust, and the trust then distributes the entire proceeds to the surviving spouse, the spouse can roll over the proceeds to his or her own IRA account just as though he or she had received them directly.

TIP   If your beneficiary is having credit difficulties or is contemplating bankruptcy, you may wish to establish a trust that distributes the IRA benefits to your beneficiary as annual distributions, as opposed to a lump sum. There may be protection for the beneficiary under your state's commercial law.

One basic rule about IRAs is that they must be held in the name of an individual. A trust cannot be the owner of an IRA account.

Therefore, when a trust is a beneficiary, it must by definition begin distributions, even though the trust may be set up for the benefit of the spouse. It does not retain benefits that would have normally been available to the spouse, simply because the spouse is the ultimate beneficiary of the trust. So the trust cannot roll over the inheritance into an IRA account. If the trustee wishes to give the spouse rollover treatment, he must distribute the inheritance to the spouse, and she must put the assets in an IRA under her control.

If the trust is the beneficiary of the IRA, the distribution rules it may apply for the benefit of the named beneficiary depend on meeting a number of conditions. The trust must be irrevocable, it must meet state legal requirements as a valid trust, the individual beneficiaries must be named in the trust document, and a copy of the trust must be given to the IRA custodian.

If these conditions are met, then the trust can apply various life-expectancy computations to determine the amount of the required distributions.

If the account holder was under the age of 70-1/2 when he died, the IRA can then be paid to the trust using either the five-year distribution rule, depleting the account. Or, the life-expectancy rule can be applied with the life expectancy of the oldest trust beneficiary used in the computation.

If the IRA account owner died after age 70-1/2, the rules are similar to other nonspouse beneficiaries:

EXAMPLE   The IRA account owner died after age 70-1/2 and was taking distributions based on her life expectancy without recalculating her life expectancy each year (the term-certain method). The distributions to the trust must be made based on the life expectancy of the IRA account holder had she lived. Each year, the life expectancy is reduced by one, not recalculated according to the life expectancy tables.

TIP   Given the complexities of distributions to trusts, the trust should be named a beneficiary only in rare circumstances. If the spouse is to be the beneficiary, and if he is capable of managing his own IRA, he should be named outright. IRA accounts can be split into multiple accounts with different beneficiaries, if necessary. Do not let the estate-planning benefits of trusts blind you to the income tax consequences.

RULES FOR THE DISABLED

If you are disabled, the tax penalties for pre-59-1/2 distributions don't apply. Once disabled, you can take any amount you wish each year without tax penalty no matter what your age. You are, however, still bound by the 70-1/2 distribution rules and must begin distributions then as would any other taxpayer.

If you have begun taking distributions under the pre-59-1/2 rules to avoid the 10 percent tax penalty and then become disabled, you do not have to continue under those rules. Your disability takes precedence.

There are certain procedures you should follow to have yourself classified as disabled. There is a specific definition of "disabled" in the tax code:

". . . unable to engage in any substantial gainful activity by reason of any medically determinable physical or mental impairment which can be expected to result in death or to be of long-continued and indefinite duration" (IRC Section 72(m)(7)).

If disabled for Social Security or insurance purposes, you probably need not worry about proving your disability. If not, here is a suggested course of action to get your disability classification:

1. Visit with your accountant and outline your desire to take distributions without the 10 percent tax penalty through a disability waiver.

2. Visit with your doctor, armed with the disability definition as provided by your accountant. Ask her if she can certify you disabled under the definition.

3. Have your doctor write a letter to you, and to your accountant, detailing your infirmity and discussing why it disables you. Her letter should directly relate to the tax code definition of disabled.

4. Then your accountant will want to use your doctor's letter and have a qualified tax attorney who specializes in pension law give a written opinion that you meet the disability rules under the tax code.

This will not guarantee favorable tax treatment by the IRS. However, if you are audited, you will have ample proof from the appropriate professionals that you are indeed disabled under the code.

Take all that documentation to your IRA custodian and ask him to code your distributions under the "disability" exception when he reports to the IRS. Your custodian may not be willing to do so, but it is worth the try.

Beyond the tax implications of disability are the emotional and psychological aspects. If your disability raises the possibility of heavy medical expense in the future, you need to remember that in some states an IRA can be attached by creditors.

And if your disability means that you have long lapses in judgment or in the ability to focus on your investments, you need to be sure your investment plan will run without your input. Professional managers are a must for you.

I can't stress enough the need for you to be absolutely candid with your advisors. Inform them fully about the nature of your disability and its effects on your behavior and judgment. They need to be aware that you may not always be functioning at 100 percent. If left in the dark, they may ask you for approvals on investments or tax returns, unaware that your responses might not be coherent or well considered.

If your disability points to long-term, steady deterioration, you need to discuss this with your beneficiaries. Make sure that a durable power of attorney exists to allow a loved one to run your affairs if you become incapable of doing so. You want to avoid triggering an unnecessary distribution of the IRA before your death because of the heavy income tax consequences. So, a trust accepting your IRA assets when you become incompetent creates major income-tax liabilities and should be avoided. Again, the power of attorney is your best way to handle it. The IRA can remain in place, yet a trusted individual can run it for you.

HOW YOUR CUSTODIAN REPORTS ACTIVITY

Your IRA custodian will report your taxable income to you from the IRA at the close of the year on Form 1099-R. It is important to remember that the IRS will be furnished a copy of this form by your custodian.

If you decide to transfer your IRA to another custodian, do the transfer directly as a trustee-to-trustee transfer. Otherwise your IRA custodian will report the distribution as such on the Form 1099-R and withhold tax on it.

You will use this form to verify for the IRS the income you report on your tax return.

SPECIAL EVENTS AND THE IRA

Divorce, nursing homes, lawsuits, physical deterioration can all wreak havoc on any financial plan. These events can be catastrophic or mere inconveniences, but they always create anxiety and fear. How do you handle these to survive them financially?

Divorce

If you have spent the better part of your adult years working to develop a pension benefit, your spouse has been involved in that process as well. Courts generally take the position that your spouse has an interest in your pension benefit, even though it may be held in your name only. Whether you hold a pension at your company or it has been paid in a lump sum to an IRA, you can expect your spouse to sue for it and the courts to lend a sympathetic ear.

> **TIP** In community-property states your retirement plan assets can become part of your marital assets—assets that are divided equally between the two of you. These states, including California, Louisiana, Texas, and Arizona, among several others, can also play a factor if you have ever lived in them while accruing your benefits.

This point is driven home by the existence of a court order known as a Qualified Domestic Relations Order, or QDRO (pronounced "quad-row").

The Retirement Equity Act of 1984 established alternate recipients under Qualified Domestic Relations Orders. Simply put, it establishes the right of someone other than the original recipient to receive funds from a qualified benefit plan if the right circumstances are present. And this other person is not limited to spouses. Children, former spouses, or other dependents of the plan recipient are eligible to receive a payout representing some or all of a vested benefit.

A QDRO is part of the divorce decree granted by a judge that establishes the payout to the alternate payee (your spouse). Under a QDRO, your spouse retains the right to apply favorable tax treatment to the distribution. An IRA may be used to carry out a QDRO. For instance, if your spouse is successful in suing for one half of your IRA, one half of your account can be transferred to an IRA for her benefit, and your ex can then use a personal IRA with all the tax benefits in place. This same rule applies to any amount distributed under a QDRO.

In effect, the government allows the normal IRA tax rules to be bent for a QDRO. By placing one half of your IRA in your spouse's name under a QDRO, you do not have to pay income tax on the distribution, nor does your spouse have to claim it as income. Of course, if it is not rolled over, she will have to pay income tax, but you will not have to claim it as a taxable distribution.

And, if you take a lump sum from your employer and pay any amount to your spouse under a QDRO, your ex can roll that portion to an IRA to continue to defer tax. Remember, however, that the QDRO is the only means by which your spouse can take and roll over part of your lump sum. If you stay married, it cannot be split into a separate IRA for your spouse.

When a large lump-sum benefit is present, either as a future payment or in an IRA, both parties need to work together, if possible, to structure a settlement that will recognize the heavy income-tax consequences of distributions. For instance, if the spouse sues for monthly support, and the only source of funds is an IRA, the amount requested will need to be adjusted for the taxes that would be paid from the IRA.

EXAMPLE   Beth sues for $2,000-per-month support payments. Since her husband is retired, the only source of support is from his $600,000 IRA, which generates about $45,000 per year in interest income. In order to provide $2,000 per month, he must distribute

$3,000 per month from the IRA. After paying his income taxes, he has $2,000 left for her.

It may be in both parties' interest to minimize the tax bite and thereby maximize the funds available to apply to a settlement. There is little point in using the IRA as a weapon to punish by requiring heavy income tax payments.

You should also remember that when your spouse takes a lump sum, the employer may ask you to sign off on the distribution. By doing so, you acknowledge that your spouse is taking a lump sum and you are holding the employer harmless for having made that distribution. If your spouse then loses the lump sum in the market or at blackjack, you can't go back to the employer for relief.

It is crucial for your attorney to work with your accountant to prepare the proper divorce settlement. The accountant can advise about the tax rules that apply to any vested benefits or IRAs. To ignore the tax consequences invites disaster.

Bankruptcy

Must your IRA be given up if you file for bankruptcy?

The question is not easily answered since state law, not federal, governs this issue. Some state courts have ruled that a creditor can attach an IRA since it is in your control, just as other assets you control can be attached.

Other state courts have ruled that an IRA is exempt from attachment. Remember that an IRA is generally covered by state law, while an employer-sponsored plan can fall under federal jurisdiction. For this and other reasons, it would make sense to roll over any employer distributions into a fresh IRA and not mingle the lump sum with contributory IRA money. This may help protect the funds from creditors, in addition to preserving your right to roll over the funds to another employer's plan.

However, the Supreme Court did rule in *Patterson* v. *Shumata* that an interest in a qualified plan can be excluded from bankruptcy proceedings. Don't confuse this with an IRA. The distinction may appear to be minor, but it is important. A qualified plan is sponsored by and run by an employer for your benefit. An IRA is yours and is directly under your control.

Such fine distinctions show that the only way to get a good answer is to consult an attorney in your community. This is an area of the law that requires expert opinion. You can't plan on thumbing your nose at your creditors simply because the money is in an IRA. They may be able to get at it.

Nursing-Home Expense

When you or your spouse enter a nursing home, you are entering into a contract with a private supplier of care. As you use those services, you must pay for them. If you don't, you can be sued just as any other creditor would sue you. Then, commercial law in your state would decide if your IRA could be attached.

When you are destitute, Medicaid will pick up the cost of the nursing home. In at least one instance that I have seen (in Ohio), the state took the attitude that the IRA had to be depleted first before Medicaid would kick in. And, if the spouse of the nursing-home resident was living on a lifetime annuity from the IRA, the annuity could be attached to pay the nursing home, as could the IRA of the spouse. The IRA is a countable resource, and its value may not be reduced by any taxes due on the distributions.

It is not likely that you could preserve a large IRA and ask the government to pick up a nursing-home expense. Once again, legal counsel is necessary to get at the rules in your state.

> **TIP** Because of this devastating possibility, you should seriously explore long-term care insurance, especially if you have income not spent. That income can be applied to the coverage and insure you against depletion of your estate, including your IRA.

Emergency Loans

You may have read that some benefit plans, like 401(k) plans, allow for emergency loans for medical or educational expense. An IRA cannot be used in the same way.

You cannot use your IRA as collateral for a loan. Doing so makes that portion used immediately taxable. Nor can you borrow money from an IRA, except that you can use the money for 60 days and then replace it without penalty.

You cannot lend money from the IRA to one of your children, even if you have a promissory note and are being paid a reasonable rate of interest and a set repayment schedule. The tax code prohibits such "self-serving" transactions. It may seem ironic that you can invest in a mortgage certificate through your broker and so lend your IRA money to complete strangers, but you can't lend to your children, even at a higher interest rate.

The fact is that personal lending can eventually be abused. That "loan" to your children can wind up in your pocket. You pulled money from the IRA without having to pay the income tax on it. If your child then went bankrupt, the tax would be permanently avoided since the IRA loan would become a bad debt. Other potential abuses are the reasons why direct loans from your IRA are prohibited.

The Taxpayer Relief Act of 1997 allows some exceptions to the 10 percent tax penalty for early withdrawals for certain housing, medical, or educational needs:

1. Up to $10,000 can be withdrawn for first-time home purchase by the IRA owners.

2. Medical expenses that exceed 7.5 percent of your adjusted gross income (AGI)

3. Higher-education expenses for you, your spouse, children, or grandchildren

4. To some unemployed, funds for payment of health-insurance premiums

Remember, this liberalization of the tax code simply removes the 10 percent tax penalty on the withdrawal—you must still pay income taxes on the distributions. It would be a good idea to check with a qualified tax specialist to be sure you fall within the rules for the waiver of the penalty.

TIP   If you need cash for an emergency, see your banker for a loan. You can show him the IRA as a potential source of income, should you need it to repay the loan. Bring your most recent statement to show him the income the account generates. Although you're not taking it as income, it is available should you need it. So your potential income is often much higher than your recent tax returns show. Be careful, however, not to pledge it as collateral.

Now you see that state and not federal law governs many aspects of IRA vulnerability. And there is nothing sacred about an IRA. It can be attached by creditors, taken by a nursing home, or given to your spouse. Only qualified legal counsel, familiar with the laws of your state, can provide the definitive answers you need. Forewarned is forearmed.

SUMMARY

A lump-sum recipient always needs to remember that a lump-sum distribution comes with a built-in tax liability that must be paid at some point. In addition, special situations, such as divorce or disability, can further complicate tax payment.

A basic goal of any lump-sum recipient is to pay income tax on the lump sum in the most efficient way possible, and this can include accelerating or postponing taxable income.

First, you need to establish the income-tax rules for your age. Often, you'll have several choices of how to compute distributions and pay tax on them. Many times, these calculations will be quite complicated, and so the services of a qualified tax advisor is usually required. After all, income taxes and possible penalties can consume up to 60 percent of the distribution, so a bit of prevention before taking a distribution is a wise thing.

In addition, your beneficiaries can be bound by many of the tax rules that applied to you, so tax planning is often done in a multigenerational setting.

Since income taxes are such a large embedded liability in a lump sum, proper planning for their realization is a must.

CHAPTER SIX

Financial Planning for the IRA

If you are going to realize your dreams for retirement, it won't happen by accident. You need a well-thought-out plan. Before you can begin selecting investments or ordering mutual-fund brochures, you need to do a great deal of financial thinking. And once you have established a plan, you need to execute it.

A financial plan gives you a road map to direct you along the journey. It is essential if you are to get to where you want to be. You should have a specific procedure for accomplishing this. In order:

1. Fact finding
2. Goal setting
3. Asset allocation
4. Investment selection
5. Implementation
6. Performance analysis

Throughout the process you will want to keep five major issues always in mind:

1. The need for income
2. The need for security

3. Tax issues
4. Inheritance issues
5. Growth of capital

By following this outline, you are able to put discipline in the process. Too often, people fall into hit-and-miss investment. You may be offered products or investments that, while perfectly sound, may also be perfectly wrong for your particular situation. Investments should fit the needs established by fact finding and goal setting. You certainly wouldn't take your car to your mechanic and ask him (or her) what he's offering that particular day.

Instead, you talk with him (fact finding) and establish that the car needs an oil change (goal setting). Five quarts of oil and one filter are needed (asset allocation). The right filter and proper weight oil are selected (investment selection), and the oil change is done (implementation). Before you leave, the mechanic tells you to check the oil every once in a while (performance analysis) and bring the car back in 6,000 miles (a check-up to be sure all is well).

It is important that this process is circular in nature. It reinforces itself constantly over time. When you bring the car back, the cycle is repeated all over again. Performance analysis forces recycling on a regular basis. In this chapter, we examine each of the six components in detail.

THE FINANCIAL FACT FIND

Your first step is to fill out a financial-fact form. This is a way of taking a snapshot of your situation. I have seen many different forms over the years. Most are too complicated. It's better to use one that is easy to complete. A sample is found in Appendix 3. Enlarge it on a copier and use it.

> **TIP** Don't do the work and then hand it over to your spouse as if it were the Ten Commandments. Work as a team. This is the only way to ensure that the numbers are accurate and that you are both committed to the process.

The form is broken up into three sections. The first contains biographic data of you and your family. Next is a list of assets and liabilities, then a section for special comments. Even if you don't retain professional advisors, you should complete a financial fact find. If you interview for an accountant or broker, take it with you and show it to him.

Complete each question to the best of your knowledge. Don't worry about being accurate to the penny, but be as exact as you can. If your circumstances don't quite fit the form, change the form. Once you have filled in as many blanks as are relevant, make sure you add up the asset and liability totals and compute your net worth (assets minus liabilities).

Analyze Your Debt

Strive for a debt-free lifestyle. The psychology of living in retirement is quite different from working full time. Your income tends to be fixed, and as an investor you fret a bit more about interest rates and your income.

Take off some of the pressure. Clean up your debt, and don't take on any more. And if it feels good to pay it off, even if it doesn't make a great deal of financial sense, pay it off. People tend to get so wrapped up in numbers and taxes that they often overlook peace of mind as an important part of the equation. We think nothing of spending money on a vacation because it makes us happy. If paying off your debt makes you happy, think of it as a daily vacation for the rest of your life.

Once you've hit retirement, debt becomes a real anchor around your neck. How much do you have, and at what rates of interest? If it's nonmortgage debt, you should almost certainly pay it off. It is very difficult to invest money and earn more than companies charge on nonmortgage debt.

EXAMPLE   You have $5,000 in debt on credit cards and a few payments left on your car. The interest payments total $50 per month. The rates of interest you pay range from 9.5 percent on the auto loan to 16.5 percent on your credit cards. What do you do with your savings? You can invest in bonds and earn 6 percent. You decide instead to pay off your loans. You reduce your expenses by $400 per month (the amount of the monthly payments), and instead of earning $29 per month on your investment, you save $50 per month in interest expense.

Think of debt repayment as investment in reverse. Reducing expenses has the same effect as earning interest. And since debt is never forgiven, paying it off is always a sure thing. You can't say that for every investment.

Do You Have Credit Problems?

You have to be careful to analyze your nonmortgage debt. Large credit-card balances or personal loans used to make purchases should be warning signs. Are your spending habits out of control? Did you roll up credit-card debt into a home-equity line of credit? Do you borrow from one card to pay off another? You can't afford that behavior once you're on a fixed income. You won't have pay raises or bonuses to bail you out each year.

If you show any of these credit-abuse symptoms, you may need credit counseling. Every community has credit-counseling agencies. Look in the Yellow Pages and make sure you go to a nonprofit agency.

You also need to think through whether you should take a lump sum. The lump sum is a loaded gun in the hands of someone who can't control spending habits. Remember that an IRA can be attached by creditors.

Mortgage Debt

By the time you reach retirement, you should have paid off your mortgage. If you haven't, the first thing to do is to find out whether refinancing would make sense. If you can't afford to pay it off, then at least try to reduce the amount of interest you have to pay out. What interest rate are you currently paying, and what rates are available if you refinance?

Many people assume that because they're entering retirement, banks won't lend to them, especially on a long-term debt such as a mortgage. This is not true. The bank looks at your income to make sure you can service the debt, and the property is collateral in case you can't.

The general rule of thumb is that you need to get a new mortgage rate 2 percentage points below your current rate. If you're now paying 9 percent, you need to get 7 percent for it to make sense. Reason? Closing costs and mortgage taxes are expenses that you must pay when you refinance but that you don't recoup. This can amount to several thousand dollars. (When I refinanced a $190,000 mortgage, closing costs and taxes amounted to nearly $2,000, and I didn't pay any points.) So you need several years of significant interest savings to pay for them. Anything less than a 2 percent swing probably won't do it.

When you refinance, there are a few things to keep in mind:

Don't add to the debt. It is always tempting to roll other debt into the mortgage since the mortgage interest is tax-deductible. A mortgage is a long-term debt. If you have credit-card debt, pay it off from savings. Don't burden yourself with higher mortgage payments for the next 20 years.

EXAMPLE   You decide to roll $5,000 in credit-card debt into a 20-year mortgage at 8 percent. Over the life of the loan, that $5,000 will cost you over $5,000 in interest payments.

Take a 7-year mortgage or a 15-year mortgage if you can afford the higher monthly payments. There is no sense refinancing at a lower rate and then burdening yourself with 30 years of payments.

If you are a fixed-income investor with a lump sum, you may find that the corrosive effects of inflation can be a bigger problem as you get older. Give yourself a break. If your mortgage payments stop in 7 years or 15 years, that reduction in monthly expense can be a big boost to your spendable income as you can see in Table 6.1. Get the double benefit of a lower rate and a short payoff schedule.

TABLE 6.1 Monthly Mortgage Payment on $100,000 Loan

7 Years	15 Years	30 Years
$1,558.62	$955.65	$733.76

Don't take a floating-rate mortgage. If it makes sense to refinance you'll be paying at a lower interest rate than you are now. And since you'll be living on a fixed income, you should stabilize your liabilities as well.

> **EXAMPLE**   You have a $100,000 mortgage and a $200,000 lump sum. Enticed by a floating rate of only 5.5 percent you see advertised, you refinance. You also invest your lump sum in ten-year bonds at 6.5 percent, noting that your mortgage interest is only $5,500 per year, while your lump sum earns $13,000 per year. However, two years later interest rates have risen sharply, and your mortgage now carries a rate of 10 percent. Your interest expenses have nearly doubled, almost to $10,000 (you have paid off a bit of the mortgage during the first two years) while your interest income remains static at $15,000. You find yourself being squeezed by your monthly obligations.

Always remember that as an investor in bonds, you are a lender, and with a mortgage outstanding you're also a debtor. Don't ignore your activity as a lender when considering your activity as a debtor. Like a bank, you need to make sure that if the interest rate on your debt is fixed your investments should be as well. And if your mortgage floats, you run a risk in being locked into long-term bonds in your portfolio.

Don't be blinded by the tax-deductibility of the mortgage interest. Generally, your tax bracket is lower in retirement, so the mortgage-interest deduction is worth less. And even with the deduction, you're still money out of pocket. What you need to do is compare the net-after-deduction cost of the mortgage with investment in tax-free bonds. This is an apples-to-apples comparison between paying off the mortgage with your savings or investing the money. How do you figure out which to do?

EXAMPLE You have $60,000 in savings in addition to your lump sum to invest. Your tax bracket is 30 percent. Your mortgage is at 8 percent. You check with your broker and find that you could earn 5 percent tax-free in municipal bonds. After your mortgage-interest deduction, your mortgage costs you 5.6 percent (.08 × (1 - .3) = .08 × 0.7 = .056 = 5.6%). Since there is always investment risk in a bond, and since the mortgage is costing you a bit more than you could earn by investing the money, you pay it off rather than invest.

In this way, you have the advantage of not having to worry about a monthly mortgage payment. You live in your own home, free of debt. If an emergency arises in the future, you can always get a home-equity line of credit to raise cash.

When interest rates rise above your mortgage rate, explore paying it off at a discount. You may have a golden opportunity to retire your mortgage at substantial savings.

EXAMPLE You refinance your $100,000 mortgage to a 15-year mortgage at 7.75 percent. Two years later, interest rates have risen to 9 percent. A quick check with your broker confirms that 13-year bonds with a 7.75 percent interest rate are selling at around 86 cents on the dollar. So, you purchase $100,000 worth of bonds for $86,000. The $100,000 in bonds will generate $7,750 in interest each year. Although you will pay on your mortgage principal each month, you've locked in all the interest income you need to equal the mortgage interest, and you've purchased $100,000 worth of principal for $86,000, a $14,000 savings. In effect, you've paid off the mortgage by buying enough bonds to cover the debt. It's no longer a concern. And, if interest rates fall dramatically, you can sell the bonds for a profit and simply continue the payments as before.

- If you refinance, take a higher interest rate instead of paying points. Once you've paid out points, you can't recoup the expense. Make your refinancing as cheap as possible by avoiding points. This leaves open the opportunity to refinance again because you haven't paid a lot to refinance the first time. Think of it this way: Do you really believe that current interest rates are as low as they'll get in the next four or five years? If not, keep your costs down and leave open the option to do it again.

- Don't pay off debt in a lump sum from your lump sum if you have other choices. Extracting cash from a lump sum is a very expensive proposition. Whether from the initial check from your employer or from an IRA rollover account, you generally need to pull $1.40 to raise one dollar.

EXAMPLE   Harry has credit-card debt of $10,000 at a 15 percent interest rate. He decides to pay it off from his IRA. He takes $14,000 from the IRA. After paying his income taxes, he has only $10,000 left (his combined state and federal rate is 40 percent). Had he left the $14,000 in the IRA, at 8 percent it would have grown to $28,000, or $20,000 net after taxes in nine years.

What if you have credit-card debt at a high interest rate and no savings? Do you pay it off from the IRA? The answer is often yes. If your debt is the double-digit interest-rate variety, you can save money even if you have to pay taxes to get your hands on the cash from your IRA.

Warning! If you have a spending problem, paying off the debt may be only a Band-Aid on a much bigger problem. Your problem isn't cleaning up debt for retirement. Your problem is controlling your impulses and working within a budget. You can't pledge an IRA as collateral for a loan, so don't count it in your borrowing-power calculations. You may choose to pay off debt from savings when you retire to reduce your monthly burden, reasoning that you can always borrow money if you have to using the IRA as collateral. The IRA is off-limits as a pledge to a lender. Pledging it as collateral can result in the IRS declaring the entire account taxable income. You should note that when you do apply for a loan, you should list the IRA as an asset. And take the time to explain to the loan officer that even though you aren't tapping the IRA for income, the income it is generating is available, if you need it. This will show that your sources of income are much higher than reflected on your current tax return.

Total Your Assets

Look at your fact find. Take out a piece of paper. Divide your assets into two categories: those that produce income and those that don't. Your primary residence is an asset, but is not income producing. Your vacation home may produce income, but you have to net it against your expenses in maintaining the property. Generally, your income-producing assets will consist of stocks, bonds, and cash. Once you have isolated your income-producing assets, add them up. Then, using a reasonable rate of interest, find out what your potential income from them will be.

> **EXAMPLE**   You have $260,000 in stocks, bonds, and cash, including $140,000 in your IRA rollover account. Your broker tells you that good quality seven-to-ten-year bonds are yielding 7 percent. Your potential income is $18,200 from your investment assets.

Most people figure out just their current income. What you really need to know is how much you could earn if you had to. For the moment, you want to ignore inflation, the return possibilities of common stocks, and other mitigating effects. Just use a reasonable investment rate to arrive at a rough estimate. Armed with this figure, you can now add in your Social Security and other pension benefits to arrive at a retirement-income scenario.

> **EXAMPLE**   You have a Social Security benefit of $8,000 per year and a pension of $4,000 from a previous employer. Added to your investment income of $18,200, your total potential retirement income is $30,200.

> Social Security + Pension + Investment Income = Total Income

> This may be much more than you need, or not. But you now know your potential.

WORK UP YOUR BUDGET

There is only one way to estimate your expenses. Pull out your checkbook and your credit-card statements for the last 12 months and add them up. If you try to figure it off the top of your head, you'll miss a lot of places you spend money. Even $20 a week adds up to $1,000 a year.

Armed with your records, you want to break up your expenses into two categories:

Absolute Necessities
Food
Rent or mortgage
Medical-insurance payments
Automobile expenses
Clothing
Utilities
Taxes (property and income)
Nice to Have but Could Be Done Without in a Real Pinch
Life insurance (if in excess of what is truly needed)
Vacations
Entertainment (includes eating out)
Gifts
Charitable contributions

Create two budgets. The first is your basic budget, your absolute bottom line, the amount of money you must have. The second is the amount you'd like to have—a supplemental budget. As you write down your expenses from your records, put them on two separate lists.

Once you have your basic budget, make sure you have enough in pension, Social Security, and interest payments to meet that basic budget. You're making sure that no matter what may happen, you can meet your needs. Then look at your supplemental budget. Since you now know how much your income will be and how much your basic budget will require, you can whittle down the supplemental items to eliminate those you can't afford.

EXAMPLE   Mary has $42,000 in retirement income. Her basic budget totals $36,000 and her supplemental budget $10,000. She needs to pare $4,000 from her supplemental budget. On closer examination, she finds that nearly $5,000 of last year's expenses went for various expenses related to her job in sales. Since she's no longer working, she can easily eliminate $4,000.

Combined with your estimate of annual expenses, this gives you a pretty good idea of how much to put into bonds and how much into growth investment.

EXAMPLE   Your annual expenses are $20,000. You decide to set aside enough money in bonds that, combined with Social Security and your pension, will cover your expenses. Since your Social Security and pension total $12,000 per year, you need $8,000 from investment income to cover them. You find that Treasury bonds are yielding 6 percent. By purchasing $135,000 in bonds, you will generate $8,000-per-year income. Your expenses are covered. The balance of your investment assets will go into common stocks for growth.

Once you have arrived at your asset and liability totals, you can decide how much of your capital to apply to debt repayment. The balance is available for retirement income investment. This process will also focus on exactly what you are earning from your investments. Stocks not paying a dividend will be less attractive to you than ones that are. But the basic goal here is to pencil out the broad picture of how much you have, how much you owe, and the resources you can marshall to see your way through.

Life Insurance

How necessary is life insurance in retirement? It depends on your circumstances. The value of life insurance to a retired couple often boils down to how much money the beneficiary could earn from the benefit.

EXAMPLE   Joe dies and leaves Kathy $150,000 in insurance, Now that she's alone, she has a strong need for security, so she is unwilling to spend the principal. She invests the money and earns $9,000 per year tax-free from municipal bonds.

So, Joe's policy was worth $9,000 per year to his spouse. It is also true that their children will probably inherit $150,000, but this is not our main concern. If Kathy will need that $9,000 because her survivor's pension will be reduced on Joe's death, then the policy should be kept in force.

If, on the other hand, Kathy will have adequate income even after her husband's death, then the policy must be analyzed, as is any other investment. How much has to be paid in and how much will come back out? If the policy has been in force for many years it can probably be kept, even if the dividends the policy earns are used to make the annual premium payments.

Include the Effects of Taxes

When you figure your budget or compute your income, you must always take into account the effect of income taxes. For many retirees, taxes are the single biggest expense they have. Your income has to be reduced for income tax before you can apply it to your budget. Money you spend is after-tax income.

Add in the Effects of Inflation

You can't ignore the effects of inflation. Over many years it slowly but surely eats into your income. It is a silent tax. See Table 6.2.

Inflation in the United States has averaged around 4 percent during the last 25 years. You can use a planning rate of 3 to 4 percent in estimating future needs. A simple calculator will do the trick.

EXAMPLE   Bob's budget calls for $45,000 per year in expenses. This is fairly close to the income he currently earns. He applies a 3 percent inflation rate to this income by multiplying $45,000 by

1.03 to get next year's figure. He then multiplies $46,350 by 1.03 to get the second year's number, and so on for ten years. In ten years, Bob will need just over $60,000.

This calculation is always a real eye-opener. How will you cover the effects of inflation?

TABLE 6.2 **Effect of Various Rates of Annual Inflation on the Value of One Dollar**

Value of $1	3 percent	4 percent	5 percent
5 years	86 cents	82 cents	77 cents
10 years	74 cents	66 cents	60 cents
15 years	63 cents	54 cents	46 cents
20 years	54 cents	44 cents	36 cents

Social Security is indexed for inflation so you can assume that it will keep up. Most monthly pension checks are not inflation indexed, so that pension will be worth less as time goes on. Your bond portfolio will keep pace as long as you don't invest in lengthy maturities. Interest rates and inflation are broadly linked, so you can assume interest rates will rise if inflation increases, and vice versa. Structure your bond portfolio to take advantage of this. (See Chapter 9.)

Keep some money set aside as an "inflation bank." This will be savings that you'll use to help ease the inflation squeeze down the road. If your income is currently more than adequate, set aside some for use in later years when it may be a closer call.

If your income is barely adequate, consider taking part-time work. Go into partial retirement instead of full retirement. This will ease your current spending requirements and allow you to set aside some money. And if you're facing an early-retirement decision, don't take it if your income is currently just enough. Inflation can put you behind the eight ball later on.

Take heart. Inflation tends to hit hardest on families with children where price increases can't be dodged. As a retiree, many of your expenses are not inflation-sensitive. Your mortgage payment is fixed, and the increased cost of medical care is somewhat eased by Medicare. Food and fuel are your main inflation-sensitive expenses.

Inflation is not always a given. While it appears to be the trend for the foreseeable future, economies tend to self-correct for long periods of inflation with periods of deflation, or falling prices. The 1930s were a good example of this. While nobody wants to see that Great Depression repeated, chances are you'll see a period of deflation or stagnant prices during your retirement.

The Fact-Finding Follow-Up

You should track your progress on a quarterly basis. Monthly is much too often because some expenses, such as income taxes, are paid on a quarterly basis.

All you need do is sit down once each quarter and add up your actual expenses, comparing them against your budget. If you are over budget, you need to figure out if the budget is unrealistic or if your discipline has slipped. By doing this together with your spouse, you develop a commitment to the budget and to the process. And by analyzing your position quarterly you stay on track year after year.

The Annual Review

Once each year, you should complete a new financial fact find. Compare the new figures on it to the old ones. This will allow you to observe the longer-term trend in income, savings, and debt. It will point out strengths and weaknesses to you. Here are a list of questions to pose during each annual review:

1. Are we dipping into savings?
2. Are we saving too much and spending too little?
3. Is our debt increasing?
4. Are we worth more, less, or the same as a year ago?
5. Should we pay off any debt?
6. Should we refinance any debt?
7. Is our investment portfolio structured for growth and income?

8. Are we staying ahead of inflation?
9. Is our budget current and in line?
10. All in all, are we satisfied with our financial situation?

By asking these simple questions, you are considering all aspects of your financial situation. This review and rethinking each year keeps you current on what you have and what you should be doing.

WHAT IF YOUR INCOME BEGINS TO DEPLETE YOUR CAPITAL?

Despite best efforts, sometimes income needs to begin to run down the available capital. This can stem from many sources, but there are three that are the most common culprits:

1. You began retirement with inadequate savings.
2. Unanticipated expenses balloon your income needs.
3. Poor investment returns created a shortfall.

Whatever the reason, you need to apply some Band-Aids to the problem. First, you need to be realistic about your situation. Take a hard-nosed and clear-eyed look at your financial circumstances. Work up a budget and make sure it is realistic.

Think about what caused the shortfall. If it was unanticipated expense, identify it as recurring or a one-time occurrence. If it was a one-time, you can work within the budget you've set up. If it is a recurring problem (medical expense, for instance) then you have to add it into your budget. Don't substitute hope for reality.

If your expenses are under control, apply a 7 percent or 8 percent withdrawal rate to your entire savings base (IRA plus other investments) and see if that will cover your expenses. If not, you have a chronic problem that needs to be addressed. Not doing so merely postpones an inevitable day of reckoning.

If poor investment returns are the culprit, identify the source of the problem. If you have been doing your investments yourself, you probably need the help of a professional. If you have a professional, has the advice been good, and ignored by you, or has the advice been poor? If poor advice, then you need to find another advisor, or consider going on your own, if competent help is not at hand. (See Chapter 4.)

There are many strategies you can apply to address the income shortfall. Some are obvious, others not. While some of these may appear to be drastic, remember that running out of money is even more so. If you get to the point where your survival is at stake, everything goes on the table for consideration. (Preretirees take note: Make sure you can afford retirement!) Here are a few you can use:

1. *Sell your home.* If you have a mortgage on your home, consider selling your house, paying off the mortgage, and applying the cash left over for your new residence. This will mean a downsizing in your home, but what good is a home that you can't afford? If your home is worth $250,000 and has a $150,000 mortgage on it, sell it and take the $90,000 to $100,000 proceeds and buy a place for cash. And, when you do so, pay some attention to public transportation. If you can't close your budget gap, you may need to reduce your traveling expenses.

2. *Sell your second home.* Second homes have, in some cases, more attachment than first homes. Many people view them as a true reward for years of sacrifice and effort. If you can't afford two, one has to go. Now, you may want to sell your primary residence, but if it's near your children, it's probably the second one that will go. That's OK. Take a deep breath and sell it. Second homes are significant expenses, even when you receive rental income. If you actually sit down and figure out what your condo really costs you, you'd be surprised. Add in insurance, dues, the costs incurred in traveling to it and back, upkeep, and annual maintainance. It all adds up.

3. *Pay off credit-card debt.* If you're carrying credit-card debts at 18 or 19 or 20 percent interest, pay them off. Maybe you've got money invested in stocks that you believe can beat those returns. Not a good bet. Clear out the credit cards and eliminate those monthly payments.

4. *Get rid of the second car.* Two cars are a nice luxury, but frankly, retirees can get along with one. Sell the oldest one, or sell the most expensive, but sell it. Not only will you have the cash for expenses but you can reduce your automobile-insurance expense, and the cost of keeping two vehicles on the road.

5. *Eat at home.* Eating out is a luxury. Make sure everyone is pitching in with the dishes, and use your kitchen.

6. *Eliminate vacations.* Again, nice to have when you have the dough, but not a necessity. There's lots to do around town. Visit your kids instead of the Grand Canyon or the Grand Canal.

7. *Cash out your life insurance.* You may have built up substantial cash value. Get an update on your policy and explore unlocking the cash. You can often keep the policy in force, while putting the cash to good use at home. If you bought the insurance for estate-tax reasons, remember that there is not estate tax on a depleted estate. A legacy for your kids? That's admirable, but it may not be a realistic goal.

8. *Get a job.* Yes, I know you didn't sign up for that when you retired, but sometimes you don't have a choice. There's no shame in staying afloat financially.

9. *Consider a reverse mortgage.* In a reverse mortgage, you trade off your home for a line of credit, a lump sum, or monthly annuity. The bill is due when you move or die. As long as you stay in the house, you don't have to pay on the loan or the accumulated interest. And, if the house is worth less than the debt when you die, the holder of the reverse mortgage can't get more than the value of the property—the rest of your estate is off limits. Two caveats: Have your lawyer review the documents, and be aware that the reverse mortgage can cost upwards of $5,000 to prepare.

10. *Tell your children—nyet!* Many parents and grandparents just can't say no. They feel a tremendous sense of guilt if they don't pitch in with a few bucks at every opportunity. Remember that the first order of business is to secure your own retirement, not to pass a

legacy. Much as we might want to help, sometimes we just can't afford it.

You're better off, and your family is better off, if you simply tell your kids that you're comfortable, but if you don't watch your expenses, you're going to spend their inheritance. Ask for some slack on requests, and you'll find that you'll get it. If you don't, lay down the law. Again, its no shame to have that kind of conversation. Younger people are all too aware of the problem of saving for retirement. It's better than suffering in silence. Besides, if your kids aren't sympathetic and understanding, then I would question why you help them.

11. *Cancel out the leakers.* There are a million things that leak wealth out of a household. They're the little things that, over time, can make a difference. I know that some of these may sound petty, but we're dealing in a crisis situation—you're going to run out of money. The idea is to change your habits at the margins and avoid wholesale downsizing of your life.

Stop buying books (use the library), wash your own car, mow your own lawn, clean your own house, eat more pasta (and less meat—good for you anyhow), turn down the thermostat when you go away, offer your time as a gift, clip coupons. In short, find those 100 little ways to whittle down your expenses. They accumulate to your benefit, just as they have been causing part of the problem.

You'd be surprised to learn that if you did just the things I listed in the last paragraph, you'd save over $2,000 per year, assuming you're an average consumer of these items. (Housecleaning every other week at $50 per visit is $1,250 per year.)

Income shortfall is a difficult situation. It seems so unfair after a life spent in labor, yet you must remember that life offers no guarantees. You may have made a mistake retiring when you did. Unfortunately, that mistake is one that can reverberate for years.

Certainly, unforeseen difficulty can't be avoided. The illness of a grandchild, a fire, or an accident can all wreak havoc with the best-laid plans. However, excessive and unneccessary expense, poor investment results, and inattention to detail can all be avoided. The retiree must always take prime responsibility for the quality of his or her retirement. You can delegate the tasks but you can't delegate your own responsibility.

A WORD ABOUT INVESTMENT RETURNS

If I can't make a retirement plan work with a 7 or 8 percent return assumption (even if we will be more aggressive and will earn more than that over time) I do not endorse the plan.

One crucial mistake many people make is they overestimate how much they can earn on their portfolio and thereby close a retirement shortfall. And recent market history has lent credence to the idea that you can assume a return of 10 percent or 11 percent or even higher. A little work with a simple calculator and a yellow pad will help dispel that notion.

Consider the individual with a $500,000 lump sum. The problem he faces is that he needs $50,000 per year from his lump sum or he can't make ends meet. Furthermore, he is unwilling to spend principal and therefore must take his withdrawal from investment earnings. Since U.S. stocks have averaged more than 10 percent per year over time, he decides to invest 100 percent of his lump sum in good-quality stocks (no speculation for him!) in order to make the plan work. After all, the stock market has been earning 15 to 20 percent per year for several years. He feels he's being conservative.

At the end of the first year, the market did indeed give him a 10 percent return, and he happily pulled that out and still had his original $500,000 lump sum. Unfortunately, in year two, the market paused and dropped a mere 5 percent—a very modest decline. After withdrawing $50,000 and taking the $25,000 market hit, his lump sum has dropped to $425,000. In year three, the very mild bear market wipes another 10 percent off his lump sum and then stabilizes. Including his withdrawal of $50,000, and a decline of $42,000 in the value of the account, his lump sum has now shrunk to $333,000. A $50,000 withdrawal now represents, not 10 percent of his account, but a full 15 percent of the account. And, instead of having to earn 10 percent per year, he now has to earn 15 percent per year, just to cover his withdrawals. In order to get back to $500,000, he must earn over

20 percent per year, year after year, and hope that he never sees a bad market again.

You can see that using even modestly higher return assumptions can be devastating to a retirement experience. Here, a mild 15 percent bear market wiped out over one third of his entire retirement nest egg in only two years—and he still has 25 years more to go.

SUMMARY

Good financial planning must precede the receipt of the lump sum and its investment. Only with a sound plan in place can the right mix of tax and investment treatment maximize the income needed for retirement.

Financial planning requires the application of a set of tasks that, when done properly, can assure the emergence of the right course of action.

Fact finding is done first to organize the relevant data about your financial situation.

Then, reasonable goals can be set, utilizing reasonable assumptions about spending and rates of return on invested assets.

Once goals are in place, the right mix of investment assets, called asset allocation, is set in place. This is the "big picture" view of your portfolio and has the greatest impact on performance.

Then, and only then, can you select the vehicles to carry out the asset allocation: stocks, bonds, mutual funds, money managers, and so forth.

Implementation of the process then begins, and regular monitoring of performance helps keep the entire program on track.

While on the lookout for various pitfalls and common mistakes, you take the opportunity to recheck your planning on an annual basis, gathering your facts, analyzing your progress, and making adjustments.

In reality, the first financial plan becomes the blueprint and is the most important. However, a regular checkup is a must and ensures that the assumptions originally made are still valid.

If planning is simply beyond your skill set, a financial planner can assist. Alternatively, your accountant can work with you, or you can seek investment advisors with financial-planning abilities.

Without a doubt, it has been my experience that those people who engage in sound financial planning have better retirement experiences than those who "wing it."

Forewarned is forearmed.

CHAPTER SEVEN

Asset Allocation and the Lump Sum

Proper asset allocation is crucial to investing. Without it, success is impossible. It is generally accepted that asset allocation accounts for over 90 percent of the investment return of a portfolio!

Therefore, it is crucial that you pick the right mix of assets when investing your lump sum. This will have more of an effect on your investment returns, and therefore, your income, than any other investment decision.

Asset allocation is the process by which you select the mix of assets for your portfolio. These include stocks, bonds, and cash. No other investments will offer the characteristics you need for growth, income, and liquidity.

Real estate, for instance, can be very attractive but lacks liquidity. If you are interested in real estate, it's better to buy a piece of property that you'll use rather than make a passive real estate investment.

Your need for income can best be met with bonds and your need for growth by common stocks. Cash, which generally has the lowest return, will be used only to meet current income needs or because stocks and bonds are unattractive.

Don't confuse the investment uses of these classes. While it is true that utility stocks can be used for income, blurring the line between stocks and bonds, you want to think of them as growth vehicles. If you begin to confuse growth and income, you'll find yourself running higher degrees of risk than you assumed when you invested.

This means that you won't try to buy bonds for capital gains. While artful investment in bonds about to experience a credit upgrade (which leads to an increase in price) can be very profitable, it isn't practical for most investors. Such credit analysis is a highly specialized activity.

You're better off putting your time into proper asset allocation. And, with unlimited profit potential in common stocks, you should make them your investment of choice for gain.

Most investors spend their time trying to pick a "good" stock. I think that's a mistake. It has been estimated that 80 percent of the price movement in an individual stock can be attributed to the over-all movement of the stock market, and the remaining 20 percent can generally be found in the movement of the specific industry.

For example, if a stock were to move from $40 to $60, a $20 increase, it is likely that about $16 of that move would be attributable to a rise in the stock market, with another $2.50 or so a result of that stock's industry's strength.

As you can see, only a very small portion of the move is a result of the individual success of the company. The bulk of your efforts should be expended deciding whether to be in stocks rather than stressing over what stocks to pick. And it is more important to be in the right industries than it is worrying about the right companies.

If the stock market is going to be strong and retailing stocks are going to be a market leader, it is not as important to decide whether to buy J. C. Penney or Sears. It is crucial, however, to be in stocks and to own retailers. You're better off buying both Sears and Penney.

Yet most investors spend most of their time looking for individual stocks rather than considering the market as a whole. You should do the opposite. Don't be concerned with what stocks to buy as much as to whether you should be buying stocks at all. If, for instance, you feel that the market is going to be strong and that airlines are going to be market leaders, you should buy equal dollar amounts of the three largest airlines. You can be quite confident that a strong market and a strong airline group will include at least two of these three stocks, After all, they ARE the airline industry.

This same philosophy holds true with bonds and cash. It is much more important to decide whether to be in cash or bonds than which money-market fund or what bond you should buy. If bonds are strong, all investment-grade bonds will move together, almost in lockstep.

SHAPING YOUR PORTFOLIO

There are two main issues to address in asset allocation:

1. What are your overall asset allocation guidelines?
2. What are your current allocations?

For instance, you may decide that on an overall basis, you will have the following asset allocations in your portfolio:

Stocks	25 to 50 percent
Bonds	40 to 70 percent
Cash	5 to 35 percent

That is, common stocks will never exceed 50 percent of your portfolio, nor comprise less than 25 percent. This is your overall asset allocation. But should you currently be at 25 or 35 or 50 percent? This frames the second question—current allocations.

To arrive at your overall allocation, you need to explore the expected returns for each asset class over time. You can figure some likely returns over long periods of time and then apply the appropriate risk profile for each class of asset, helping you determine precisely how much risk you are willing to take for what reward. You then need to think a bit about how each of the asset classes acts in relationship to others, to give you some idea of best- and worst-case scenarios.

Viewing historic returns helps give you a framework in which to work. Here are the annual returns of each asset class for most of the twentieth century (covering 50 years of investing through March 1998):

Common stocks	13.4 percent
Long-term bonds	5.7 percent

Cash (T-bills)   5.0 percent
Inflation   3.9 percent

You can now estimate the annual return on your portfolio by mixing various asset classes together.
For example:

50 percent stock, 30 percent bonds, 20 percent cash = 9.4 percent return
30 percent stock, 50 percent bonds, 20 percent cash = 7.8 percent return

Of course, it would be easy to say that you should be 100 percent in stocks, because that asset class historically offers the highest returns. And for younger investors, that allocation might not be completely inaccurate. But so far you have taken into account only the returns of each asset class. You must now flesh out the formula by examining the risk that each investment possesses.

ESTIMATING PORTFOLIO RISK

Only when you measure risk against reward can you be comfortable with your allocation. You need to remember that constructing a portfolio must be done within the context of your risk tolerance. Once you have gauged your tolerance for risk, the balance falls nicely into place. However, most people are entirely unfamiliar with the concept of estimating a portfolio's risk before they commit their funds.

That is, most people make several investments and then hope that they haven't taken too much risk. This creates anxiety because the proper groundwork hasn't been established. They are unaware of how to measure the risk of a portfolio.

Figure 7.1 shows how to measure the risk of a portfolio. It is an example of two-way asset allocation. That is, you are examining a portfolio comprised of two asset classes: stocks and bonds. A graph of three-way asset allocation would do the same thing except it would measure the three asset classes together: cash, stocks, and bonds.

The chart is easy to read. It shows the actual returns and risk of various portfolios comprised of different mixes of stocks and bonds

FIGURE 7.1 March 1978-March 1998 Risk/Reward Analysis

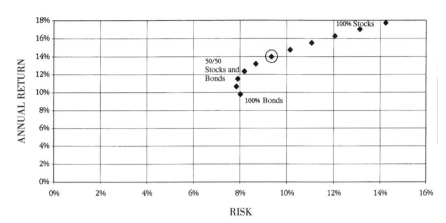

over 15 years. I have highlighted 100 percent stocks, as represented by the S&P 500, and 100 percent bonds, as measured by the U. S. Treasury bond. I have also inserted a label at 50/50, stocks and bonds. Each dot represents an additional 10 percent in stocks versus bonds, as you move up the chart.

You can see that as you add more stocks to the portfolio your return increases, and your risk increases. In this graph, risk is measured by the Annualized Percent Standard Deviation based on each quarter's return. This is a fancy way of saying that you measure risk by how much the portfolio fluctuates from quarter to quarter.

When you own a Treasury bill, your portfolio fluctuates very little from quarter to quarter, reflecting the low risk of a Treasury bill. You don't expect your Treasury bill to vary that much in value. You do expect it to quietly appreciate to full value as you hold it.

However, if you own a high-risk over-the-counter stock, you wouldn't be at all surprised to see it fluctuate wildly as you held it. It might start the year at $24, fall to $18, then rise to $30. That high level of fluctuation represents the higher risk of the investment.

The highest risk of all is that which can fluctuate all the way to zero—100 percent fluctuation. And while it may seem that holding cash poses no risk at all (a dollar is always a dollar), it is the erosion caused by inflation that actually does create a fluctuation in the value—steadily down. So by measuring the fluctuation of the asset class over time, you can apply a measure of how much risk you are assuming for commensurate return.

The notation "100% stocks" on the chart refers to the stock market as measured by the S&P 500. For the 10 years measured by this graph, the Standard & Poor's 500 had a high rate of return (17.7 percent per year) along with a high level of risk as measured by a Standard Deviation of 14.2.

Treasury bills, on the other hand, showed a low return of 5.4 percent per year, with a very low-risk profile (1.0 Standard Deviation).

As you can see, the more you increased the proportion of stock in the portfolio, the higher your risk and the higher your reward, as you would expect. One should expect higher risk for the potential for higher reward.

In my mind, the most crucial number is at 30/70. Note that a portfolio of 30 percent stocks and 70 percent bonds had a higher return than all bonds. Yet the risk is no higher. This is a crucial concept. If history is any guide, over longer periods of time, an investor should be able to earn a higher rate of return, without a corresponding increase in risk, by using an allocation of 30 percent stock and 70 percent bonds. Note that at 40 percent stocks the risk increases.

So, if you are more conservative you should maintain 30 percent of your funds in common stocks. Although you can have negative years in the stock market, the 30 percent stock allocation will serve you well.

Consider that a 20 percent decrease in common stock prices is by any measure a bad year. Let's assume you had 30 percent of your money in stocks and 70 percent in bonds earning 7 percent. How would you have fared?

Stocks totaling $30,000 drop 20 percent to $24,000.
Bonds totaling $70,000 gain 7 percent to $74,900.

Your $100,000 portfolio went down a total of $1,100, or just 1.1 percent for the year. The interest on the bond-portfolio ($4,900) overcame nearly all of the $6,000 loss in the stock portion of the portfolio.

Now, let's look at a year in which the stock market rises 20 percent:

Stocks totaling $30,000 gain 20 percent to $36,000.
Bonds totaling $70,000 gain 7 percent to $74,900.

Your $100,000 just gained $10,900, or 10.9 percent. You can see how your portfolio is cushioned for a bad year in the market, yet shows better than a bond-only gain in a good market. Applying your long term returns for stocks (13.4 percent) and bonds (5.7 percent) in the 30/70 mix would give you an annual average return of 8.0 percent. Compared with the 3.9 percent rate of inflation during these same 50 years, your portfolio would have returned, in excess of inflation, 4.1 percent per year. Keep in mind that an allocation of 100 percent bonds would have returned 5.7 percent or 1.8 percent per year more than inflation. You would have increased your after-inflation return without a meaningful increase in risk by including an equity component. This is superior asset allocation.

A younger individual might increase her stock allocation to 70 percent to take advantage of many years of compounded growth at a higher rate of return. Such an investor has many years to weather bad markets. If you are near retirement, on the other hand, you don't really have enough time to handle such adversity, and so a lower stock allocation is recommended.

Let's pause here. Can you see how you are applying a rational study of risk and reward to gauge how much risk to take? Instead of blindly hoping for good luck, you are generating a logical study of your tolerance for risk and your potential return for the tolerance you have. This lessens anxiety and increases your comfort because you have a clear program with a well-thought-out basis for action. You know that a bad market is a natural and expected part of your long-term strategy for coping with the markets and your need to increase your capital base. You have a discipline that helps to keep you straight when times are difficult.

Compare this to the investor who enters a poor market without a frame of reference. He feels isolated, out of control, and vulnerable. Without a discipline, he acts more on emotion and fear than from a well-planned strategy. Without the anchor to steady him in rough waters, he too often blindly bails out to lessen his anxiety and reduce his fear. The price paid is illustrated in poor investment performance.

DECIDING ON YOUR ASSET ALLOCATION

You have seen how the asset-allocation decision is the most important investment decision you make. Deciding what asset classes to own is an important component of the investment decision.

In deciding on the specific asset allocation, you must analyze your circumstances to arrive at a satisfactory model. The basic question to answer is: What asset allocation will produce the maximum return within your risk tolerance?

Several issues must be explored:

1. Your overall wealth
2. Your age
3. Your need for current income, versus long-term total return
4. Your goals
5. Your prior investing experiences

1. Your overall wealth. If you have greater wealth or net worth, you can tolerate more risk. An individual with a home and $50,000 in investment assets near retirement cannot tolerate the same risk as a multimillionaire with a diverse portfolio.

2. Your age. A 40 year old can use a 20- to 25-year time horizon for investment and so can afford the risk of up-and-down market cycles to ride the long-term positive trend. A 58 year old with four years until retirement will enjoy only one four-year market cycle before funds are needed. He can't afford the risk of a wrong decision because he doesn't have the luxury of time to bail him out and consequently must be more conservative.

3. Your need for current income, versus long-term total return. Lifespans of 80 or 85 years are not at all uncommon. So, a 60 year old can look forward to 20 to 25 years of investing. That's hardly the short time frame generally associated with the elderly. There is a tendency to bury one's head in the sand at age 60 and limit investment strictly to government and other high-quality bonds. Given the length of retirement, this is clearly a mistake. While the percentage of common stocks may be reduced, it should be eliminated only in cases when your wealth overwhelms the need to maintain a good overall return.

For instance, an individual with $2 million in investment assets who needs only $100,000 per year in income must achieve only a 5 percent return to meet his objectives. He may very well opt for the quiet assurance of bonds and make up any shortfall from principal. He has chosen the lesser worry over inflation and interest rates rather than fretting over common stocks and the market. So, the inclusion of common stocks isn't automatic.

4. Your goals. You need to be clear about why you are investing. For some, the generation of a secure source of income is the only task. A portfolio concentrated in bonds and other fixed income investments would make the most sense.

For others who do not need current income, long-term growth of capital is paramount. Common stocks would be the vehicle of choice.

And, if your goal is a combination of both current income and long-term growth of capital, then a more balanced portfolio of stocks and bonds is appropriate.

If you are confused about your primary investment goal, then you will find yourself confused about how to allocate your resources. For instance, if you seek current income and invest in common stocks, you will become frustrated in a negative-equity environment. You will be taking money from your principal and watching your account balance drop.

Conversely, if you really want long-term growth and you invest in bonds, you'll become unhappy with the slow rate of progress.

You need to have your primary goal firmly in mind. All else will flow from that.

5. *Your prior investing experience.* There are few experiences worse than investing your lump sum just as the stock market turns down. A benefit that took 30 years to accumulate can be reduced by 10 or 20 percent in a matter of weeks. And, unfortunately, neophyte investors tend to be drawn into the stock market after it has had a long and profitable run and it appears "safe" to invest in stocks. Of course, the chances of a market reversal are also very high, just at that time.

In my experience, the decision to invest a lump sum on one's own is rarely a fee issue. An individual investing in no-load mutual funds will still pay from 3/4 of 1 percent to 1 1/2 percent per year in management fees—about the same as the fees charged by a balanced portfolio manager. Therefore, the decision is not an economic one. Be clear on that.

It usually boils down to a question of trust and control. Some people need to control everything and so find it difficult to trust anyone else with the investment task. While they may point to fees as the issue, a close analysis of fees shows that is usually not the case.

If you have very limited investment experience, don't learn about investing with your lump sum. You're going to make mistakes, and your retirement assets aren't the proper classroom. Let a professional handle your lump sum, and if you want to eventually take over the management of it, keep a fraction, say 10 percent, and manage that yourself. Over time, your mistakes will cost you less, and you may find that you're simply not cut out for the investing game. Or, you may find that you can do very well and so can gradually take over investment responsibility.

On the other hand, if you have a great deal of investment experience and investment success, you are probably perfectly comfortable doing the investing yourself. In that case, asset allocation is your primary task, and you can use a wide array of investment vehicles to reach your goals.

GUIDELINES FOR VARIOUS INVESTORS

Let's look at some asset-allocation guidelines for various investors. Remember that your process is dynamic. You will be adjusting your allocation as you experience various investment returns on your asset classes.

The Young Investor—Ages 25 to 40

As investors go, 25 to 40 is pretty young. During these years most people are spending money buying homes and raising children, with only modest amounts left over for investment.

Nevertheless, if you're one of those people who are fortunate enough to generate fair amounts of investment dollars during these years, your investment of choice is clearly common stocks. An allocation might be:

Common stocks   80-100 percent

Bonds   0-20 percent

Given your extended time frame and the superior returns on common stocks over long periods of time, you have the ability to ride the overall trend. You will undoubtedly experience down markets, but they should be viewed as opportunities to increase your stock investment. Since markets seem to run in three- to five-year cycles, you will enjoy the benefits of five to ten market cycles before retirement.

Your longevity affords you the opportunity to aggressively seek capital gain. Your biggest enemy here will be yourself, your natural tendency to back away from common stocks in poor markets.

Remind yourself to rebalance your allocations when the stock market is down by adding to your equity portfolio.

Stock selection should include a mix of blue-chip and other large-capitalization issues along with aggressive growth stocks.

The Affluent Middle-Aged Investor—Ages 41 to 55

Allocation:

Retirement is only a glimmer in the eye at 41, but a real prospect at age 55, so as your middle years unfold you begin to scale back common-stock exposure to half the portfolio. A workable allocation might be:

Common stocks   50-70 percent

Bonds   30-50 percent

This is aggressive enough to continue to reap market gains, yet the larger bond portfolio has a greater cushioning effect in down years.

Your stock selection is more limited, focusing on large-capitalization blue chips and winding down the more aggressive portfolio of your earlier years.

Your 30 to 50 percent bond exposure helps generate cash to cushion poor years in the market, while providing a fairly substantial anchor to windward. Although you will use the four- to seven-year area for bond investment, you will extend maturities to ten years when rates look particularly attractive.

The Preretirment Investor—Ages 55 to 62

Allocation:
For investors in this age group, a good asset allocation might be:

Common stocks	20-35 percent
Bonds	65-80 percent

Depending on your risk tolerance, equities are reduced to the point where a 20 percent down year in the stock market would be completely offset by the interest earned in the bond portfolio. With a shortened span until retirement, you really don't want to have a down year on an overall basis. Yet you can still participate in one to two complete market cycles, generating additional gains.

Stock selection is limited to blue chips and bonds that carry a higher-credit quality level, with a prevalence of government-backed issues and others having AA and AAA credit quality. No bonds should be purchased with less than a single A credit rating.

The Retired Investor—Ages 62 and Older

Allocation:
If you have retired, your asset allocation should look like this:

Common stocks	20-25 percent
Bonds	75-80 percent

You carry enough in common stocks to generate incremental returns in good years while offering little risk in poor ones. Since you anticipate bond interest being spent for living expenses, you can let your equities compound over the years without the need to disturb the portfolio for withdrawals.

Of course, if an emergency arises or bond yields prove inadequate, the equities can be converted to higher yielding bonds, or the proceeds from stock sales can be used to cover any shortfalls.

The individual stock-and-bond selection is quite similar to the pre-retirement individual, although advanced age may require a shortening of the average bond-portfolio maturity. As you advance in age, a growing desire for liquidity and safety is quite natural.

MAKE THE PROCESS DYNAMIC

Once you have decided on your asset allocation, you should analyze the portfolio every quarter or twice per year and readjust the allocation to account for the performance of the asset classes. By making a course correction on a regular basis, you have now made the asset-allocation process a dynamic one; it changes with time and circumstances.

One of the basic rules of good investing is that you should put money into investments that have fallen in price (buy low) and take money out of them once they have risen (sell high).

Let's say you have decided that you are going to maintain a 70-percent-bond, 30-percent-stock exposure in your portfolio. You invest $70,000 in government bonds and $30,000 in common stocks. Three months later, your stocks have done very well, rising to $35,000. The bond portfolio has increased by 2 percent to $71,400. The entire portfolio is now valued at $106,400. The stock portion of the account is now 32.8 percent, an increase from 30 percent due to the strong performance of your stocks. You now want to bring your equity portion back down to 30 percent, so you take $3,620 out of stocks and put it into bonds. This brings your mix back to the 70/30 ideal you decided to maintain. Note how money came out of stocks as their value rose.

Let's take the opposite case. Once you open the account, let's say the market takes a hit and your stocks drop to $25,000. The bonds again rise to $71,400, so the portfolio is now worth $96,400. Thirty percent of that amount in stocks would be $28,920, so you move $3,920 out of bonds and into stocks. You have bought more stock at lower prices.

This is a simple system, yet over time, the effect of buying low and selling high creates added value. And this technique meets your need to keep your discipline simple and easily understood. It is an automatic way to take profits and to buy when markets have fallen and prices are low. Your asset allocation, then, is an orderly progression that takes into account both the historic performance of the various asset classes as well as your age and circumstances; it is a dynamic and yet simple process that changes over time to serve your needs.

The more detailed work of selecting individual issues is done within this overall asset-allocation framework.

SUMMARY

We began by saying that asset allocation is the single most important investment issue you face. With over 90 percent of all investment returns explained by asset allocation, it is easy to see why this is so. And, it is equally true that most investors put the cart before the horse—they spend endless time picking individual investments and very little time on asset allocation.

Asset allocation sets the amount of risk and the amount of reward you can expect from your portfolio over longer periods of time. In order to be done properly, you need to be clear on your primary investment goal, whether income or capital growth or a combination of the two.

In arriving at that decision, you must take into account your tolerance for risk, the amount of time you have to invest the funds, your needs for current income, your investment experience, and your overall financial situation.

Often, investors mistake a fee issue for a trust or control issue. Whether you invest yourself or have others do it, you will generally find that fees are not grossly different, and so you need to be clear on why you want others to invest for you, or why you invest yourself.

With proper asset allocation, the achievement of long-term investment goals is much easier to accomplish. Without it, it is nearly impossible.

CHAPTER EIGHT

Common Stocks and the IRA

Since you want to position some of your IRA portfolio in common stocks for growth, you need to focus on several strategies that will help you achieve that goal without exposing your account to high levels of risk. There are several techniques you can use for common-stock selection that can be beneficial.

It cannot be emphasized too much that preservation of capital is the first goal of any IRA investment strategy. You always want to live to fight another day. When you are in full retirement, or close to it, opportunities to replace lost capital from wages are limited. Go-for-broke strategies can be devastating—there simply isn't time and money left to rectify the errors.

There is little doubt that picking stocks is the most popular subject in investing. People are fascinated with the possibility of making a lot of money in the market. The advice ranges from the time-tested and worthy to the obscure and silly. You can invest based on the stars, or perceived cycles in the natural world, or on the winner of the Super Bowl. Each method actually has its adherents and comes with assorted newsletters to fuel the faithful.

Other methods have proven successful over time. Investing in stocks with low price-earnings multiples comes to mind—a technique now copied by dozens if not hundreds of professional money managers. While small-capitalization stocks may come in and out of favor, they do tend to outperform their bigger brethren over time.

No matter how sound the approach, however, it will fall in and out of favor. No investment style will be successful in all markets, and that is a source of endless difficulty for investors when their particular style goes sour. The inevitable reaction is to dump that style in favor of one that seems to be enjoying greater success. It has been my experience that, generally, just when people feel compelled to take action to sell out either a stock or a style, they have done so precisely at the wrong time.

Much of this is rooted in psychology, both individual and group. Study after study has shown that investors tend to follow the market and the crowd instead of acting independently to discern a change coming in the trend. Investors, for all their protestations, tend not to anticipate but to follow.

Analysts will often continue to raise earnings forecasts the more their forecasts prove to be true. Never mind that stocks and their industries tend to be cyclical. Never mind that two or three good years tend to be followed by a bad one.

LOOKING BACKWARD: THE PITFALL OF REAR-VIEW INVESTING

Many forecasts are not forecasts at all; they're merely a straight line drawn from recent past experience. I have a chart that I developed about Elvis Presley impersonators. In 1960, it was reliably estimated that there were slightly over 200 Elvis impersonators in the United States. By 1990, that figure had grown to 14,000. By carrying forward that rate of growth, I estimated that by the middle of the twenty-first century, there would be more than 58 million Elvis impersonators, or one of every six Americans. The offensive unit of the Chicago Bears would have two on the field, perhaps at left tackle and center. A jury would have two, while a four-man bobsled team one.

Naturally, these are ridiculous assumptions. I simply took the recent history of Presley impersonators and continued the same growth curve into the future. And, despite a lot of research to the contrary, many people assume that because a company's earnings have been growing at 10 percent per year for three years, next year will be the same. I would suggest that the longer a trend holds in place, the more likely it is that next year will be entirely different. Good analysts recognize this, and instead of estimates that merely fake good analytical work, they actually do attempt to posit an accurate forecast, based more on the future than on the past.

People would save a lot of money if they would stop investing with their eyes planted in the rear-view mirror. Instead of looking at the history of Elvis impersonators and multiplying based on the historic record, they would be better advised to think independently. Better to ask the question, "What could make this year different from last year?" than to put money at risk based on what is little more than an assumption that good things will continue without change.

We all know instinctively that change is the normal course of events. This is especially true in dynamic and progressive societies. Only dead or dying systems remain static and resistant to change. And, since we live in a robust and changing world, we should rarely bet on yesterday becoming the way of the future.

Here are a few of the most striking examples of rear-view investing at major turning points in the market:

- In 1929, it was assumed that the United States had reached a new, permanent level of prosperity. The stock market lost 90 percent of its value over the following three years.
- In 1972, accepted wisdom meant buying stocks that would grow forever—the so called "Nifty 50." They became so grossly inflated in price that, some two decades later, many had yet to beat their 1972 highs.
- In 1981, it was widely assumed that given the increases seen in the price of crude oil, it would easily surpass $100 per barrel before the end of the century. (Some felt it would happen before the end of the decade.)
- In 1982, just before the market began a move that would see a 350 percent increase in stock prices over the span of the 1980s, most were bemoaning the worst recession since the Depression.

- In late 1987, it was generally assumed that the market would continue to break to new highs with very little to stop it. What followed was the greatest crash in the history of the markets. Then, what followed were equally dire forecasts that also proved incorrect.

- Finally, the great bull market of the 1990s has spawned a host of "this will last for years" mentality, despite the tendency of markets to self-correct for sometimes long periods of time.

I could go on and on for quite a while about predictions and assumptions. (Who anticipated the breathtaking collapse of the Soviet Union?) In case you think that wrong-way prediction is a thing of the past, focus on how many people didn't have the foggiest notion of how we would fight a war against Iraq. Many, including retired generals and veteran war correspondents who covered the Vietnam War were basing their commentary and assumptions on the last war. The strides made in both military hardware and doctrine got by them. As a result, their view was much more pessimistic than it should have been,

This was especially evident on the day the invasion of Iraq began. Most market analysts were predicting a 100- to 200-point fall in the Dow Industrials when the war started. Instead, the stock market roared ahead over 100 points.

Not everyone, of course, was bearish. Some pointed out, correctly, that so much despair and fear could only lead to a higher market. Rationally, however, it would have been difficult to make the argument that the market could head higher. An impending war created the worst kind of uncertainty. Had Iraq prevailed, its strangle hold on oil would certainly have led to further recession and inflation. And, since the country was heading into a recession, everything looked pretty bad.

This is very confusing for people. How can the market be believed when it heads higher when all about is bad news, worse news, and uncertainty? The answer is relatively simple.

If everything looks bad, and the bottom appears far off in the mist, it is a logical assumption to make that anyone who would sell securities based on that negative view of the future would have already done so. That fact is usually confirmed by looking at a chart of the Dow Industrials or the S&P 500. The chart will typically show a significant market sell-off in the recent past—the evidence of wholesale liquidation of stocks. When the actual event comes to pass, it has already been anticipated by people selling based on fear of the event actually happening. The event itself is anticlimactic.

If everyone who would sell has done so, doesn't it stand to reason that the more aggressive market participants will now be those anticipating a positive turn of events? And so, these more aggressive investors act on their anticipation by purchasing securities. The market moves higher, and most simply don't believe it. They look at current events as proof that purchasing securities is a risky and foolish venture. The market moves higher still, frustrating them even more. Only weeks later, as the doom and gloom lifts, do they see what the market sensed weeks before: that all is not so bad and in fact was due for a change for the better.

Sadly, they now buy stock, even as the market begins to retreat. Once again, they refuse to believe that the market should go down (Look at how good things are!), and they purchase from those who are now anticipating a turn for the worse. So it goes. Some people never get the hang of it.

This kind of frustrating experience is common to many people and accounts for more market casualties than any other reason. We have learned, perversely, that the lowest amount of risk will be found in those situations that appear to have the greatest amount of risk.

This seems to be a contradiction. After all, if something looks like a duck and quacks like a duck, isn't it always a duck? If something seems to have a lot of risk, doesn't it then? Not necessarily—not in the hard realities of the investment world. Let's examine why.

DEFINING RISK IN A COMMON STOCK

Risk, in relation to purchasing stock, is the chance that your investment will show a loss or a return not commensurate with the risk assumed. Let's use a game of dice as an example.

If you bet $1 to earn 10 cents on the chance that a throw of the dice would show double sixes, we would both agree that was a poor bet. The odds are overwhelming that you'll throw anything but a twelve, since only one combination of the 12 sides of two dice will produce a twelve. We would characterize that as a high-risk bet.

On the other hand, if throwing a twelve on a $1 bet would earn you $100, we would consider that a low-risk bet. We would expect to throw a twelve long before we had lost $100 betting $1 per throw.

This illustrates a measure of risk that takes into account the risk taken for the reward earned. All risk should be defined with the potential reward for assuming that risk. When a situation becomes increasingly fraught with risk, the potential reward must be increased. The way to increase the potential reward in a stock is to reduce the price of the stock. As the perceived risk increases, the price continues to drop, reflecting the increase of sellers wishing to avoid that risk. This process continues until the anticipated risk is so great as to cause the price of the stock to drop to nothing. At that point, the risk is so high (infinite) that the reward has to be infinite to reward the investor. An example would be a company that has gone out of business.

Remember this the next time you are tempted to buy a stock that looks cheap. It will look cheap only relative to the price at which it used to trade. A stock that has dropped from $40 to $5 may look cheap, but a rational view would be that something drastic has happened, and the change may be permanent. And while $5 may look cheap in absolute terms (it looks cheap compared to stocks trading at $100 per share), you should remind yourself that $5 is composed of 40 eighths, or 20 quarters. If you view it now at 40, or at 20, it looks much more expensive. And a drop of only $1 in the price is a 20 percent hit to your capital.

Such are the tricks our minds play on us when we invest in the market. Keeping these in mind, we try to profit from the mistakes of others. But one of the devilish things about investing in the market is that many situations that in most circumstances would warn you away can be viewed in precisely opposite terms.

We avoid stocks that look cheap relative to their recent past trading history. Yet the most profitable places to invest are in those areas that investors perceive carry the highest levels of risk. In those situations, stock prices have already been hammered down to reflect that perception of risk. Because they have been brought down, and because so many investors have sold their stock, those areas, paradoxically, carry lower levels of risk than areas that have yet to be marked down.

In purchasing depressed issues, however, it is a mistake to buy only individual securities. While you may fathom, correctly, that a particular industry will come out of the doldrums, you may buy a stock in that industry that, for completely different reasons, fails to move. Or you may jump early and overpay for the stock. Because of these pitfalls, I have developed an approach to investing that I call the "basket."

BUYING BASKETS

Most IRA account holders are better equipped to sense the trend of an industry, as opposed to an individual stock. We hear about the auto business or the homebuilding industry having tough times. Maybe computer stocks are soaring, or crashing.

And so, investors might be better served by finding industries that are attractive and then buying a representative sampling of that industry.

I believe that it is easier to predict the movement of an entire industry than a particular company within that industry. Let's use airlines as an example.

The Airline Industry

We all know that when fuel prices are high and the country is in recession, airlines tend to lose money, and their stock prices are severely marked down. The risk in airline stocks is perceived to be high. They are losing money and some may even go out of business. This is probably all true. Who wants to buy an airline stock only to lose the entire investment? Yet, investment in airlines is compelling, since eventually the industry will fly again into profits.

The way to take advantage of the opportunity is to buy, not one, but several airline stocks. While you can argue that an individual airline may go out of business, you can't argue that the airline industry will go out of business. People will continue to fly in airplanes as the most cost-effective way of traveling long distances. Therefore, it is a simple matter to isolate the three strongest industry leaders and buy equal dollar amounts in all three stocks. It is quite impossible to imagine a recovery in the airline industry without all three of the industry leaders participating. Although a particular region may continue to have difficulty, the general recovery of the economy will have a great impact on airlines that fly to most of the major metropolitan areas.

There may be individual quirks that can cause one of the three to lag behind. Although recovery helps the industry, perhaps one of the three has a labor problem, or a safety problem that causes a curtailment of operations. Nevertheless, with three horses pulling your cart, you can have one lame and still get the cart to market. By buying three stocks instead of one, you have significantly reduced your risk.

When you buy an airline stock, you're buying it because you've made a decision about the industry, and you've picked that particular stock to help translate your view into action. Go the extra step and buy two, or three, or four stocks from that industry.

Other Industries

A similar situation can exist in almost any industry. When copper prices are depressed and the copper industry is really in the pits, purchase three of the industry leaders. When copper recovers, you'll have handsome profits.

When the banking industry appeared to be flat on its back in late 1990, we had accounts that purchased as many as 20 banks, all of them either national or super regional banks. Our reasoning was quite simple: While the odds were fairly good that any single bank could have gone out of business, the odds were much higher that the banking industry would survive. So we could expect that from the 20 we purchased, one or two or three could go bankrupt, but the survivors would show such high profits on our investment that we would more than make up for the losers. Within months, we accrued profits of 30 percent to 100 percent on nearly every issue we purchased. Since we limited our purchases to the biggest banks (the area precisely where the greatest risk was perceived), we felt secure because we knew the country would need a national banking system. Again, a particular region or small bank might not do particularly well, but if the banking system would survive, those 20 banks would probably be the cornerstones.

You don't want to be deluded by the idea that you don't do as well if you buy fewer shares than if you concentrate on one stock.

For some reason, people are reluctant to buy 50 shares of an $80 stock, preferring 100 shares of a $40 stock. Either position has an equal potential for gain. A 20 percent move in an $80 stock is just as profitable as a 20 percent move in a $40 stock, if the dollar investment is the same.

I could give many examples, but you get the idea.

Spread Out the Investment

You want to invest between $10,000 and $25,000 in a single basket. In purchasing three different stocks (that tends to be a good average) you may wind up with odd lots (holdings of less than 100 shares) here and there. If you buy stocks on the New York or American Stock Exchanges or the NASDAQ market, they are not difficult to sell. The important thing is that you spend equal dollar amounts on each stock, so that you have no bias toward any individual issue.

What to Look for

In deciding which stocks to buy within an industry look for:

1. *Leadership.* You want stocks that are industry leaders and so will participate in the industry's recovery.
2. *Strong financials.* Companies heavily burdened with debt can show the greatest percentage gains. But since you're buying in an atmosphere of crisis and difficulty, you may be early. That is, you're buying before the company has put its troubles behind it. And so the company should have a strong financial condition to weather the storm. You don't want to buy one with a high potential for bankruptcy.

3. *Broad industry participation.* If you're buying drug stocks, for instance, you want companies that market a broad spectrum of product, not a narrow one. Again, you don't want to be blindsided with a problem that can derail the recovery for that stock.

4. *Dividends.* Since anticipating a turn can mean the investment does not perform for some period of time, you can at least earn a dividend while you wait. This provides some ongoing return and so helps earn a profit. This, however, is not as important as the other three criteria.

Isolating names is no more difficult than a trip through the Value Line Investment Survey or Standard & Poor's guides. The information is easily accessible, although interpreting the relevant financial data is beyond the ability of many investors. In its place, a Standard & Poor's stock ranking (A, B, and so on) or the Value Line Safety Ranking is good to use. I would suggest a Value Line Safety Ranking of 3 or better, and a Standard & Poor's rating of B or better.

If you're out of your depth, ask your broker for good stocks within the industry of interest. He or she will have that information readily available.

Mutual-fund investors can consider groups such as Sector funds. Funds that limit investment to a single industry accomplish the same thing as buying the individual stocks of an industry. These funds offer the convenience of one-purchase-buys-all, dividend reinvestment, and switching between funds. But convenience comes at a price. Many fund groups of this type carry various fees, as well as annual fund expenses and management fees.

If you like to buy and hold, it may be less expensive to pay a one-time commission and buy individual stocks.

Finding Industry Ideas

How do you find these ideas and focus in on likely candidates? There are several ways, and some may appear to be haphazard. It is my experience that there are always good ideas around and stocks to buy, so a strictly regimented discipline may blind you to some particularly creative ideas. Experience has taught me there are situations that can trigger profitable investment.

Here's a list of things that should focus your interest:

1. *The atmosphere is generally gloomy.* This typically occurs in recession, or after the market has really taken a beating. Whatever the atmosphere, you need to see it reflected in . . .

2. *Lower stock prices.* You want to see prices in that particular industry marked down between 30 percent and 50 percent from previous highs. Those highs may have occurred earlier in the year or several years ago. It should be obvious that today's prices are a considerable disappointment from prior levels. For instance, if the industry price index is currently down 30 percent from its high but up 30 percent from its low, you might continue looking. If, however, the price represents a new low, your interest may continue, especially if accompanied by . . .

3. *Broad media coverage of the industry's woes.* Coverage by nationally circulated publications insures that everyone knows the story and that enough time has elapsed to flush out sellers. When the doom and gloom is widely recognized across the country, a lot of the risk has already been wrung out of stocks. Of course, the best of all worlds is when . . .

4. *You read an article in a national publication that questions the very survivability of the industry.* While there are always articles questioning the viability of individual companies, articles that question the survival of an entire industry are much more rare and reflect an even deeper level of pessimism. Since most industries survive their difficulties, such reportage is usually a pretty good buy signal.

What you will see is a general picture of pessimism, depression, and a general assumption that risk is very high. I have seen these situations arise with utilities, telephones, drugs, airlines, banks, and other equally necessary businesses.

There are some pitfalls in this approach.

Once you try a basket, and it works, there is a tendency to rush out to find another. Fortunately, because industries tend to move at different times, it's usually not too difficult to find another opportunity. You have to keep in mind, however, that you may have had a stunning success because the market as a whole had a good move up. In that atmosphere risk has increased, since stocks are not selling at bargain-basement lows.

Your response is to pick more carefully and rein in your profit expectations. While the first basket may have returned 20 percent or 25 percent in fairly short order, your next basket may only return 15 percent. Be aware of where stock prices are in the cycle and adjust your expectations accordingly.

Another problem is that after the market has had a healthy advance there is a tendency to buy groups that haven't moved. This can be a mistake, because if a group doesn't participate in an overall market move, you could be so early as to lock up your money without hope of near-term profit. After all, a basket purchase should be a fairly quick hit. You're looking for profits within six months to one year of purchase. A basket isn't designed as a multiyear, long-term buy-and-hold strategy.

Like good food or a pleasant wine, a successful investment move creates a desire for more. You have to realize that the very success you have enjoyed due to higher stock prices reduces the chances of success on the next go-around. There is an old saying on Wall Street: Bears make money, and Bulls make money, but pigs don't.

WHEN DO YOU SELL THE BASKET?

Selling is usually more difficult than buying. But, there are several ways in which you can judge when to sell.

First, establish your profit potential when you enter the positions, then sell the basket when you've reached your profit goal. How much profit to expect? Look at the old highs for the stocks and the industry, then pick a target somewhere between where they are now and the old highs. Unless you can make a reasonable argument for a 25 percent gain, you shouldn't enter the basket; 30 percent to 50 percent is a reasonable profit goal.

Your broker can give you assistance through her firm's research department, or you can check other resources, such as the ValueLine

Investment Survey to get an idea of the immediate prospects for that industry.

Or, you can sell positions as they appreciate in relation to your account. Since any single industry shouldn't comprise more than 15 percent of your portfolio, you can sell down the positions once they become 20 percent or more of the account. This way, you sell as they rise, taking profits as you go.

DOING THE DOW

One excellent way for individual investors to invest is to use the 30 stocks comprising the Dow Jones Industrial Average. Dow Jones, the keeper of the index, designs the Dow to mimic the American economy by constructing a portfolio of 30 large "blue-chip" corporations in many different industries. If you were to buy all 30 of the Dow stocks in equal *share* amounts, you would own the Dow Jones Industrial Average. This indexing of your portfolio would assure you the return of the Dow over time. And the Dow has usually outperformed all major stock indexes over longer periods of time.

But, perhaps you don't have enough capital to buy all 30 stocks. In that case, you can buy a subset of the Dow.

One of the more popular strategies has been to buy the 10 highest yielding stocks in the Dow—euphemistically called the "Dogs of the Dow." The idea behind this is that the highest yielding stocks represent true value, whether through beaten-down price or high payouts of earnings to shareholders. While performance has varied from year to year, this has proven to be a good market strategy.

Conversely, there is evidence that buying the 10 *lowest* yielding stocks in the Dow works also. This strategy concentrates the portfolio on stocks that are more growth oriented, hence the lower dividend yields.

It is statistically accurate to say that if you own 7 to 15 Dow stocks, your chances of performing within 10 percent of the Dow industrials over time is fairly high and so, a strategy that limits purchasing to a select group of Dow stocks would probably work fairly well.

The key point here is that for the IRA investor, a portfolio laden with America's largest corporations is not a bad idea. In a down market, you can probably sleep easier than with a portfolio of hot-shot ideas, some of which may not have the staying power to make it through bad times. And, limiting purchases to Dow stocks means that you can usually have a lower turnover, so, lower expense.

Finally, since you are buying only the highest-quality stocks, you are sticking to one of my main investing maxims for IRA investors—buy only quality issues.

STICK TO YOUR PLAN

Once you've entered the position with a plan, stick to it. If you wind up selling a position and it then reverses and goes much higher, you should shrug if off and go on to the next opportunity. But for every stock that does that, you'll have two or three that will prove to be good selling opportunities. Keep your greed under control. If you abandon the strategy midstream, you're back to investing on emotion and guess.

There are times when you buy a basket and the mistake quickly becomes evident: The stocks fall from the first day you own them and then continue to be weak. There are times when you goof. You have to recognize this as a normal part of the investment process. You take your lumps and look for another idea.

If you really have picked a depressed industry, prices should be near bottom. A further drop exceeding 10 or 15 percent could signal that you've misjudged things and that the bottom is still out there somewhere.

The next time you have an investment idea about a stock go the next step and analyze whether your opinion is really an industry opinion or an opinion on an individual stock. More often than not, you'll find that your investment scenario is about the industry, and you've picked a stock that will play that through. If so, expand to a basket. Your performance will improve over time, and you'll reduce your risk in the process.

BUYING INDIVIDUAL STOCKS

Don't buy individual positions when you can afford a basket. The basket approach is a superior way to invest and will fulfill most of your needs to invest when you're not using a professional manager.

Nevertheless, there are times when a special situation arises and you want to own a particular stock. I must emphasize that this shouldn't happen too often. In the course of a year, you might find one or two that you'd want to own.

There has been so much written about how to pick individual common stocks that it is difficult to add anything new. There are many good books on the market that cover the subject in great detail, and I've listed some in Appendix 2. When you do find a stock you want to own, it should be because it fills some niche that can't be filled in any other way. A few concrete examples might help illustrate this.

- You can purchase a Real Estate Investment Trust (REIT) as a way of investing in real estate markets. This is an especially good way to buy real estate exposure for your IRA.
- In attempting to find good yield, you can look at preferred stocks.
- There are other limited uses for individual stocks, but it is more accurate to say that you buy a single stock when you can't find a basket to fill your needs.

Again, it's not that there aren't profitable opportunities in individual stocks. It's just that investors are usually making an industry judgment but mistake it for an individual stock idea. Think about some of the stocks you may have bought in the past. Weren't you really focusing more on the industry than on the company?

STOCK OPTIONS AND COMPANY STOCK

Many people accumulate both shares and options on the shares of their employer. Sometimes, this accumulation is through a payroll-deduction savings plan, often with a discount for purchase. In other cases, the employer has granted options or stock to the employee. And, the more shares and options accumulated, the more difficult it can become to decide what to do.

The difficulty of the decision lies in the size of the problem. If you retire with, say, 50 percent of your benefit in stock, the size of the position makes decision difficult. One of the basic tenets of investing to remember is to always try to make the small decision. There is less pressure that way, and you can therefore think more clearly.

So it is with concentrated positions. If you try and make an all-or-none decision on the sale of the stock, you will find it difficult to do the right thing. And so, you should follow an orderly thought process in this regard.

An Employer-Stock Game Plan

After working with clients for 20 years, many of whom retired with concentrated stock positions, I have formed some clear guidelines I encourage people to follow. The important thing to remember in all of this is that no one really knows where the price of your employer's stock is going to go, and so you should concentrate your efforts on formulating your investment portfolio. That will tell you what to do about your employer's stock.

For instance, if you are interested only in current income and don't want any risk, you sell the stock . . . all of it. But, you say, I think the stock is going to go up. That may be, but your goal is current income, not capital appreciation. Wrestling with this issue may lead you to conclude that you really are after some capital appreciation, and so perhaps some stock should be held.

If you try to fathom the future movement of the stock, you will generally find it a fruitless exercise if you are carrying a large position. This is because the pressure of the decision prevents clear thinking. How large is large? It varies for each person, but my rule of thumb is more than 30 percent of your investment assets in your employer's stock is a large position. This is because at the 30 percent level, if the stock drops 20 percent, it would represent only a loss of

6 percent in your entire portfolio. This is a manageable loss and would not jeopardize your retirement.

That 30 percent threshold is one I encourage clients to use. If you are bullish on the stock, nevertheless you should sell it down to about 30 percent of your investment portfolio. Exceptions do abound, however. If you have a very high net worth, say, $5 million or more, you can hold onto a larger amount, up to 40 percent. Why 40 percent? Because even if the stock is completely wiped out, you'll still have a $3 million portfolio, and I consider that to be the threshold portfolio for highly compensated people to continue a reasonably affluent lifestyle.

Once in a while, I will run into an individual who wants to make the big bet on his company's stock—a 50 percent or more position. That is all well and good, but I question the wisdom of attempting to significantly increase your net worth once you've retired. It's not that it can't be done. It's just that if you are wrong, you've inalterably reduced the quality of your life for the two or three decades of retirement. If you want to try it, just be sure that you've got adequate resources to carry you through if you're wrong.

Psychological Pitfalls

There are several pitfalls that you need to avoid in deciding whether or not to hold onto the stock.

1. *I don't want to be disloyal.* If you have enjoyed a good career at your company, and if the company has allowed you to build your family's net worth, it is a natural thing to feel a sense of loyalty to the company. And so some people are hesitant to sell their stock because they feel they would, in some way, be betraying the hand that fed them.

Nothing could be further from the truth. If you were to ask your company's CEO what he or she would advise, the person would almost certainly tell you to worry about yourself and your family and do the right thing for them. They would not ask you to think about the needs of the company. Companies give stock and options to retain good employees. And they know that eventually that stock will be sold.

You can still be loyal to your former employer without holding onto the stock.

2. What if I sell it and the price skyrockets? Well, that is a reasonable question and a realistic problem. It invokes the "greed" side of our personalities.

You need to be clear on your financial goals. If your goal is for maximum capital gain, holding onto the stock is one way to meet that goal. On the other hand, you have concentrated the risk into one single stock, and that is probably not a wise thing to do. Better to sell some stock and diversify into other stocks as well.

If you are seeking maximum current income, then the stock position runs counter to that goal and should be sold, with the proceeds put into bonds.

3. What if I hold it and the price plummets? This is the other side of the equation and invokes our "fear" response.

If you are concerned about a fall in the price, you are signaling to yourself that you are probably carrying too much risk; so sell enough stock to reduce that fear to a manageable level.

4. I really like the prospects of the company, but I'm holding a lot of stock. This is essentially a fear of loss. You like what you see, but are uncomfortable with the size of your position.

Again, you need to be clear on your investment/retirement goals. If you have capital gain as part of your game plan, then holding onto a reasonable amount of stock would make some sense.

5. If I sell the stock, I will have to pay a lot of tax. Taxes are the cost of doing business in the investment world. Any time you own an investment-for-capital gain, capital-gains taxes go along with that investment. Don't let the tax bite sway you—one market swoon could drop the price of the stock the equivalent of the taxes you would pay by selling early.

Before selling, however, you should explore with your attorney, accountant, or advisor the variety of strategies available in charitable giving, setting up irrevocable trusts, and getting stepped-up cost-basis treatment if the stock eventually winds up in your estate. Sometimes, an outright sale is not the best course of action.

Of course, if the stock is sold inside an IRA, no current tax is due.

> **TIP**   There is an interesting investment vehicle called an *exchange fund*. In an exchange fund, you contribute your shares of company stock to the fund, and in return, you get partial ownership of the fund, which is typically a diversified common-stock fund. You pay no tax on the contribution to the fund, but the taxes don't go away. Eventually, when the fund, closes down, you'll get your share of the common stocks in the fund, and they will reflect your original cost basis in the stock you contributed.
>
> Exchange funds are typically for the affluent investor, and minimum investments of $2 million or more are not unusual. They are offered by very few companies, and you usually need to contact a broker to find one.
>
> Exchange funds allow you to diversify your portfolio without incurring current taxes.

6. *The stock is down and it's only a paper loss until I sell it.* The plain fact of the matter is that you have the loss. It is not just a paper one. It's a real one. The question is, are you going to earn back the money in the position you currently have, or in something else? The fact that it is a loss should signal to you that perhaps there may be a better investment than the holding of the company stock.

7. *I can't sell. I've taken 20 years to accumulate the position.* It doesn't matter if it took 20 years or one year. The reality is that you have a certain number of shares and you need to make a decision about them. You accumulated the shares because you wanted to increase your net worth to help fund retirement. Well, you're now there, and you need to put that money to work in the best way possible.

8. *I want to hold the stock, but I think the price will be weak for the next year or so.* You should explore using various options strategies, called *collars,* to protect the position.

While a discussion of collars is beyond the scope of this book, they involve selling a call option and simultaneously buying a put option on the stock as protection.

For instance, if your stock is trading at $40, you could sell a call option with a price of $40 and expiring in six-months. Then, you would take the money you received and buy a put option with a six-month expiration. By selling the call, you allow the buyer of the option to call away your stock at $40 within the next six months. However, the seller of the put allows you to put the stock to them at $40 within the next six months. In effect, you have removed any downside, or any upside, in the stock.

If you are correct, and the price falls, you could sell your puts for a profit, or put the stock to the put seller at $40 and be done with it.

As you can see, this is a complicated transaction, and the services of a professional are a must. You also need to explore the tax consequences of this transaction with your accountant.

9. *I want to hold the stock, but I need some cash to finance purchase.* If the stock is not held in an IRA, you can simply pledge it as collateral and borrow the money from your bank or broker. Your broker is limited by Federal Reserve regulations in how much he or she can lend against the stock, but the broker will sometimes have a better lending interest rate than the bank.

The bank, on the other hand, can be more flexible in how much they lend, and the terms of the loan. Check with both before deciding.

Stock Options

Stock options are a more complicated issue, but made simpler when you remember that they are simply another form of stock ownership.

The tax issues surrounding stock options are fairly simple, but I strongly urge my clients to see their accountant to be clear on their tax strategy before they decide to hold or exercise options. However, it has been my experience that individuals holding stock options are quite clear on the basic rules, and so we'll assume that you already know them, and if not, you'll see your accountant for help.

What if you retire with a number of options of varying expiration date? First, you should value the options based on the actual economic value.

1. *You hold options on 1000 shares with an option price of $20. The stock is currently trading at $60. The value for planning purposes is $40,000.* Then you want to compute whether or not the value of the options exceeds the 30 percent ownership threshold. That is, you compare the economic value of the options to your total investment portfolio and see if that is more than 30 percent. If it is, you need to decide how much risk you're willing to take. Presumably, if you have a number of options, you were senior enough in your corporation to have a well-informed opinion about the company. But, no matter how highly you regard the prospects of your former employer, the industry can go cold or the stock market can drop, so you won't be immune from those problems.

Use as your rule of thumb, the 20 percent loss rule. Compute what a 20 percent hit to the stock would do and judge whether or not you could sustain it. And, remember, that options leverage your position, and so, a 20 percent hit to the stock hits your options a lot harder:

2. *The stock drops from $60 to $48, a 20 percent decline. However, based on your option price of $20, the 20 percent stock decline has wiped off 30 percent of your profit ($40 profit has been cut to $28).* As in concentrated ownership of the stock, a large option position is difficult to deal with since large decisions tend to paralyze our thinking. And, given the leverage of the option, small moves in the price of the underlying shares is magnified:

3. *You own 12,000 shares on option. A price change of $1 in the stock is a $12,000 gain or loss to your net worth.* Unless you have a very strong opinion on the stock (that is, sell it all or hold it all), you can use almost any strategy that will take you out of the position in a

piecemeal way. Building upon the ideas offered earlier about concentrated stock positions, you can consider the following:

a. Simply exercise and sell a specific percentage of your options each year, say, 20 percent.

b. Exercise and sell as each option reaches expiration.

c. Exercise and sell enough options to keep your position at no more than 20 percent or 30 percent of your net worth.

As you can see, all of these strategies will sell you out over a period of time and so, you will average the price of the stock over that period.

If, on the other hand, you have a very strong opinion, you may decide to get rid of your entire option position, or keep all of it. Just remember that as far as the investment decision is concerned, you are in essentially the same position as a concentrated stock position. While the taxes on option-exercise frame different issues, it is still, at heart, an investment issue.

INTERACTING WITH THE MARKET

Investing in the stock market entails risk. As such, it can be an emotionally difficult process. I have found very few situations that will bring out an individual's true character more than putting his or her money at risk.

When your capital is on the line, all kinds of psychological hang-ups, foibles, and fears come into play. At times, people can be irrational about the whole thing. Fear of loss can stress certain people beyond their ability to cope.

It is important, then, for you to know yourself very well. You should be concerned with overstepping your ability to handle risk.

This is not to say that once you've gotten a handle on your risk tolerance you simply invest based on that. You may have experienced many investment setbacks due to poor advice. You may have never had a game plan and investment discipline. So there is an educational process that must be applied. Strategies and concepts must be made clear and adhered to.

If you have a long history of investment failure, your first task is to rebuild confidence. This may mean investing only in high-grade bonds for some period of time. The idea is to begin to develop a consistent record of portfolio growth. As the portfolio grows, so grows your confidence. Once you feel that you've made some headway and that investment success can be yours, then revisit the idea of taking risk.

Like a person learning how to walk again after having a leg in a cast, the first steps are always taken carefully. Start with a small position. These small investment moves are intended to serve a dual purpose: to make a profit and to test your reactions to money at risk. Perhaps for the first time, you are becoming aware of how your mind works for and against your investment strategy.

When you react in an irrational way, your thoughts should center around your reaction. It does little good for you to give in to emotion and sell out losing positions. By doing so, you simply reinforce the negative behavior that has hurt your performance in the past. Much more difficult, but much more beneficial, is to take the time to explore your reaction to events.

This kind of interaction and exploration of motive and emotion is the only way you can progress. To blindly repeat yesterday's mistakes wastes both energy and money.

Can You Handle Risk?

Now, it may be that you really are incapable of taking risk. The trauma of past loss may be so great that the problem is not going to go away. People who experienced the depression of the 1930s often react this way. Their experience was so humiliating and painful that they find it impossible to run the risk of losing capital.

However, whether you change your attitude toward risk, and whether you improve your technique, at least you have made a good attempt to do so. If you have to revert to U.S. Treasuries or certificates of deposit, you do so with the knowledge that you have fully explored alternatives and found them impossible to use.

If you overcome your fears and begin to enjoy investment success, you have made a substantial contribution to your well-being. You develop the confidence to be more creative in your investing. You have a discipline and a sense that while you may not make money on every move, you are making a concerted and intelligent effort.

Why Be In the Stock Market?

There is another problem in immersing yourself in the stock market. You may tend to lose sight of why you're doing it at all.

Over long periods of time, common stocks have shown superior returns versus other investment classes. They have done so because common stock ownership represents ownership in business, and businesses generally earn higher returns on their stockholders' invested capital than does money invested in bonds or precious metals. The only reason management borrows money from the bank is because they believe they can earn more than the interest expense paid out.

We tend to forget all of that in our search for winners. We forget that all the effort is being made to find businesses that can earn superior rates of return on their stockholders' invested money. If that were not the case, a fixed rate of interest offered by a bond would be a better alternative.

Since active human endeavor (running a business) tends to produce better results than collecting interest (investing in bonds), you shouldn't be daunted by trying to pick common stocks. The most important aspect of the strategy is to be in common stocks. If the quality you pick is good, and if you diversify your holdings in several different issues, you'll do well enough.

Keep It Simple

We're pointing to one of the basic tenets of investment philosophy: Keep it simple. If the market is going to have a major up-leg, you'll participate if you own five or six big stocks. A lot of energy is expended trying to get the edge, trying to do just a little bit better.

Much of this effort is best left to professionals. Trying to decide whether an auto stock is going to move before a telephone stock is an inexact art at best. Most investors would be better off buying both and hedging the bet. It's a much more important call deciding whether you should be in the market at all.

If you can't find a way to invest in stocks that makes sense to you, but you want to be in the market, buy an index mutual fund. An index fund attempts to mirror one of the major stock market indices, usually the S&P 500. While you'll never beat the market in an index fund, you can at least be assured that you'll be close to the returns of the market. Being close and in the market is a far sight better than abandoning the potentially high returns of common stocks altogether because you don't believe you can beat the market.

SUMMARY

Once the overall asset allocation of your portfolio has been set, you need to position some of your money in the stock market. If you want to pick your own stocks, you're much better off purchasing baskets that reflect better times ahead for depressed industries.

Don't spend a lot of time fine-tuning your stock picks. Focus more on the question of whether you should be in the market and with what portion of your portfolio.

Buy industry leaders in a group. If you think the market is going higher, buy six or seven blue chips in different industries that will ride the general trend.

Examine your motives and reactions continuously so that you learn from your mistakes.

If you can't pick stocks on your own, hire a money manager or find a good general common stock fund and let others do the work. Sometimes, admitting that you can't do something well is most of the battle.

Pick up and study any one of the books on the stock market listed in Appendix 2, even if you are going to have others invest for you. You need to understand something about the market and how it works if you are going to be able to make sense of what others advise you to do.

Finally, remember that over time, common stocks have historically outperformed all other major asset classes and so have a definite place in your IRA portfolio. Growth of capital from common-stock investment is important to any long-term IRA investment plan.

CHAPTER NINE

Bonds in the IRA

Fixed-income investments tend to be the overwhelming choice for IRA investors. Faced with the prospect of living on a fixed income and the need for security, these investments are a natural pick. They provide a steady stream of interest income and a fixed maturity date when funds will be returned. This combination of income and certainty of principal repayment make them attractive for lump-sum investment.

What exactly is a fixed-income investment? It is an investment that returns a stated rate of interest to the investor, with a stated maturity or return of principal. These include:

- Certificates of deposit
- U.S. Treasury bills, notes, and bonds
- Federal Agency Bonds
- Mortgage-backed securities
- Corporate bonds
- Municipal bonds
- Money-market funds and other day-to-day investments

For simplicity, investors refer to the bond market as the fixed-income market.

Much has been written about the bond market and how to invest successfully in it. So much has been done, in fact, that we need to simplify the abundance of advice given about bond investing. Since your bond portfolio is only part of your planning and investment process, you need to develop a proven strategy for handling your bonds. This will allow you to focus time and energy on other areas where you can exert more control.

We will learn to use a strategy called bond laddering that will not only simplify your bond investing but will greatly increase your chances of being successful.

JUDGING A BOND

All bond investments have three properties:

1. The credit quality of the instrument
2. The date of maturity
3. The terms of the interest payments

Learn to judge each bond by these three simple attributes. Once you break down a bond by these three components, it is easy to decide on how the bond will fit into your strategy.

The credit quality and maturity of a bond are the two yardsticks you need to use when executing a bond-laddering strategy. I mention these now so you can keep them in mind when we discuss bond laddering.

A Bond Investor Is a Lender

When you buy a bond, you are lending your money to the issuer of that bond. Whether it is the U.S. Treasury or Ford Motor Company, your purchase of that bond has made you a creditor of the issuer. They owe you interest on your loan, and they agree to pay your money back to you on the stated date of maturity. The exact terms of this "loan" are set forth in the indenture, a document created when the bond was issued.

When a company issues bonds, investors (lenders) want to know the credit quality of the bond before they buy. So issuers (the borrowers) find it worthwhile to pay for an independent credit appraisal that investors can use to judge the bond's quality.

Standard & Poor's, Moody's, and Fitch's are the "Who's Who" of bond-rating organizations. These companies are paid by the bond issuer to apply a credit rating to bonds as they are issued. Once the rating has been given, the rating company continues to follow the creditworthiness of the bond and, if necessary, change its rating, sometimes years after it was first issued.

Again, this allows investors to follow the quality of their bonds as long as the issue is outstanding.

The rating companies use a system of letter symbols to express their opinion about the bond.

The U.S. government carries an AAA credit rating because of its unlimited taxing ability. Companies with lower credit ratings may be rated AA, A, BBB, BB, B, CCC, CC, or C if they are rated by Standard & Poor's. Moody's follows a slightly different system. For instance, a BBB rating by Standard & Poor's is equivalent to a BAA Moody's rating.

There are also shades of meaning associated with these ratings. Bonds rated A- are better than bonds rated BBB+. Likewise, an AA+ rating is slightly better than AA, but not as good as AAA.

How these ratings are set is a complicated subject. There are a number of financial tests that ratings agencies apply in order to create a rating on a bond. If you want to examine these in more detail, your broker should be able to provide this information to you. In addition, you can write directly to any of the rating companies for this information.

CREDIT QUALITY AND RISK IMPLICATIONS

The lower the credit quality of a bond, the higher the investment risk. After all, if there is some doubt that you'll be paid back, you will want to demand a higher rate of interest, or return, for your trouble. If a bond is very safe, you'll settle for a lower rate, reflecting the higher quality of the investment. You need to determine just how much risk you're willing to run in your bond portfolio. Remember, higher returns don't come without higher risk.

As a general rule, when you use a bond-ladder strategy, you shouldn't settle for bonds with a credit rating lower than A-. Bonds rated A- or better carry good rates of interest without high levels of credit risk. You should know that bonds rated BBB or better are referred to as "investment-grade" bonds. Bank trust departments, for instance, can buy them.

If you buy a bond rated A- or better, your bond can undergo a bond credit downgrade, while still leaving you with an investment-grade instrument. If you start with a BBB-rated bond, and it is downgraded to BB, you'll find that not only has the bond developed serious problems, but if you try to sell it you'll have to accept a substantial markdown in price. Since many institutions won't buy bonds below BBB quality, there is a much smaller pool of buyers for BB bonds. The BB rating also carries the handle of "junk bond." It's more trouble than it's worth for you.

By sticking to bonds rated A-, or higher, you'll find that the issuers are among America's largest corporations. You'll have every reason to believe that all payments due to you, both principal and interest, will come to you on time.

I don't believe you need to stick with AAA issues either. At the AAA level, there is a reduction in the interest rate you can earn. AAA bonds are as risk-free as the market acknowledges, so rates of interest are correspondingly low. By buying only AAA bonds, you are paying a very high insurance premium against default.

EXAMPLE You have a $100,000 bond portfolio. Bonds with A ratings are currently yielding 1 percent more than bonds rated AAA. By purchasing AAA-rated bonds, you are giving up $1,000 per year in interest to reduce your risk against default.

Sell on a Credit Downgrade

Once you have put your portfolio in place, you'll want to monitor credit quality. If your broker's statements don't carry the credit rating of each bond on the statement, ask him for a credit report every three months. The ratings companies publish handy credit-rating guides that your broker subscribes to, so it isn't difficult to gather together this information. If you want, you can subscribe to the Standard & Poor's Bond Guide. Issued monthly, it carries credit ratings and changes on hundreds of bond issues (Standard & Poor's Corporation, 25 Broadway, New York, NY 10004).

Once your bond is downgraded to BBB, you should seriously consider selling the bond. If you have established A- as your lowest credit rating, you'll want to adhere to this rule. The rating company has downgraded the bond for a reason, and you need some guideline to trigger a sale.

Keeping in mind that BBB is still investment-grade quality, why would you sell? Because, if you are surprised by a further downgrade to BB, then the price markdown on your bond will be considerable. While the price difference between A- and BBB is fairly small, it is quite large between BBB and BB. Bond-rating companies tend to drop the rating on a bond a notch at a time (A- to BBB+, then to BBB, then to BBB-, and so on), so you'll usually have some time to decide.

There are times when you'll hold your BBB bond. If, for instance, the downgrade occurs at the end of a recession and the bond you hold was issued by an automobile company, it is reasonable to expect that with improved business conditions the auto company will enjoy stronger profits. It is even possible that the credit rating will be upgraded instead of downgraded.

When in doubt, sell the bond. Maintain the quality of the portfolio.

Diversify Your Risk

Keep in mind that bond issuers can default. You want to spread around your money so that you don't have too much lent to one borrower. Just as a bank will diversify its loan portfolio, you will want to do the same.

As a general rule, you should limit each issuer to 5 percent of your bond portfolio. This means that on a $100,000 portfolio, you'll want to have 20 different bond issuers. In this way, a default on a bond affects only 5 percent of your portfolio. It will hurt, but it won't be fatal.

If you are holding an AA- or AAA-rated bond, you could bump your exposure up to 10 percent. U.S. government issues, of course, can comprise 100 percent of your portfolio, if you are very risk-averse.

You also want to keep diversified by industry. It wouldn't be prudent to have 20 different bank bonds in your portfolio. (We're talking about bonds issued and backed by the bank, not about certificates of deposit, which carry government insurance.) While you don't have more than 5 percent of your portfolio in any one bank's notes, you do have 100 percent of your portfolio exposed to the banking industry. Since companies in any one industry tend to move in tandem, you actually have a higher risk than may first be apparent. The factors that could endanger one bank would probably affect all banks.

By diversifying your portfolio by industry and issuer, and by maintaining at least A- credit ratings, you have diversified your portfolio with good-quality bonds. This will provide the best compromise between high yield and low risk.

Don't Speculate in the Bond Market

Many investors speculate in the bond market to earn additional return. This is generally not a good idea because the risk/reward relationship in the bond market is rarely in your favor as an individual investor.

A lower-rated bond will carry a higher rate of interest than a highly rated one. If the risk is contained and manageable, say in A-rated bonds, the higher interest rate they provide is worth considering. However, when the risk of default becomes very real, as in the case of BB or CCC bonds, a higher interest rate offers little compensation.

If you are wrong about the bond, you risk 100 percent of your investment. If you are right, you may earn 3 percent or 5 percent more per year on the bond than you would earn on an investment-grade bond. Why risk 100 percent to earn an extra 5 percent? If you wish to speculate, do so in the stock market where you can take on equal or higher risk, but can earn 20 or 50 or 100 percent on your money.

MATURITY AND PRICE RISK

The second component of any bond, its maturity date, has to be considered before purchase. The longer the maturity date, the longer you'll wait for your principal investment to be paid back to you. Although you will receive regular interest payments until then, only the maturity date insures the payback of your principal at a specific time.

This payback creates another form of risk in bond investment. Although credit risk involves getting the money back, maturity risk deals with the value of your investment at any point in time. In order to illustrate this risk, we need to deal with two separate subjects—inflation and bond math.

Inflation

Inflation, as almost everyone knows, is the erosion of the value of money by the increasing cost of goods. If a loaf of bread costs one dollar, and if that same loaf of bread costs $1.05 one year later, we could say that bread inflation ran at a 5 percent rate for that year. That is, it takes an additional 5 percent to purchase the same loaf of bread.

If you had purchased a $1.00 one-year bond paying 5 percent interest, then you would have found that one year later, you could still buy one loaf of bread. You would have your original dollar, plus five cents in interest. We would say that you kept pace with inflation. However, if you bought a 4 percent bond, even though you had more money one year later ($1.04) you would no longer be able to afford a loaf of bread. You have fallen behind inflation.

Investors, and bond investors in particular, know that inflation is a fact of life in the modern world. They demand a rate of interest on their investments that keeps pace with inflation and gives them a couple of percentage points to boot. This "inflation premium" is always adjusting as economic news indicates whether or not inflation is speeding up or slowing down. If you estimate that a loaf of bread will cost $1.05 in one year, you'll want at least 5 percent for your money, and probably a couple of points more just in case you estimate too low.

If your bond matures in one year, you know that no matter what happens, you'll be able to readjust in one year when you get your interest and your dollar back. So, you won't feel a need to demand too high a premium for your inflation guess. But the longer the maturity of your bond, the more you'll have to be compensated for your inflation risk.

If you're buying a 30-year bond, you'll have to estimate roughly what inflation will average over 30 years. Then you'll need an additional return aside from inflation just to be sure you're making some progress. Otherwise, you'll just meet inflation but not really get ahead. You'll be able to buy the bread, but you won't be able to buy a bigger loaf. Since the guess you're making is a 30-year estimate, you'll need a higher "wrong-guess" return than on a one-year bond. What if you estimate inflation will be 5 percent and it turns out to be 10 percent?

The Risk of Trying to Sell

Let's say you guess wrong. You've held your 30-year bond for five years, and inflation accelerates to 7 percent per year. While that may seem impossible, recent devaluations of currencies around the world continue to illustrate the risk of the bond investor—a weakening currency increases inflation. Your bond is paying the 7 percent you got when you bought it: 5 percent for your inflation guess and another 2 percent in case you guessed wrong. Since 7 percent now only keeps pace with inflation, you decide to find another bond to replace the one you have.

Good news! Twenty-five-year bonds are now yielding 10 percent. This rate of interest covers the 7 percent rate of inflation, but since inflation is accelerating (inflation was only 6 percent the prior year) investors are now demanding an extra 3 percent in case they guess wrong.

When you call your broker to sell your bond you find, much to your surprise, that you can get only 73 cents on the dollar for your 7 percent bond. Your $10,000 bond is worth only $7,300. And why? New bonds pay 10 percent. Why should someone pay you full value for a bond offering less interest than a new bond?

This is the price risk in the maturity of the bond. The longer the maturity, the greater the potential loss or profit on that bond if you decide to cash it in early.

To illustrate this in more detail, we need to know some bond math.

Bond Math

In order to make a judgment about a bond and determine the efficiency of your bond portfolio, you'll need to master a bit of math. People instinctively understand that if a company shows better and better earnings, the price of the stock should go up. But people have a great deal of difficulty understanding how a bond moves in price and how to compute return. We'll try to offer some insight.

Bond prices are quoted as a percentage of their face amount. A price of 100 means 100 percent of the face amount. A $10,000 bond is quoted to you at a price of 100 (also called par). The bond will cost you $10,000 (100 percent can be expressed as 1.0. Then, $10,000 × 1.00 = $10,000).

Bonds can be priced above or below their value at maturity:

A $10,000 bond is quoted to you at 98 (.98). You will pay $9,800 for the bond ($10,000 × .98 = $9,800). Another bond is offered at 102. It will cost $10,200 ($10,000 × 1,02 = $10,200).

By varying the price, the bond market can allow investors to buy and sell all kinds of bonds. Why is this so? Think about two bonds. Each bond is due in one year. One bond will pay 4 percent interest, or $400. Another bond, also due in one year, will pay 8.25 percent interest, or $825. Wouldn't you rather have the 8.25 percent bond? Let's say that new bonds being issued are paying 6.12 percent. The 4 percent bond was issued years ago when rates were very low, but now it only has one year until maturity. The 8.25 percent bond was issued two years ago when rates were high, but also has one year to go.

Which bond to buy?

4 percent bond at a price of 98

8.25 percent bond at a price of 102

6.12 percent bond at a price of 100 (par)

To make that decision, you need to know the total return on each bond. This will allow you to make an apples-to-apples comparison of the three bonds. Total return puts all three bonds on the same footing.

The total return of a bond has two components: the interest it pays and the gain or loss on the bond itself.

> **EXAMPLE**   You purchase a one-year, 4 percent bond for a price of 98. That is, you paid 98 cents for each dollar returned to you in one year. So, your $10,000 bond cost you $9,800. Your total return is 6.12 percent. You earned $400 interest, and a profit of $200 on the bond. This $600 total profit was earned on an investment of $9,800 ($600 + $9,800 = 6.12%).

As you can see, total return is the combined return of the interest the bond pays and the profit you earned on the bond. The interest the bond pays is called its coupon return. This term originated from the days when bonds were issued as paper certificates and little coupons were clipped off the bond on each payment date and deposited in the owner's checking account. The coupon return is the stated interest paid on the face amount of the bond:

> A $10,000 bond has an interest rate of 4 percent. The coupon is 4 percent and the coupon return is 4 percent.

Of course, total return cuts two ways.

> **EXAMPLE**   You purchase a one-year, 8.25 percent bond for a price of 102. That is, you paid $1.02 for each dollar returned to you in one year, So, your $10,000 bond cost you $10,200. Your total

return is also 6.12 percent. You earned $825 interest, but had a loss of $200 on the bond. So, your total profit of $625 was earned on an investment of $10,200 ($625 ÷ $10,200 = 6.12%).

Of course, if you buy the 6.12 percent bond at par, your total return will be 6.12 percent on your $10,000 investment. You will earn $612 interest and have zero profit/loss on the bond ($612 ÷ $10,000 = 6.12%).

So, all three bonds had the same total return.

This is an important point about bond investing. The total return is the one on which to focus. It is the only number that gives you your net return on the investment. Whether you bought the 4 percent bond at 98, or the 8.25 percent bond at 102, your return was the same.

Most investors have trouble with this point. They instinctively prefer the 8.25 percent bond, but feel uncomfortable about the $200 loss on the bond itself. They shouldn't. It is the net return on the combination of interest and principal that is important.

When you enter the bond market, you'll find that bonds trade at all kinds of prices, all quoted as a percentage of the face amount. You can see from our preceding example that, by adjusting the price of the bond, any bond can be bought or sold, no matter how high or how low the original coupon on the bond.

PUTTING CREDIT RISK AND MATURITY RISK TOGETHER

Credit Risk + Maturity Risk + Bond Math = Total Risk. Now that we understand credit risk and maturity risk, we can put those together with our bond math and get a good handle on the risks we face when we buy a bond.

If you plan on holding a bond until maturity, you don't have to concern yourself too much with price risk. The bond price will fluctuate from day to day, but those fluctuations are meaningless. On the day of maturity the face amount of the bond will be returned to you; no more and no less.

You may have to sell the bond before it matures, however. If you face a credit downgrade and have to liquidate the bond, you'll get the prevailing price in the open market. Your broker will obtain a bid for the bond, and that bid price will reflect not only the new lower credit quality of your bond but current interest rates as well. If interest rates have risen since you bought the bond, the bond will fetch a lower price, as shown in Table 9.1.

TABLE 9.1   Market Value of $10,000, 7 Percent Bonds of Different Maturities If Interest Rates Move Up or Down 1 or 2 Percentage Points After Purchase

	1 Year	5 Years	7 Years	10 Years	30 Years
+2 percent	$ 9,800	$ 9,200	$ 8,900	$ 8,700	$ 7,900
+1 percent	$ 9,900	$ 9,600	$ 9,500	$ 9,300	$ 8,800
-1 percent	$10,100	$10,400	$10,600	$10,700	$11,400
-2 percent	$10,200	$10,900	$11,200	$11,600	$13,100

And, if the credit quality has been downgraded, you face an additional hit to the price of the bond.

You have to be aware of price risk. If you buy bonds with long maturities and interest rates rise, you know you won't be able to get full price for your bond if you want to sell it and buy another bond.

> **EXAMPLE**   You own a 7 percent bond due in 10 years. Interest rates rise shortly after you buy it, with new bonds now at 9 percent. Deciding that you want to buy a new bond with a 9 percent yield, you try to sell the bond you have. A 7 percent, 10-year bond is worth only $8,700. Rather than take the $1,300 hit, you decide to hold the bond until maturity.

And since rising inflation is a negative for bond prices, you'll find yourself locked into bonds with not only a low rate of interest but a low market value as well. Even though you intend to hold your bonds until maturity, you can't ignore the threat posed by inflation and credit risk.

This is a problem. On the one hand, you want to be assured of an adequate income stream. So you don't want to buy short-term, low-yielding bonds. On the other hand, you recognize the risk to your income if inflation rises and the risk it poses to the value of your bond portfolio. So you don't want to buy all long-term bonds.

THE TERMS OF THE INTEREST PAYMENTS

All bonds pay interest at regular intervals. The length of the interval can vary.

Most bonds pay interest semi-annually. Every six months you get an interest payment. Many certificates of deposit, especially if bought through a broker, pay this way as well.

Mortgages tend to run on a monthly or quarterly cycle. Finally, very short-term paper, such as six-month U.S. Treasury bills or six-month CDs, pay on maturity.

The payment interval of a fixed-income investment shouldn't be a major concern in deciding whether to purchase that investment.

USING YIELD CURVES TO FIND VALUE

The graph in Figure 9.1 is known as a yield curve. To create a yield curve, you plot the yield of 1- to 30-year U.S. Treasury bonds on a graph. Further, Figure 9.1 illustrates a normal yield curve. Absent of any artificial pressures, we would expect to see a curve like this one. You can see that yields rise rather sharply up to the seven-year mark, where the curve begins to flatten out. In other words, you get a lot more yield for going out to the five-, six-, or seven-year maturity, but not as much by going out an additional 5 or 10 or even 20 years. This area around the 5- to 7-year maturity I call the meat of the yield curve.

Invest in shorter maturities and you give up a lot of yield. Invest longer and you take on a lot more risk.

Yield curves can often anticipate future interest-rate movements. While they're not infallible, and it does take some skill to learn how to interpret them, there are some basic ideas any investor can use.

The normal yield curve illustrated here exists most of the time. However, pressures in the economy or financial markets can create

FIGURE 9.1 Yield Curve

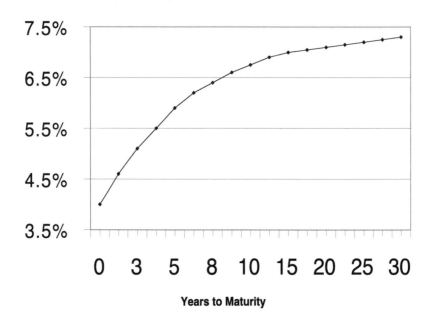

some odd-looking yield curves. An inverted curve means that short-term interest rates are higher than longer-term rates. This can happen when the Federal Reserve is attempting to cool the economy by keeping short-term interest rates high. A flat-yield curve means that interest rates are nearly the same across the entire maturity spectrum. Sometimes the curve is humped, with the highest rates in the intermediate part of the maturity scale.

> **TIP** Invest by paying attention to the current yield curve. It can be found every day in *The Wall Street Journal* Credit Column. When the yield curve is inverted, buy longer-term bonds. An inverted curve signals that the Fed is tightening money, which eventually leads to a fall in interest rates. When the yield curve slopes upward very steeply, you can generally anticipate that interest rates will rise. When the yield curve is flat, buy intermediate-term bonds. When the yield curve slopes normally, buy your usual maturity of choice: the curve is neutral for signaling interest rate movements.

Some of this advice is often difficult to use. After all, when the yield curve is inverted, the highest interest rates can be found in the shortest (safest) maturities. So it takes a certain amount of courage to invest in a longer maturity for a lower yield. But if you do so you'll be well rewarded. Higher yields in the short end of the market will tumble when the Fed is finished leaning on the supply of money. And, as the economy inevitably slows, interest rates across the board will fall. So, by ignoring those juicy short-term yields, you are anticipating a fall in rates:

> **EXAMPLE**   Six-month CDs are yielding 7 percent. Five-year CDs, by contrast, yield 6 percent. You buy the five-year CD. In six months, the new six-month CD has fallen to 4 percent, and the new five year to 5.7 percent.

To repeat: Over time you will find that the meat of the yield curve exists in the three- to ten-year area of the bond market. If you confine your purchases to this area, you'll find your returns acceptable for both risk and yield.

As you can see, there are many factors to consider in putting together a bond portfolio. Price risk, credit risk, and various maturities and terms can confuse you. There is a solution to this dilemma. It is a compromise between the risk of low interest rates and the dangers posed by inflation. The bond-ladder strategy should be your strategy of choice in bond investment.

THE BOND-LADDER STRATEGY

> Charlie Fowler has a problem. Newly retired from his job as an engineer for a major equipment manufacturer, he has a $300,000 lump sum as his pension benefit. Since the income from the lump sum will provide most of his retirement income, how can he invest it in a way that will give him good income while protecting him against inflation? The answer is a bond ladder.

Think of a ladder. Rung after rung ascends, letting you climb step by step. Each rung is roughly the same distance apart, but the ladder doesn't go on forever. There is a definite limit to the number of rungs and the distance they cover. Picture someone climbing a ladder. Some people start at the first rung and go up a step at a time. Some begin with the second rung.

Think of each bond you own as the rung on a ladder. Think of the distance between rungs as the time until maturity between each bond. Think of your shortest-term bond as the first rung on your ladder and the longest maturity as the final rung.

The idea is to stagger your maturities in roughly equal increments over a specific time period and then reinvest money by purchasing the farthest rung on the ladder. You have to decide on the length of the ladder and the credit quality of your bonds. That's it.

EXAMPLE Marlene has $200,000 for investment. She settles on a three- to seven-year ladder, with a minimum credit quality of A- for each of the bonds she will buy. She will spend all the interest and roll the principal as it matures. Table 9.2 shows what her portfolio looks like.

TABLE 9.2 Marlene's $200,000 Bond Portfolio

Year of Maturity	Amount	Yield
1999	$ 40,000	5 percent
2000	$ 40,000	6 percent
2001	$ 40,000	6.5 percent
2002	$ 40,000	7 percent
2003	$ 40,000	7.5 percent
Average = 2001 (5 years)	$200,000	Average = 6.4 percent

As each bond matures, she purchases a new seven-year bond. By 1999, interest rates have stayed the same, and Table 9.3 shows what her portfolio looks like.

Several interesting things are worth noting. First, you can see that when Marlene's first $40,000 matured, she rolled it to the farthest rung on her ladder: seven years, or the year 2006. Every time she has money to invest, she'll buy seven-year bonds. By doing so, she is able to increase her yield toward the seven-year yield, which is much higher than the one-, two-, or three-year yield.

TABLE 9.3

Year of Maturity	Amount	Yield
2000	$ 40,000	6 percent
2001	$ 40,000	6.5 percent
2002	$ 40,000	7 percent
2003	$ 40,000	7.5 percent
2006	$ 40,000	7.75 percent
Average = 2002 (3.4 years)	$200,000	Average = 6.95 percent

She always has her money coming due within seven years, while she is averaging the seven-year yield. And, her average maturity tends to hover between three and five years.

If interest rates rise, she'll have some money coming due regularly to roll over to higher rates. If rates fall, she won't have all her funds coming due at the same time to be rolled over at low rates. This strategy cuts off the highs and the lows. She'll never suffer from earning the lowest rates, nor will she ever earn the highest rates.

This is a compromise, playing off the risk of low rates against the risk of inflation and high rates. Look at what happened to Phil.

Phil had a lump sum of $50,000 from his 401(k) plan. Convinced that interest rates were heading higher, he put all his money in a one-year bond at 5 percent. A year later, interest rates had fallen a full percentage point. Convinced even more that they would rise, Phil bought another one-year bond at 4 percent. A year later, new bonds were paying 1 percentage point more; back up to 5 percent.

Poor Phil! For two years he's averaged 4.5 percent on his money. Had he followed Marlene's strategy, he would have earned an extra 1.9 percent, or $950 per year, for the two years—an extra $1,900. Phil has paid a heavy price for a bad guess on interest rates.

> Convinced that rates will now fall, Phil locks all the money into seven-year bonds at 7.75 percent. A year later, interest rates have surged 2 percentage points. Marlene is rolling over $40,000 in new seven-year bonds at nearly 10 percent. Phil is stuck at 7.75 percent. The loss from selling his bonds would be too great; he can't afford the roll up to new bonds.

It doesn't pay to try to guess interest-rate movements. While I can concede that a few professionals have pretty good judgment about these things, they are the rare exception to the rule. If you are going to be successful as a bond-market investor, buy good-quality bond ladders, hold the bonds until maturity, and roll the funds to the farthest rung on your ladder. The only exception to this is in the case of a credit downgrade on one of your positions. In that case, sell the position and buy a new bond either with the same maturity or go to the farthest rung once again.

Setting Up Your Bond Ladder

As you can see, setting up a bond ladder requires only three decisions:

1. The maturities of the ladder
2. The minimum acceptable credit rating on the positions
3. The amount to invest on each rung

You can see from our yield-curve discussion that the "meat" of the yield curve is generally found in three- to ten-year maturities. Any maturities shorter than three or four years and there is a significant decrease in interest paid. Any maturities longer than ten years increase price risk due to inflation and credit risk due to the longer time frame of the position. This increase in risk is generally not accompanied by an equally large increase in yield.

The best policy is to stick to ladders of three to ten years, or four to eight years, or any reasonable combination between three and ten years. You could have a 3-5-7-9-year ladder, or a 3-4-5-6-7-10-year ladder. In either case, you always buy new bonds at the longest rung.

You'll always average the intermediate-term yield in the market—the best trade-off between yield and risk. This is a reasonable expectation for your bond portfolio and your best opportunity to maximize your return over time. There can be some pleasant surprises.

> **EXAMPLE**   You began with a four- to ten-year ladder, investing $20,000 in each rung on the ladder. Two years later interest rates have moved 5 percentage points higher. Your first bonds aren't due for two years. However, a quick check with your broker reveals that while you'll take a hit on your two-year bonds (they were four years originally, but two years have passed), you'll be able to lock in the much higher current yields and extend your maturity to ten years. The additional interest will repay you the loss on your bonds in three years. After that, you'll be money ahead.

If you use a bond-laddering strategy, you must be prepared for the fact that you'll never be able to get all your money invested at the highest yields. If you establish your ladder and a year later interest rates have risen, you'll find that most of your bonds will have to stay in place, especially the longer-term ones. This is a fair concession. After all, anticipating interest rates and the peaks and valleys of those movements is exceedingly difficult.

The bond ladder should be constructed using intermediate-term maturities and A- or higher rated bonds. It succeeds in minimizing risk and maximizing yields. Because it is passive in nature, the expense to run a ladder is very small. You pay a commission to buy a bond and then hold the bonds for several years. If you pay a 1 percent commission to buy a five-year bond, that bond costs you only .2 percent per year.

What About Bond Funds?

Bond mutual funds are an excellent alternative for small accounts. Once you have $25,000 to invest, you have enough to consider a bond ladder.

The big drawback with a bond fund is to try and avoid high expense levels. Bond investing carries a lower potential return than equities, so you don't want expenses eating into your interest income. A fund charging .5 percent to 1.25 percent of your account value per year in management fees or a broker selling and replacing bonds every year has a higher performance hurdle to jump to overcome this expense.

> **EXAMPLE**   You have $100,000 in a bond fund paying 6 percent. The management fee is .75 percent per year. You earn $6,000 in interest and pay out $750 in management fees. This cuts your return to 5.25 percent.

If you can create your own bond ladders, by all means do so. If you lack the expertise or can't find someone to help, use a fund.

Buying individual bonds and holding them to maturity is usually a lot less costly than other alternatives.

Be Creative

Investors will vary their ladders according to their outlook on the future and their level of comfort. Some will allow only AAA paper into their portfolios, and others will accept bonds rated as low as BBB-. The AAA investor must accept lower yields as the price for safety. And the BBB- investor will enjoy higher yields but must be resigned to an occasional credit problem in the portfolio.

If you drop your credit quality to BBB-, you must be more vigilant in keeping current with credit-rating changes.

Some investors will place a bet once in a while if interest rates have reached what appears to be an extreme. If rates hit 10 percent and you have a three- to ten-year ladder, you might take half of your maturing bonds and buy twelve-year bonds. If rates have hit a new low, you might extend only half your available funds to ten years, and the balance to six months, waiting for a better opportunity.

> **TIP**   One way to judge how much lower interest rates can go is to subtract income taxes and inflation from the one-year CD rate. When that calculation results in a negative number, it means that investors are getting a negative return for investing. That simply can't persist over time. Either inflation must fall, or interest rates must rise.

One-year CD rate	3.5 percent
Less income taxes at 33 percent	-1.2 percent
Less current inflation	-2.0 percent
Equals a return of	0.3 percent

Interest rates probably won't fall much further.

Whatever you do, however, don't try to outguess the market. I can't emphasize enough how difficult it is to time interest-rate movements. Just when you think rates are about to take off, the economy can slip into recession and you'll find yourself with a lot of cash, waiting for an opportunity that may be years away.

OTHER THOUGHTS

1. *Be more careful about credit quality after the economy has been in a growth phase.* Good times hide problems that companies may be having. Tighten up your credit quality when times are good. The ensuing recession will always cause credit downgrades.

2. *Be more willing to take credit risk after a recession.* Recessions expose most of the problems that companies have. Credit downgrades are frequent and result in higher yields. The economic recovery will cause credit upgrades in many areas. If a company has been downgraded to A- in a recession, it is reasonable to assume that an economic recovery will stabilize the ratings of most bonds and, in some cases, make an improvement.

3. *Don't confuse quarterly-earnings reports with credit quality.* A company may be having near-term difficulties in turning a profit but may

have great staying power as a credit risk. Just because a manufacturing company is losing money doesn't mean that their bonds aren't good. Bond holders stand in line ahead of stockholders. Even if a dividend is cut on the common stock, interest payments usually continue without interruption. Not sure? Let the credit rating be your guide.

4. *If given a choice, always take a lower yield and better quality.* If you want to speculate, go in the stock market. Your bonds should not keep you awake at night. If you're unsure about a choice of bonds, stick to better quality. The yield you give up by taking higher quality won't make a difference in your life.

5. *Get a good broker. Bonds are a specialized area and require specialized knowledge.* There are many brokers who love the bond market and will be happy to help you construct a good bond portfolio. Seek them out, especially if they believe in the ladder approach. Bonds generally carry lower commission revenue than stocks, but a dyed-in-the-wool bond broker understands that and is willing to work with that compensation schedule in mind.

6. *Don't ignore swap opportunities.* At times you'll be able to improve your position by selling a bond and simultaneously buying a replacement. However, swaps shouldn't be a frequent habit. There are opportunities, but they usually come with a price. For example, you can often swap into a higher-yielding bond for the same money as the bond you would sell, but the give-up is a longer maturity.

7. *Concentrate on credit quality more than on price fluctuation.* It always feels better when your bonds are going up because interest rates are going down. What is important, however, is that you maintain your income, not count phantom profits that you'll never take. Spend your time making sure you'll be paid on time and paid off on time.

8. *Don't let your money-fund balances build.* Investors lose large amounts of money simply sitting in money-market funds, waiting for interest rates to go up. Even if rates do rise, they must rise fast enough to overcome the low rates that money funds pay. Sitting in a money fund at 4 percent waiting for interest rates to go up may not make a lot of sense if you can earn 9 percent on the money elsewhere. Rates have to go up in a hurry to overcome a 5 percent annual differential.

9. *As a general rule, remember that interest rates go down in a recession and up in a recovery.* There are exceptions to this, but over time the

rule will prove true. You should always know where you are in the economic cycle when you are investing in bonds.

10. *Look at the trend of rates over the past six months as a good guide to where they'll go in the next six months.* If rates have been rising, especially if the economy is in recovery, chances are pretty good that they'll continue to rise. And if they have been falling, especially in a recession, odds are they'll continue to fall.

11. *Don't fight the Fed.* The Federal Reserve Board has a great deal of influence over the direction of interest rates. If the Fed has been easing, your hopes for higher rates will be futile. If the Fed has been increasing interest rates to slow the economy, you can postpone your purchases for a little bit.

12. *Don't let success go to your head.* Once in a while you'll get a hunch that'll prove correct. Consider it luck, or serendipity. Whatever you do, don't anoint yourself a new bond-market guru.

13. *Don't forget the muddle factor.* Companies and countries in trouble tend to muddle through. We all tend to muddle through. The worst rarely comes to pass.

14. *Don't forget the wrench factor.* Someone or something always throws a wrench into a good thing. Countries and companies tend to fall short of their aspirations. The most optimistic forecasts rarely come to pass.

SUMMARY

Buy a book about bonds. Study how bonds work, especially mortgage issues. A credit rating is crucial to understanding a bond's worth; learn what they mean. The more you absorb about the bond market and how it works, the more interesting it becomes.

CHAPTER TEN

Municipal Bonds and the Companion Account

Along with your IRA, you should maintain a second investment account I call the "companion account." The companion account is where you will house your more liquid, shorter-term investing. In order to make your life less complicated and to give you easier access to your funds, your companion account should be held at the same institution as your IRA.

Your custodian should have a cash-management account. Sometimes called a financial management account, these all-in-one accounts typically offer checking and credit-card access to the account. In addition, these accounts allow you to participate in the full range of investing.

HOW THE COMPANION ACCOUNT WORKS

The idea is to have your custodian channel funds from your IRA to your companion account once you begin taking income. Once there, you can immediately access the money with a check or credit card. No waiting for the mail to be delivered. And you can usually direct-deposit other income checks such as Social Security or pension to the account.

In addition, you can do most of your non-IRA investing in your companion account, emphasizing municipal bonds to generate tax-free income. In this way, you have both tax-deferred income from the IRA and tax-free income in the non-sheltered companion account. In order to not disturb your longer-term IRA portfolio and to avoid needless taxable income from an emergency distribution from the IRA, you want to lean toward shorter-term investment in your companion account.

> **TIP** It is now possible to get a checkbook for your IRA if you are over 59 1/2. IRA custodians are offering the service, and it's such a good idea that you should consider it.

Your companion account becomes a catchall for municipal-bond interest and IRA distributions, as well as for stock dividends, if you place stocks in the account. Since you'll open your companion account as a joint account with your spouse, this will give her access to your IRA distributions. Remember, your IRA is held only in your name, so your spouse doesn't have direct control or access to it.

It's convenient! You've reduced your account needs to just two accounts, yet retained all the investment and tax-planning flexibility you need.

> **EXAMPLE** You have $260,000 in your IRA rollover account. You consolidate your $80,000 savings in a companion account, investing in shorter-term municipal bonds. Your municipals generate $4,000 per year in tax-free income. You ask your custodian to move $1,500 per month from your IRA into your companion account. With your checkbook, you pay all your monthly bills from your companion account.

WHAT ARE MUNICIPAL BONDS?

When Ross Perot disclosed the details of his investment portfolio as required by federal law as a candidate for political office, it was noted that many investments fit the style of a self-made entrepreneur, including high-tech stocks and venture-capital commitments. Many observers were surprised to find, however, that Perot's basic bedrock investment of choice was municipal bonds. What prompted this savvy capitalist to find municipal bonds so attractive?

As one who oversees municipal-bond portfolios for clients in a dozen states, I've always found municipal bonds so attractive that they form the bedrock of many investment portfolios. Let's look at the basics of municipal bonds and then at how you can fit them into your overall investment strategy.

It is easy to identify municipal bonds. They are issued by state and local government entities: Cities, towns, counties, water districts, state agencies, industrial-development authorities all issue municipal bonds. The basic denomination for purchase is $5,000.

Municipal bonds carry a unique and compelling feature: The interest they pay is free of federal income tax, and if you purchase a bond originating in your state of residence, free from state income tax as well. This one-two tax punch provides plenty of incentive to consider these debt obligations. A tax-free municipal-bond account combined with a tax-deferred IRA can significantly reduce current investment-related income taxes.

Credit risk? As government issues, municipals have enjoyed a nearly default-free history. Default is a very rare occurrence, generally limited to small, specific-purpose bonds in isolated instances. Municipal bonds default in less than 1/10 of 1 percent of all instances.

One of the major credit-rating companies, Standard & Poor's, Moody's, or Fitch, assigns a quality rating to most municipal bonds.

This independent rating gives investors the ability to judge the bond in a quick and reliable way. Municipals are rated AAA, AA, A, BBB, BB, B, etc., following the general rating scheme applied to other types of bonds.

Two other points about credit quality. Sometimes a creditworthy issuer is too small to pay for a credit rating, or finds that it can sell its bonds without one. School districts often fall into this category. So the absence of a rating doesn't automatically mean the bond is of poor quality. Second, you may run across a bond that lacks a rating but is known as "bank qualified." Don't be misled by this term. This has nothing to do with the credit quality of the bond. "Bank Qualified" refers to bonds that meet certain criteria established by The Tax Reform Act of 1986 to enable the interest they generate to be tax-free.

Bonds issuers that need to enhance their credit rating to sell bonds may apply for bond insurance. Companies such as MBIA, FGIC, and AMBAC ensure the bond holder against default. The issuer pays the insurance premium from the proceeds of the bond sale. The bonds are then rated AAA. Note, though, that the insurance typically guarantees timely payment of principal and interest. In the event the issuer defaults, the bond holders will not see their principal prior to maturity. They can't cash in early. In the interim, interest is paid on time.

Municipal bonds come in many varieties, but in two categories—general obligation and specific use. Each has its fans and detractors.

General-obligation bonds are the obligation of the issuer and are supported by the issuer's full taxing authority. Theoretically, your state could raise as much in taxes as necessary to service its general obligations, or GO bonds. For this reason, many conservative investors prefer GOs. Of course, the additional implied safety means that the yield paid is a bit lower than other bonds of equal credit rating.

Specific-use bonds are backed by a limited source of revenue-tolls from a bridge, water bills, and so forth. Absent general taxing authority, many perceive these bonds to carry higher risk. What if no one uses the bridge? In the municipal bond market, differences in risk are small indeed and are often more theoretical than real. No one may use the bridge and the toll revenue may be inadequate to service the bond, but since the state knows it will have to borrow again for new bridges, it is not likely to let the bond holders eat a loss.

MUNI-BOND MATH

Let's say you've just purchased a new 5 percent bond for $10,000. You'll earn $500 per year in tax-free income. What is this worth? If you are in a 28 percent tax bracket, and your state imposes an additional 4 percent state income tax, your combined bracket is 32 percent. In order to walk away with 5 percent after-tax, you would have to earn 7.35 percent in taxable interest: 7.35 percent is referred to as the taxable equivalent yield. The formula is: One minus your tax bracket divided into the bond interest rate; in this example:

.05 ÷ (1 − .32) = .05 ÷ .68 = .0735 = 7.35%

Very often municipals will trade at taxable equivalent yields higher than CDs or Treasuries and equivalent to corporate bonds of equal credit rating. And at times municipals will trade "cheap" to taxables, meaning that their taxable equivalent yields are much higher than they should be relative to taxable bonds. Since the interest is tax-free, you don't have to add it on top of your other income when you do your tax return. So tax-free income can prevent you from being pushed into a higher tax bracket.

MUNICIPAL YIELDS OFFER COMPELLING VALUE

Consider this: The long-term return on common stocks in the United States as measured over the past 50 or 60 years has been between 10 percent and 11 percent per year. Everyone would consider common stocks to be pretty good vehicles for building wealth. What many fail to point out is that this is a pretax return. Whether the gain is from dividends or from capital gains, you have to pay income tax on it. When you reduce this gain to reflect the taxes that must be paid, the net-after-tax return falls to between 6.8 percent and 7.5 percent. (I recognize that the tax is often postponed because the securities are held for many years.) On a risk-adjusted basis, municipals can be a better investment than common stocks. Put another way, would you rather try for an average return of 7.25 percent, with risk, after taxes, or a nearly risk-free return of 5.5 percent? The point is not that all your capital should be in bonds, but that municipals are a much more interesting and compelling investment than they appear at first glance.

Investment Strategies

The best way to go about buying municipal bonds is to find a good broker. You need someone who specializes in municipal bonds, who understands the market for them, and who has access to adequate bond inventories. While municipals seem to be quite simple and safe, the fact is that many carry obscure or unusual terms of repayment that, if activated, can be a nasty and expensive surprise to the unaware. Mandatory puts, optional puts, sinking funds, prerefundings, and a host of other arcane terms and conditions means that you need a pro to assist you. State mortgage bonds are very attractive. Since they are usually callable at par, paying a premium (more than the face value of the bond) means that a sudden call can leave you poorer and wiser.

Bonds should be bought with the idea of holding them to maturity. Since municipal bonds are traded strictly over the counter, with many small or inactive issues, bid-ask spreads and transaction costs make them poor trading vehicles. As with other bonds, laddered portfolios work best. In a ladder you stagger your maturities and roll over new money to the farthest maturity in your ladder. By laddering, you'll have money due regularly for reinvestment, but you'll average the longest maturity in yield. This longer maturity will almost always be the higher yield available.

Since your IRA bond portfolio will emphasize four- to ten-year maturities, you can use one- to three-year maturities in your companion account. You'll have funds rolling over from one to ten years.

GETTING THE BEST FROM YOUR BOND PORTFOLIO

Since longer-term taxable bonds can offer, relatively speaking, more options for investment, your IRA can invest in them. And it will create a more stable account to generate long-term income.

You should also limit each purchase in your companion account to 5 percent of your total portfolio, with no more than 20 percent in any one issuer.

After selecting your ladder maturity, you should choose a minimum credit rating for your portfolio. More venturesome investors will go as low as BBB, since yields are noticeably higher than they are for A-rated bonds. Conservative investors will stick with AA and AAA bonds. If a bond in your portfolio drops below your minimal accepted rating, it should be sold and replaced. Your broker's statement should show you the credit rating on each bond.

Even though your approach is passive, you need to be vigilant. Don't hold your bonds in a safe deposit box. You aren't at risk by having your broker hold them, and by placing them with her, you can be assured of being informed about call provisions or tender offers. Your coupons will automatically be cashed for you. With many issues going to "book entry" issuance, many bonds now exist only in electronic memory. No paper is actually issued.

Keep informed about call dates, sinking funds, credit ratings, and put features. Any one of these may provide an opportunity to "swap" into a better position. In a swap, your broker simultaneously sells your bond and purchases a replacement. Since there are two transactions, she will often swap for you at a reduced commission rate. For instance, if you know that one of your bonds may be called away from you next year, you may want to swap out of it now while you can still get a premium for the bond.

My Personal Preferences

How do I invest my clients' municipal bond money? Like all investors, I have personal preferences that I have built into my thinking over time.

For long-term investors, I prefer ladders of three to ten years; shorter and I lose some yield, longer and I have increased price risk if interest rates rise. Given the need for liquidity, you might want to shorten your municipal-bond ladder.

I like bonds rated A or better if shorter than five years, AA or better if longer. This gives me some room for a credit downgrade while still retaining an investment-grade bond.

I'll often buy longer-term bonds if there is a call feature within my ladder horizon: A 20-year bond with an 8-year call provision. Odds are, somewhere 8 to 12 years out, my bond will be called away. So I can enjoy a 20-year yield with a shorter expected maturity.

I will buy insured bonds, but I limit myself to one third of the portfolio in insured bonds. Insurers are, after all, private corporations without a government guarantee. While all the major municipal-bond insurers continue to earn AAA ratings when they insure, I don't like to place too much money in insured bonds.

I do like state mortgage-agency bonds. They typically pay a high yield, and because they are callable, tend to trade relatively close to par value. Good medical-care-facility bonds, especially geriatric facilities, are worth considering. But you have to be careful; some hospitals are operating in the red.

School districts are always worth a look, as are state general obligations (known as GOs), and state power authorities. Nonstate issuers such as Puerto Rico, the Virgin Islands, and Guam are state as well as federally tax-exempt and should be considered. Finally, bonds subject to the alternative minimum tax, or AMT, trade at higher yield levels and are, therefore, timely.

SUMMARY

All in all, municipal bonds provide a profitable and tax-wise use of capital in any portfolio. No wonder a self-made billionaire made them his investment of choice.

Along with your IRA, the companion account becomes a valuable tool in both simplifying your life and helping you plan your income and tax needs.

CHAPTER ELEVEN

IRA Inflation Hedges

Precious metals and real estate are the two most common investment types known as "inflation hedges." These are investments that flourish when inflation is high. Conversely, they languish when inflation is low or when inflationary expectations are low. Since they will perform well when more traditional IRA investments (stocks and bonds) are performing poorly, they are often incorporated into IRA portfolios. You need to treat these two investments just like salt and pepper: A little bit can go a long way, but too much can ruin a meal.

PRECIOUS METALS

The precious metals consist of gold, silver, and platinum. They have three primary uses: industrial applications, jewelry, and investment. While industrial and jewelry use remain relatively constant from year to year, wide swings can be seen in investment demand. It is this wild card in investment demand that can create tremendous price movement in metals. In fast markets it is not unusual to see the price of metals move several percentage points in one day.

So a portfolio too heavily laden with metals can experience sickening price swings when metals fall from favor. Since metals don't pay any dividends or interest, an investment in metals can represent dead money in a quiet market.

Traditionally, investors have been encouraged to keep between 3 percent and 5 percent of their portfolio in precious metals. I subscribe to this advice, preferring a 4 percent to 5 percent mix in IRA portfolios. Because of the large swings that the metals can have, profits (or losses) of 30 percent or 50 percent are not unusual. Remember, a 50 percent profit on 4 percent of your portfolio adds two full percentage points to your overall account yield.

Precious metals will generally advance in price under the following circumstances:

1. Inflation is rising.
2. Inflationary expectations are rising.
3. There is political unrest.
4. There is general uncertainty or fear.
5. The U.S. dollar is weakening.
6. Common stocks are falling.

Metals prices tend to advance well into an economic recovery when industrial demand strengthens and investors become concerned about rising inflation due to a strong economy. If you are going to buy precious metals, wait until the stock market has had a good advance while the economy was still in recession. This market advance signals an imminent economic recovery. If you wait until you see a recovery in the newspapers, chances are the price of precious metals have already advanced.

Once you have metals in your portfolio, you should not sell them unless you have a very strong conviction that inflation is a dead duck and that metals will have no room for price appreciation. Even so, remember that war and other unpredictable events can have a dramatic impact on the price of precious metals. This upward move in the metals will come at a time when your stocks and bonds are having rough sledding. At such a time you'll appreciate the hedge that metals give you in a portfolio.

How to Invest in Metals in an IRA

It is perfectly legal to buy U.S. gold Eagle coins in your IRA. An American Eagle is a coin minted with nearly pure gold and sold in denominations of one ounce and fractions of one ounce of gold. It has no collector's value, and you can expect to pay a premium of a few dollars over the gold value of the coin. It is not legal to put collector's items (numismatic items) such as rare coins in an IRA. Collectibles, in general, and rare coins, in particular, are not allowed in an IRA. However, coins are not the most profitable way to invest in the metals. Gold-mining stocks, whether purchased outright or through a mutual fund, are the investment of choice. When you look at some simple math, you'll see why.

EXAMPLE   The price of gold is at $300 per ounce. Amalgamated Mines produces gold at a cost of $200 per ounce. Amalgamated earns $100 profit for each ounce it sells.

Two years later, the price of gold has risen 25 percent to $375. Amalgamated still produces at a cost of $200, but its profits have nearly doubled to $175 per ounce.

You can see that a 25 percent move in the price of gold resulted in a 75 percent rise in mining profits. Since stock prices move in relation to earnings, the rise in the price of a mining stock will be much more pronounced than the simultaneous move in the metals. Mining companies offer a leveraged way to invest in the metals market without borrowing to do so. Put another way, a $10,000 investment in gold Eagle coins can be the equivalent of only $5,000, or less, invested in mining shares.

Precious Metals Mutual Funds

Since your metals exposure is a specialized investment area, a gold or precious-metals mutual fund makes the most sense for IRA investors. There are very few funds from which to pick, so you don't have to plow through hundreds of offerings. At most, there are two dozen funds worth your consideration. When searching out a gold fund, be prepared for some strange-looking track records. A fund might be down 15 percent one year and up 42 percent the following year. It is most important to compare that fund against other metals funds—never against stock or bond funds.

Once you've done the comparison, read the fund's investment objectives and investment restrictions carefully. You want a fund that is going to keep you invested in the metals market at all times. You do not want a fund that may be invested in short-term bonds on occasion. You're controlling your risk by how much you are investing in metals, so you want to be sure the fund will keep the investment exposed to the metals market.

Gold? Silver? Platinum? My bias is toward gold. Silver and platinum are more heavily tied to the economic/industrial cycle than is gold. Gold is more of a pure inflation/uncertainty hedge than either silver or platinum. Also, since nearly all of the world's platinum comes from Russia and South Africa, price swings can be much more violent than that of gold because of the concentration of the world's known supply in two sometimes volatile countries. And, investments in platinum are particularly scarce since they are limited to mining companies almost exclusively located in South Africa.

If you want to buy individual gold stocks, look for companies located in North America with large estimated gold reserves. As with oil companies, you'd also like to see a history of success in the effort to replace gold reserves. A good place to start is the Gold Industry Review in the Value Line Investment Survey. (You should be able to find it in your public library.) Once you've found a few you like, try to put together a portfolio of three to five (or more) good-quality mining stocks. Buy equal dollar amounts of each and hold them. You'll find dividends will be very low. But you're not buying these stocks for dividend income. You're buying them as an insurance policy to protect your account against the vagaries of the future.

You can also ask your broker to find convertible issues from mining companies. Typically, these take the form of bonds or preferred stocks that not only pay a good rate of interest but are convertible into the common stock of the company. They don't have as much bang for the gold buck but they do pay you a reasonable return while you wait. Warning—credit quality is generally below average.

REAL-ESTATE INVESTING

Real-estate investing reached frenzied proportions during the 1970s and 1980s. The longer inflation took its toll, the more real estate appreciated, the more accepted it became as a matter of faith that real estate was a "can't-lose" proposition. Worse, most real-estate plungers borrowed as much money as they could, using very little of their own. This leverage was accommodated by most banks who would lend up to 90 percent of the purchase price to the buyer.

Real-estate speculators learned that no market moves up forever and that leverage is a double-edged sword. When you put down only 10 percent of the price in cash, it doesn't take much of a move down in price to wipe you out.

> **EXAMPLE**   Joe Pressing buys a small commercial office build-
> ing for $400,000, putting 10 percent, or $40,000, in as a down pay-
> ment. He borrows the remaining $360,000 as a mortgage from his
> bank. A real estate slump brought on by overbuilding hits his city.
> His property is appraised at only $360,000. Since this is what he
> owes the bank, Joe will lose his entire investment of $40,000 if he
> sells. He's stuck.

After the difficult real-estate markets of the late 1980s, real estate recovered along with the rest of the economy. If you want to put real estate in your IRA, it is difficult to do so. There are specific prohibitions in the internal Revenue Code against self-serving transactions. Therefore, you can't buy real estate from yourself, nor can you lend yourself a mortgage using IRA funds. You can't give your kids a mortgage from your IRA.

You can, however, invest in real estate through arms-length transactions. There are several vehicles you can use, including limited partnerships. However, I believe the best real-estate investment is a publicly traded REIT or Real Estate Investment Trust.

A REIT (pronounced to rhyme with "feet") is an organization formed for the sole purpose of engaging in real-estate investment. Management is responsible for making all decisions and running the affairs of the REIT. In order to enjoy REIT tax status, the REIT must distribute to the shareholders all the capital gains and interest earned in the form of dividends.

A REIT does not necessarily buy real estate. It may act solely as a mortgage lender and so may resemble a bond fund in operation.

Investing in REITS

REITS are bought and sold by shares listed on various stock exchanges and the NASDAQ market. Your broker can provide research on many of them, and they are widely followed by Wall Street. The Value Line Investment Survey carries an entire industry section on them.

REITS have many advantages for the IRA investor.

1. Since a REIT is publicly traded, it is easy to sell at a fair price. This eliminates one major disadvantage of real-estate investment. When you buy an individual property, it can take months to sell.

2. Since your IRA is tax sheltered, you don't have to hassle with tax reporting. Your IRA collects the dividends and any capital gains. You don't need to account for these on your tax return.

3. Dividend reinvestment is usually available, so you can let your real-estate investment compound tax-deferred in your IRA.

4. Small investment amounts present no problem. You don't need tens of thousands of dollars as in the purchase of an individual piece of property.

5. Since you are buying a security, you will get regular reports on operations, and the operations of the REIT will be audited by an independent accounting firm.

6. Because REITS come in many flavors and varieties, you can tailor your investment to shopping centers, apartment complexes, or a mix of various real-estate classes.

How Do You Select a REIT?

You select a REIT as you would any other security. Good management is the single biggest factor in REIT selection. The quality of the management will be reflected in the long-term track record of the REIT. Look for consistency: steady increases year after year in cash flow, dividends, and book value. Remember, the total return on your REIT investment will consist of current dividends and long-term appreciation of the investments in the REIT. Don't be misled by buying the REIT with the highest dividend. You want the REIT that has provided the highest total return over time.

> **TIP** Be aware of a little known tax problem called Unrelated
> Business Taxable Income. UBTI can arise in certain limited partner-
> ships. Before purchasing any limited partnership, be sure you have
> explored whether the investment will trigger UBTI. Excess UBTI is a
> taxable event, even though it occurs in an IRA. It is very rare but
> something every investor should realize as a potential problem.

SETTING UP YOUR INFLATION HEDGES

How do you decide how much of each inflation hedge to buy? Over time, an average investment of 4 percent to 6 percent of your IRA in inflation hedges is a good idea. In large IRAs, this presents little problem. After all, 5 percent of $500,000 allows for a $25,000 investment. In smaller accounts, this may not be the case.

If you have less than $10,000 set aside for inflation hedges, you should skew your investment toward REITS because of the higher income stream that will help in creating your income. Since gold stocks throw off little in the way of income, they are less attractive for smaller accounts where every single dollar counts.

Accounts over $200,000 should strive for a 50/50 mix in the inflation portion of the account: 50 percent in gold-mining stocks and 50 percent in REITS.

This can change. If the price of gold appears particularly depressed relative to your favorite REIT, perhaps gold-mining shares are more attractive, and new investment can be made in that area. In periods of low or declining inflation, REITS would be the investment of choice because of their dividend yield. When inflation is rising, gold-mining shares will react more quickly in price and will be a better choice.

You don't have to agonize too much over this. Inflation lifts the value of both real estate and precious metals. It is more important to be invested in one or both areas than not to be invested at all.

SUMMARY

Think of your inflation hedges just as you would homeowner's insurance. You can enjoy your home more knowing you've done something to hedge against fire and storm. And, just because your house doesn't burn down doesn't mean that you cancel the insurance.

Since your IRA will be generally invested in financial assets—stocks and bonds—you need to remember that you are carrying the risk of paper assets. And, those paper assets generally decline in value in an inflationary environment. So, to reduce that risk, you need to carry a bit of investment that can prosper in an inflationary environment.

Keeping in mind our need for liquidity, gold-mining stocks and REITS are usually the investment of choice. REITS offer excellent current income for your portfolio. Although they can decline in price as interest rates rise, they are eventually the beneficiaries of inflation—real-estate prices often rise along with price increases in other goods and services.

Gold-mining stocks offer a leveraged way to benefit from an increase in gold prices. And, gold prices generally increase when the U.S. dollar is decreasing and/or inflation is rising. In both scenarios, the prices of U.S. stocks and bonds often decline.

Finally, in times of extreme turmoil, gold can raise your level of comfort and offer potential for capital gain.

Keep your hedges to a small portion of your account, but keep them.

CHAPTER TWELVE

Mutual Funds and the IRA

As the shift toward employee-funded and managed-retirement plans accelerates, more and more people have become comfortable with mutual-fund investment. There are now more mutual funds than there are stocks on the New York Stock Exchange.

Mutual funds have many advantages and disadvantages for the IRA investor. Let's examine mutual funds in light of their strengths and weaknesses and look at where they should be used and where they should be avoided.

WHAT IS A MUTUAL FUND?

A mutual fund is a professionally managed portfolio with a specific investment objective. You pool your funds with those of other investors. As a shareholder in the fund, you own a piece of that portfolio. Your ownership is in the form of shares of the fund. The fund publishes its net asset value (NAV) every day. If you want to sell your shares, you will receive the NAV for that fund on the day you sell them.

There are many different types of funds: stock, bond, gold, real estate, industry group, growth, and income. Each fund will have a specific purpose or investment discipline, and so results will vary from fund to fund. In addition, domestic-stock funds will look a lot different in performance from international stock funds, and junk bond funds will perform differently from government securities funds. You have to know exactly what you are looking for before you invest.

Typically, all the details are spelled out in a document known as the prospectus. Obtaining a prospectus is easy because a fund will automatically send it to you before you invest. This may change in the future, but no matter what is required you will want to read the prospectus before investing.

You may buy shares directly from the fund and pay no sales commission to do so. These are known as "no-load" funds. If you buy shares through your broker, he will add a commission to the purchase of the fund. This commission, or "load" usually runs between 4 percent and 8.5 percent, with most around 5 percent.

And just as fund types can vary, the type of load can vary as well. Most load funds charge an up-front commission expressed as a percentage of the offering price. However, there are loads known as 12b-1 fees that the fund levies on an ongoing basis to cover various expenses of the fund. This fee is in addition to the annual management fee. Some funds that do not charge a commission, or load, will charge a 12b-1 fee, so don't assume that there is no charge other than management fee simply because the fund was no-load.

Whether you buy a no-load or a load fund, each fund will charge fees for management and operating-fund expenses. These combined costs are commonly known as the annual expense ratio. These expense ratios charged by the fund can run from a low of .25 percent per year to over 2 percent per year. Most fees fall between .5 percent and 1.50 percent per year.

Whether you should pay a commission is fiercely debated. Do-it-yourselfers prefer to select and buy their own funds, while those without that ability tend to have a broker make the selection and receive a commission for the work. Don't get too hung up on load versus no-load. What you are buying is net performance after expenses. If you believe that doing it on your own in no-load funds would give you worse performance than paying a broker for advice, then don't worry about paying a load.

In either case, once you own a fund, you can usually switch from fund to fund within that *fund family* (a fund family refers to all the mutual funds offered by one mutual-fund company) without any cost, or with a nominal charge called a *switch fee*. Fund families are easy to spot. When you look up a fund in the newspaper, you'll find them organized by family, not by individual fund.

Opening a Mutual-Fund IRA

Nothing could be easier. Simply call the fund and ask for an IRA application and prospectus. Find out how you can directly transfer your lump sum to avoid the 20 percent withholding tax. Once you have opened a fund IRA, you should be able to move from fund to fund within that family without having to complete new IRA paperwork.

If you have an IRA with a broker, you can invest in mutual funds within that IRA. Check with your broker to find out what funds are available within his IRA program.

Taking Income from a Fund IRA

Taking income is a straightforward matter. Simply request a distribution form from the fund family.

You have to keep in mind your overall asset allocation when taking income. If you take money only from your bond fund, after a while you'll have to readjust your balances based on income taken, not on investment return.

EXAMPLE   You have $15,000 in a bond fund and $10,000 in a stock fund. You decide to take $250 per month income, all from the bond fund. After six months, your bond fund has earned $600, but you have withdrawn $1,500. You need to move several hundred dollars from the stock fund to the bond fund to reestablish your asset mix.

You would have been better advised to take $150 per month from the bond fund and $100 per month from the stock fund. This

60/40 income distribution is the same percentage allocation as the investment you made in each fund. Whatever percentage you assign to each fund should be the same percentage as the income withdrawn. If 50 percent of your money is in the stock fund, 50 percent of your income should come from it as well, and so forth.

Mutual Funds Wrapped in an Annuity Contract

These contracts, known as variable annuities, can be set up as an IRA. Often there is a group of funds that you can use, and since your return varies with the return of the funds, the annuity is typed as variable. Fixed annuities offer a fixed rate of interest, guaranteed by the issuing insurance company.

In shopping for an IRA it is always important to be aware of the fees and charges as well as the liquidity of the investment. Since annuities carry an extra level of expense, be sure to read the sections in the annuity information relating to charges. In addition, be aware of the withdrawal penalties the contract carries. They can be quite stiff and may obligate you to stay with the IRA for several years or face a penalty to leave.

Like any other IRA, analyze the investment options, performance, expenses, and liquidity before making a decision.

COMMON STOCK FUNDS

Many investors, faced with the daunting task of picking stocks for their portfolio, prefer to turn that job over to a professional manager. And a mutual fund investing in common stocks does just that. Just as in any other investment, however, there are advantages and disadvantages to investing through an equity mutual fund.

Advantages

1. *Diversification.* When you own a common-stock fund, you will own a small piece of dozens or even hundreds of different stocks. Even a small investment will allow you to diversify your portfolio and thereby reduce risk.

2. *Professional management.* You have a professional manager or team watching over the account and making all buy and sell decisions. You don't have to worry about what stocks to buy, what to sell, or when to do it. You can go fishing and everything is taken care of for you. And professional managers tend to perform better than most individuals, so you have a much better chance of good performance than in doing it yourself.

3. *Low expense.* Even with a commission to purchase, mutual-fund investment can be very cost effective compared to paying commissions to buy and sell individual stocks.

4. *Automatic dividend reinvestment.* When dividends come into the fund, your dividends can be used to buy additional shares. You don't have the problem of deciding how to invest small amounts of money as they're received.

5. Performance-monitoring independent companies such as Lipper or Morningstar will publish performance statistics for funds, allowing you to keep track of how the fund is doing.

6. *Fund switching.* You can easily switch from fund to fund within the fund family. Changing your investment posture is quick and inexpensive.

Disadvantages

1. *You're not alone.* Your money isn't segregated from other investors. In a mutual fund you can fall victim to the whims of other investors. If the market takes a meaningful tumble and many shareholders redeem (sell) their shares, your fund manager may be forced to sell stocks to raise cash. This can be very frustrating for him and for you, since a market stumble is an opportunity to buy more stocks at lower prices. Your performance can suffer because of others.

2. *Managers may change.* Like any other professionally managed program, a mutual fund is only as good as those who manage the fund. If that shining star who made your fund a top performer leaves, you may not know about it for months. In the meantime, performance can suffer.

3. *Picking the right fund is tricky.* With thousands of funds available, many investors have learned the hard way that yesterday's performance is no guarantee of future performance. If you pick your funds

by buying the current hot fund, you're almost certainly doomed to failure. One of the quirks of the market is that by the time most people learn about an investment success the tide is about to turn. Many studies have elaborated on this. Given the proliferation of mutual funds, the task of picking a fund has certainly become more complex.

TIP   Remember that a professional manager can better your investment returns but she can't insulate you from loss. A manager striving for above-average capital appreciation can do so only by putting your money at risk. You can't expect those great returns without the possibility of commensurate losses.

When to Use a Stock Fund

1. *You have a small amount to invest.* Anything less than $50,000 is a strong candidate for mutual-fund investing. With smaller amounts of money, it isn't as cost effective to manage on a stock-by-stock basis. Unless you really enjoy stock picking, it's hard to make enough money on, say, $10,000 to compensate you for the hours and hours of time it takes to do a proper job.

2. *You don't like to pick stocks yourself.* If investing doesn't particularly interest you and your IRA really doesn't justify hiring a broker or financial advisor, you're better off picking a good stock fund and opening your IRA with that fund, no matter how large your account.

3. *You have had poor investment results.* If doing it yourself was less than successful, let somebody else do the driving. Whether it is a professional managing an account just for you or for a mutual fund, turn over the reins to someone who has a proven record of success. Investing talent isn't spread equally among all of us.

4. *You want to target several market niches.* Perhaps you want some of your IRA in growth stocks and some in foreign stocks. By using a mutual-fund family, you can have both kinds of funds and switch between them, depending on your strategy and outlook. This isn't as easy when you buy individual stocks.

5. *You can see the forest more clearly than the trees.* It's much more important to be right about major themes and market movements than it is to pick individual stocks. If you do have the gift of knowing when a

market is cheap, it is much better to use a fund to express your thoughts than to waste time picking stocks.

6. *You can't find a good advisor.* If you can't find a good broker or financial advisor, your money is much better off with a major fund family than having you struggle along with doubt and anxiety.

When Not to Use a Stock Fund

1. *You have enough money to hire your own manager.* An individually managed account is shielded from other investors. Although the fees will be higher, the personalized attention is often worth the price. Since you can see every stock you own, you have a better sense of how your IRA is positioned.

2. *You like to pick stocks yourself and are successful at it, or you have a broker who is.* It's not enough simply to enjoy it as a hobby. Investing your retirement money in an IRA is too serious to be a passing hobby. Play with money that isn't so important.

3. *You have a specific market niche that you want to buy and hold.* When you're interested only in owning a half dozen quality blue chips and holding onto them, there is little sense in paying fees to do so. You're better off buying the stocks and paying a one-time commission.

INVESTING IN BOND FUNDS

Our comments about stock funds hold as well for bond funds. But there are a couple of additional considerations about bonds that you need to know.

By and large, bond investment in IRA accounts does not offer a fixed-level-of-interest income that can be relied upon for living expenses. If your interest rate constantly floats, it is very difficult to work out a budget—you don't know how much you're going to earn.

In addition, and this is crucial, you can't lock in an income stream with a bond mutual fund. The rate of interest will float over time in the direction of market interest rates. As a shareholder, you own a piece of the entire bond portfolio. As new investors add money to your fund, your fund manager has to go out and buy new bonds to put the fund's cash to work.

> **EXAMPLE**   Sensing a fall in interest rates ahead, you buy a well-known government bond fund for your IRA. You are attracted by its relatively high yield of 7.5 percent. Interest rates begin to fall, Other investors, noting as well the high yield, begin pouring money into the fund many months after you purchased it. Your bond fund swells, and the manager must buy new bonds at much lower rates. Even though the value of the fund has risen, your interest income has fallen as the fund is forced to cut its dividend. You had perfect investment foresight, yet your income suffered.

If current interest rates are attractive, the only way to take advantage of it is to buy individual bonds. This is the only way to lock in your income stream.

However, when it comes to investing in more complex fixed-income instruments—convertibles, international bonds, junk bonds (also called high-yield bonds)—mutual funds are the vehicle of choice. Trying to figure out the credit quality of lower-rated bonds is an activity most of us should avoid. It takes a tremendous amount of knowledge, access to information, and hard work to be successful in high-yield bond management. Leave it to the pros.

It is also true that the annual management fees on bond funds can be a drag on your earnings. If your fund charges an annual management fee of .7 percent, and you are earning 7 percent interest, fees are chewing up 10 percent of your income. If the manager can generate capital gains by deftly timing her bond purchases and sales, she can overcome this drag imposed by the management fees. An examination of his long-term record should help establish this.

Generally, investors should use bond funds when they don't have enough money to buy a well-diversified portfolio. In that case, the benefits of interest reinvestment and diversification can outweigh the lack of a stable income stream. IRA investors who make bonds their investment of choice must strongly consider developing their own fixed-bond portfolios, holding bonds until maturity and using that interest for income.

However, it is also true that finding a good bond broker can be difficult, and since bonds generally trade over the counter, pricing can vary widely. You may find that it is worth paying the management fee to let a pro worry about it.

SWITCHING FROM FUND TO FUND

IRA owners will read about methods that encourage switching among various funds in a mutual-fund family.

As mentioned earlier, once you have invested in a mutual fund, you can usually switch to any other fund in that family without charge. Sometimes a fund will impose a charge to discourage frequent in-and-out trading. Various services sell advice on when to move from one fund to another. The idea is to be able to time your swings so that you buy stocks before they have risen and sell them before they fall. Ditto for bonds.

Usually these services are of dubious value for most IRA holders. Timing the market is notoriously difficult, and even if done successfully for some period of time, it will often prove fruitless if even one timing call is off the mark. Missing a major move in the market because you were sitting in a money-market fund is a dose of cold water on the idea of timing a move from fund to fund.

You are much better off setting your asset allocation between stocks and bonds and adjusting your allocation as one or the other investment proves timely. (See Chapter 7, "Asset Allocation and the Lump Sum.")

HOW TO PICK A GOOD FUND FAMILY

It is much more important to pick a good fund family than to pick a good individual fund. Some investors try to find the best stock fund, the best bond fund, and so forth. They end up with several IRAs at several different fund families. Over time, this is probably needless duplication. You want to be able to invest in both good bond and good stock funds within a family of funds. The fund family should offer, at a minimum, the following choices:

Stock Funds

1. A large-capitalization value fund
2. A large-capitalization growth fund
3. A small-capitalization fund (ideally both a value and a growth fund)
4. A foreign-stock fund
5. A precious-metals fund

Bond Funds

1. A general purpose intermediate-term bond fund
2. A government securities bond fund
3. A money-market fund
4. A foreign-bond fund
5. A Ginnie Mae or other mortgage fund

Other Factors

As in hiring any other money manager, you'll want to look at the five-year (or longer) track record for each fund, comparing those returns against other funds of the same type and against the appropriate market indices. You want to see how each fund has performed against its peer group and against the market in which it operates. And don't forget that the record you're looking at is only as good as the people who created it. How long has the current fund manager been there?

> **TIP**   In looking at investment returns, go beyond total five-year returns. Examine the fluctuation of the year-to-year numbers against the S&P 500. If the year-to-year variation is larger than the stock market, will you be willing to take the heat in a down year to wait for future appreciation?

Warning! Picking a fund family will be an exercise in compromise. The fund organization may have a terrific growth-stock fund, but only average bond funds. Or, it may have two excellent bond funds and several mediocre stock funds. You'll have to weigh the compromise by looking at how much you're investing in stocks and how much in bonds. If you're weighting your investment mix toward bonds, look for good bond funds first.

If you decide to pick your funds from various fund families, you'll have several different IRA accounts and IRA statements each quarter. This can create complications when computing taxable distribution requirements from your IRA. In addition, beneficiary arrangements and distribution options can vary widely, so you have to factor in these issues when picking your fund strategies.

Armed with those choices, you want to allocate your IRA among the various funds. Remember, the fund family will be the custodian of your IRA, and the funds forming your investment portfolio will all be held in that one IRA. You don't need a separate IRA for each fund.

Once you have decided on your basic asset allocation, you can apportion your money among the various funds, adjusting your fund balances twice each year as various segments of the market rise and fall.

EXAMPLE   You have $150,000 for an IRA rollover account. After settling on a 60 percent stock, 40 percent bond allocation, you deploy your IRA as follows:

60 percent:	$90,000 in stocks
30 percent:	$45,000 large capitalization stocks
20 percent:	$30,000 growth stocks
7 percent:	$10,000 small capitalization stocks
3 percent:	$5,000 foreign stocks
40 percent:	$60,000 in bonds
23 percent:	$35,000 general purpose bond fund
13 percent:	$20,000 U.S. government bond fund
3 percent:	$5,000 foreign bond fund

You have spread your investments across several different markets by setting aside fixed percentages in each investment class. All you need to do is snapshot your fund values twice each year and move money from fund to fund, readjusting the percentages.

Over time, as funds rise, you will take money out of them, and as they fall, put money in them. This buy-low, sell-high discipline is the opposite of what most investors do. Most buy the best-performing funds and sell the worst-performing ones. They wind up chasing yesterday's winners and selling yesterday's losers. It's like driving using only a rear-view mirror. (After the end of the first quarter of 1993, investors had approximately $800 million in the ten best-performing large equity funds. By contrast, they had over $3 billion in the ten worst-performing funds.)

Take a simple example.

You have $25,000 in your IRA rollover account. You decide on a 60 percent bond, 40 percent stock mix.

$15,000 invested in your bond fund: 60 percent

$10,000 Invested in your stock fund: 40 percent

Six months later, the stock market has had a dramatic rally, while your bonds have moved up slightly:

$15,600 Invested in your bond fund: 56.5 percent

$12,000 invested in your stock fund: 43.5 percent

In order to readjust your balances to a 60/40 mix, you make the following adjustment: $960 switched out of stocks and into bonds.

$16,560 invested in your bond fund: 60 percent

$11,040 invested in your stock fund: 40 percent

Notice how you moved money out of the stock market and into the bond market. You sold your stocks at a higher price. The opposite holds true. If the stock market fell, you would take money out of bonds and put it into stocks. This enforced discipline will give you additional returns over time, in addition to sparing you the month-to-month agony of deciding where to invest.

This simple system works very well (I use it for my own 401(k) plan at work) with a minimum amount of effort. And, if you have a good fund family from which to choose, you can create many different combinations of portfolios to adjust your risk and your portfolio diversification.

FINDING GOOD FUND INFORMATION

Most of the popular financial magazines offer mutual-fund rankings on a periodic basis. For completeness of information and reasonable price, *Kiplinger's* is hard to beat. *Barron's* and *Money* magazine also offer good fund surveys. The two mainstays in the fund performance-measuring business are Morningstar and Lipper. Both should be available in your public library.

If all this is more than you can handle, let your investment advisor worry about it. You'll pay a fee or commission to do so, but the advice should be worth the price you pay if you can't do it successfully on your own.

In that case, explore his methodology for moving among funds. Is it consistent and does he consistently follow it?

Finally, beware of anyone who charges you a commission to invest in a fund family, only to find a "better" family one or two years down the pike. You may be paying multiple commissions for no real purpose.

SUMMARY

With thousands of funds available today, the investor faces a bewildering choice in fund investment. However, the task can be brought down to manageable levels.

Most IRA investors utilizing mutual funds will want to pick one basic stock fund and one basic bond fund for their IRA. Then, they can build around those two funds with various niche funds . . . gold, REIT, international, and so forth. Often a single fund family offers convenience in fund investment, switching, and statement consolidation.

Several companies offer timely analysis of funds and fund groups, and this information is easily accessible on a regular basis.

It is important to remember that a mutual fund, like any other investment vehicle, is not a completely perfect choice. There are compromises that must be taken into consideration when using mutual funds.

While bond funds offer excellent diversification, income levels are not locked in and guaranteed. And the principal value will fluctuate. Stock funds offer similar diversification, but you are investing along with hundreds or thousands of other investors, and sometimes their actions in withdrawing or adding funds will affect the performance of the fund.

Smaller IRAs are almost always well-suited to fund investment. As the size of the IRA grows, other investment options become more viable. And, since fees on funds can vary widely, depending on the management fees charged by the fund and by any commissions paid to purchase, the investor needs to explore carefully the levels of service obtained for the fee.

CHAPTER THIRTEEN

Investment Taxes Outside the IRA

Not all your money will be invested in an IRA. Savings and after-tax employer distributions will not enjoy IRA treatment. Therefore, you need to be aware of your tax position when investing without IRA shelter.

Everybody knows the saying, "Nothing is sure except death and taxes." But when it comes to taxes, many investors are still not convinced.

The first bit of advice I can give you is to encourage you to pay your taxes on your investment activity as they are due. There are always a few people who believe they can beat the system, and they should be encouraged to not make the attempt.

However, there are two ways I believe you can minimize the effect of taxes on investment activity—by the timing of taxable activity and by engaging in tax-free investing. (We explored tax-free investing in the Chapter 10, Municipal Bonds and the Companion Account.)

THE TAX HANG-UP

One of the most destructive investing attitudes is to be blinded by the fact that you have to pay taxes on your profits. Whenever a client hesitates to take a good profit because of the taxes that have to be paid, I have to explain that taxes are the cost of doing business as an investor. They're part of the overhead. All investors know that if they make a good investment, they will earn a profit. When you take that profit, federal and state government is going to deduct around 30 to 50 percent in income taxes. This is the price you pay for profitable investment.

Yet when it comes time to pay that tax, some people balk. After observing this behavior for many years, I've come to the conclusion that this reluctance often stems from irrelevant government issues. The investment tax simply allows investors to channel their political frustrations.

This behavior is self-destructive. If a profit should be taken, then it should be taken. It's that simple. If you don't take it today, the tax on the profit won't go away. It can drop when it goes into long-term-gain status, but it doesn't go away.

Now, others might argue that by taking the gain and paying the tax, you actually lose because you no longer have the tax money working for you. To some extent, this is true.

EXAMPLE   You have purchased 100 shares of good old XYZ at $25 per share. Happily, it has risen to $55 per share. You have a $3,000 profit on your $2,500 investment. If you sell the stock, the $5,500 in proceeds will be reduced by paying capital gains taxes of about $600 (long-term capital gain of 20 percent of $3,000). So, you wind up with $4,900 in your pocket (less any state taxes).

The 100 shares of stock are currently paying a dividend of 5 percent, or $275 per year. Why sell and pay the tax? After all, the $600 in tax money is also earning 5 percent, or $30 per year. You'd lose that by paying the tax.

What is overlooked, of course, is that the argument to hold boils down to the anticipated movement in the price of the stock. If the stock holds at $55 or continues to rise, the postponement of sale was a good move. But consider what happens if the stock peters out and falls to $50. A sale now generates proceeds of $5,000. Your gain has shrunk to $2,500, so you have to pay tax of $500 on the gain, leaving you with net proceeds of $4,500. Instead of $4,900, you now have only $4,500.

Think of it this way. Since the government gets less than half of the profit, you stand to lose more by allowing the stock to fall than by selling at the higher price and paying the heavier tax. For every $1 fall in the price of the stock, you save only 20 cents in taxes, but you lose 80 cents of your capital invested. Doesn't make any sense at all.

This is why you shouldn't consider taxes the overriding factor in the decision to sell. Either an investment is going higher, going nowhere, or going down. You have to ask yourself where each of your investments are. If the answer is that the investment is going down, sell it and pay the tax. If going up, hold. And if going nowhere, look for a better place for the money. Whatever you do, don't be blinded by the fact that you have to pay tax on the gain. Be happy you have a gain at all.

I have seen this tax-induced blindness carried to extremes. Positions that were established years ago, with tremendous gains now built in, are held forever simply to avoid the tax. In some cases, it became obvious that the company had seen its best days. Yet the thought of paying the tax completely overwhelmed the logical decision to sell the stock to avoid a tumble in the price.

There is one general exception to this rule. If you are elderly, it may make sense to hold the stock and let your estate deal with it. If your estate avoids estate tax, your heirs can duck the capital gain entirely.

> **EXAMPLE**   You own 1,000 shares that you bought at $10 per share many years ago. The stock is now worth $80,000. On your death, the stock is valued at $80,000 as part of your estate. Since your entire estate is less than $600,000, there is no estate tax due. Your heirs received the stock with a new cost of $80 per share. The capital gain on the $70 appreciation has been wiped clean.

If your health is failing, you should think carefully before selling any appreciated property. The decision may lie in estate taxes, not in income taxes.

TO DEFER OR NOT TO DEFER, THAT IS THE QUESTION

For most of the post-World War II period, deferring tax made a lot of sense. Income tax rates were high, and the prospect of rates going lower in the future made deferral of tax the method of choice. Whether one purchased tax-deferred annuities, or purchased real estate with current deductions and recognition of income in the future, the idea was to defer taxes currently while in a high bracket and then recognize the income later on, say in retirement, when tax brackets would be lower.

That has all changed. Several tax acts over the past ten years did two things:

1. Closed many tax loopholes
2. Reduced marginal tax rates

It is more difficult to defer tax, and, given the general trend of income tax rates (up from the Reagan-era lows), deferral is increasingly a questionable practice. Why defer tax today in a 28 percent tax bracket, when you may have to pay the income tax in five years in a 40 percent bracket?

Of course, an IRA rollover is a very large tax-deferred account. One of its great attractions is that you are using the government's tax money over many years to earn additional income. This additional income provides not only retirement income, but a means of paying for the taxes eventually due.

While the advent of the Roth IRA now offers the potential for distributing funds on a tax-free basis, this is generally not advantageous for the retiree, or preretiree, except in a fairly marginal way.

CLOSING THE LOOPHOLES

Many investors grew fond of investing in government-subsidized housing tax shelters, writing off two or three times their investment and reaping large tax savings.

Many have not caught on to the fact that the government, in its desire to level the tax-playing field, has done away with most tax havens. The message found in law after law is that you'll pay your share of taxes on income earned and pay it now. If you don't want to pay it now, the government has limited the ways in which you can defer.

Take, for example, the tax-deferred annuity. In a tax-deferred annuity, you deposit a specific sum of money with an insurance company and it either invests it in a set of mutual funds or credits your contract interest on the money each year. All gains and interest are tax-deferred—you don't pay the tax until you take the money out of the contract.

For years, investors could put away unlimited amounts of money, defer all the tax on the increase, then look forward to pulling the money back out when their tax brackets had dropped.

The Tax, Equity and Fiscal Responsibility Act of 1982 (TEFRA), threw a couple of wrinkles into tax-deferred annuity rules. First, the initial layer of money you pulled out of the contract would now be considered interest income and taxed. Only after you had pulled out all your income would the government consider the balance a return of your original principal not subject to tax. This last-in-first-out (LIFO) method of accounting means that you can't tap your annuity on a tax-free basis. The first withdrawals would be taxable events. This was a complete reversal of the rules. Up to that point, withdrawals were done on a first-in-first-out (FIFO) basis; you could withdraw as a tax-free return of principal all your original deposit before you'd pay tax on the balance.

Then the clincher: Unless you were 59 1/2, any withdrawals of income would be considered "premature." In addition to paying ordinary tax, a 10 percent excise tax would be applied as a penalty. In effect, the government was now requiring taxpayers to treat tax-deferred annuities as true retirement accounts, not as a tax-deferral mechanism. If you annuitized your contract, the 10 percent tax penalty would be waived.

TEFRA changed the rules of the game for tax-deferred annuities. You can see that the effect of the legislation on an annuity contract was to discourage investment for purely tax-oriented reasons. If you wanted to purchase an annuity to help provide for your retirement, the law didn't change much for you. If you were purchasing it to defer tax only, the rules governing pre-59 1/2 distributions were ominous.

This is exactly what was intended. Tax deferral would be permitted when there was a strong economic reason. This push toward economic investing, coupled with a trend toward higher marginal tax rates, now makes the purchase of a tax-deferred annuity a much closer investment call. Do you, for instance, buy a tax-deferred annuity to earn 6.25 percent tax-deferred, or do you buy a high-quality municipal bond and earn 5 percent tax-free? The annuity carries a higher interest rate but must be reduced when the taxes have to be paid. The municipal provides less income, but it's all tax free.

MAKING THE DECISION

The answer lies in a calculation designed to measure the time value of money. In a time-value computation, several factors are introduced in comparing two investments, including interest rates, the effect of deferral in additional buildup, and the effect of taxes paid on the deferred funds. While you can do this calculation with a simple calculator, there are plenty of software programs that can compute these combinations for you.

Whatever software you use, the idea is to compare the two investments, taking into account not only the earnings of the funds but the taxes due and the timing of those taxes. In this way you can do a direct comparison of each investment to arrive at the bottom line: your net-after-tax return. This figure will point you to the right investment.

Investment of $50,000 by a 45-Year-Old Investor

Choice #1: Purchase a tax-deferred annuity with a guaranteed rate of 6.25 percent for five years, paid annually, to be cashed in at age 60 in a lump sum. The rate will float after the fifth year and be readjusted annually.

Choice #2: Purchase a $50,000, 5 percent municipal bond with a maturity at age 60.

Which is the better choice?

You first have to make some assumptions:

1. *The reinvestment rate on the municipal bond.* What rate will you earn by reinvesting the interest you receive semiannually over the next 15 years? After all, that interest will total $46,875 in payments, almost as much as your original investment. Solution? Assume the same rate on reinvestment.

2. *The reinvestment on the annuity contract.* Again, use your current rate for reinvestment.

Having made your interest-rate assumptions, you now have to estimate the income-tax rate at withdrawal on the annuity. You have to pay the deferred tax at age 60, so you need to know what your tax bracket will be at that point. You don't have to deal with that on the municipal, since all the interest earned is tax-free.

Given current tax rates, we'll assume your federal rate is 40 percent, and your state rate, 9 percent. This brings us to a 46 percent bracket on the taxation of the withdrawals at age 60. (The state tax is deductible on your federal return, so the combined rate is less than adding the two rates together.)

You now have all the numbers you need, so you plug them in and get the following calculations:

Value of the annuity contract in five years: $67,704.

Value of the municipal bond account: $63,814.

Since you have to pay taxes on the annuity interest, you have to reduce the annuity by $8,143 in state and federal taxes paid, leaving you with $59,561.

It's clear that the best choice in this example is to buy the tax-free municipal bonds, even though the pre-tax rate of the annuity is higher. Tax deferral is not always the best choice.

Other issues of deferral follow the same lines of thought and the same type of calculation. You are simply trying to decide whether it makes sense to defer tax or to find some other way of investing that reduces the tax bill. It's important not to lose sight of your goal. You are trying to get the highest net-after-tax return on your funds. If common stocks appear to offer higher returns, even after paying capital-gains taxes, then you shouldn't be too concerned with the taxes due.

Short-Term Deferrals

Some deferrals are short term in nature. In short-term deferral, you aren't trying to accumulate years of interest income, you're simply trying to put off for one tax year the paying of tax due on a transaction.

> **EXAMPLE** You wish to sell stock for a $30,000 gain in December of year one. By waiting two weeks until January of year two, you postpone paying the taxes until April 15 of year three. You then deposit the $9,000 of tax due in a one-year certificate of deposit at 5 percent and earn $450 interest on the funds. This interest earned is a result of timing the transaction to occur after the first of the year. By waiting only a couple of weeks, you postpone paying taxes for an entire year.
>
> *Note:* If you are on quarterly estimated payments, you must take this taxable event into account.

While the Taxpayer Relief Act of 1997 did away with the strategy known as "shorting against the box," it is still possible to recognize a loss in a stock and still keep the position. This is known as "doubling up." In doubling up, you purchase an identical number of shares that you're interested in selling. You then wait 30 days and sell half the position.

> **EXAMPLE** You own 200 shares of XYZ at $35 per share. The stock is currently trading at $25. You would like to recognize the $10 capital loss in December. It is now November 15. You purchase an additional 200 shares of XYZ at $25. On December 15, you sell 200 shares of XYZ at $26. For tax purposes, you can claim $35 as

your cost on the sold position. You have realized a loss of $1,800 and now have a new cost of $25 per share, with the stock trading at $26.

Since you can take up to $3,000 in capital losses each year without an offsetting capital gain, you try to take advantage of that by doubling up if you have losses. Of course, when you double up you recognize the gain or loss currently, but in doing so you set yourself up for an opposite gain or loss in the future. In our example your new cost is $25, so a rise back to $35 generates a $10 capital gain. Had you held onto the original position and not doubled up, you would be back to a break-even position with no tax due. Once again, you see that taxes can be postponed but not eliminated.

Doubling up is a timing technique. It recognizes gain or loss for tax purposes and postpones the tax consequences of the transaction. In doubling up, you have also doubled your market risk: If the stock declines further during the 30-day doubling up period, your losses will be twice as large. Doubling up works best when you believe that the stock has bottomed. By doubling up, you get the advantage of twice as many shares working in your favor if the stock rises.

A second strategy recognizes a gain or loss immediately without materially changing your portfolio.

Using Similar Securities

Often, it is possible to find an investment that is similar to the one you own and use that investment as a replacement for the one you have.

EXAMPLE   You own 100 shares of XYZ, a major utility. You wish to sell the 100 shares to generate a loss for tax purposes, yet you want to maintain your exposure in utility stocks. You sell your 100 shares of XYZ and simultaneously purchase 100 shares of WXY, another major utility.

Given the fact that utility stocks tend to move in tandem based on interest rates and cost of energy, a switch from XYZ to WXY will have a minimal impact on the portfolio strategy being used. The loss is taken for tax purposes, and the exposure to utilities is maintained. Since a switch from one company to another was made, the wash-sale rule does not apply.

This switch does come with a caveat: You can get into gray areas depending on how you make the switch. For instance, the sale of a particular company's bond for another bond issued by the same company, even though at a different interest rate and maturity, might not fly. The securities are just too similar. The best advice is to ask your accountant before entering into the transaction.

These timing strategies are all viable, and most important, easy to do. All they require is a call to order the purchase or sale. Again, your strategy here is to postpone the payment of tax to earn interest on the tax money for a year. A second reason is to take advantage of the $3,000 annual capital-loss deduction. Depending on whether you wish to maintain the position in the security, you will select one method over another.

TIMING GAINS AND LOSSES AND IRA INCOME

Various timing techniques for recognizing or postponing taxable events can be used in conjunction with taking income distributions from your IRA.

If you take a distribution that puts you into a higher tax bracket, postpone taking a profit in the same year on an appreciated security. Also, consider taking a loss that year to offset the taxable IRA distribution.

> **EXAMPLE**   You take a $2,000 distribution from your IRA. This last bit of income for the year means that it will be taxed in a higher bracket. You take a $3,000 capital loss on a stock you wanted to sell. Since you can use up to $3,000 in capital losses each year without having offsetting capital gains, you effectively wipe off the $2,000 IRA distribution as a tax item by playing the capital loss against it.

Using the Capital Gains Brackets to Your Advantage

The Taxpayer Relief Act of 1997 changed capital-gain tax rates and broke them into three brackets, but amendments in 1998 reverted back to two rates.

Classification	Holding Period	Maximum Tax Rate
Short-term capital gains	Less than 12 months	Ordinary income tax, 39.6%
Long-term capital gains	Longer than 12 months	20%

In order to reap maximum benefit from these rates, you want to engage in investment strategies that encourage long-term capital gains. After all, if you can get long-term treatment, instead of short-term treatment, the tax can be literally cut in half.

So, you want to avoid in-and-out trading strategies and focus instead on core stock holdings that can be held for two to three years, or more. If you have some shorter-term investment strategies, use the IRA for those since the gain is tax-deferred.

Just consider a stock you buy at $10 that rises to $18. While congratulating yourself on an 80 percent gain, you need to slow down and remember that nearly half of that gain will be paid in taxes (39.6 percent federal, plus state income tax), cutting your profit to 48 percent. As a long-term gain, the tax bite would preserve a net-after-tax gain of about 64 percent. Big difference.

Another important point to make is that since long-term capital gain taxes are now down to 20 percent, it often makes no sense to generate long-term capital gains in an IRA and then pay 39.6 percent tax on the distribution from the IRA. This converts long-term capital gains into ordinary income. Better to generate long-term gains outside the IRA and get that lower tax rate.

So, you should consider doing your fixed income investing in the IRA, where you can go for maximum interest income without current tax and use long-term-equity investment strategies outside the IRA.

SUMMARY

Given the strengthening of the tax code and reporting requirements, as well as the elimination of many tax loopholes, there are fewer ways to avoid paying tax on interest and capital gains.

Generally, tax deferral is possible through a variety of strategies designed to postpone the recognition of the gain for tax purposes. The tax due on a profit realized through investment is one of the costs of doing business as an investor. Investors should not be blinded by the emotional reaction inherent in paying tax. Instead, effort should be focused on retaining good investments in a portfolio and weeding out those that have seen their best days.

Generally speaking, tax issues should not drive an investment decision. Either an investment is a good one or it is not. A poor investment is not radically improved by a tax break.

CHAPTER FOURTEEN

The Lump Sum and Your Estate

Bill Jameson thought the idea made sense. After attending a seminar at his Senior Citizens' Center, he contacted an attorney he met on the golf course and had him draft a living trust. Bill felt that the avoidance of probate expense on his estate was a good thing to shoot for, and the living trust was something he heard mentioned by several guys in his golf league. After setting up the trust, Bill contacted his IRA custodian and had the beneficiary on his $400,000 IRA changed to the trust. After all, the trust was set up with his wife, Joan, as beneficiary. Wasn't that the idea? To get the money to her?

Bill's heart gave out while he was flailing away in a sand trap on the fifteenth hole. Much to Joan's surprise, income taxes on the $400,000 IRA were suddenly an issue. What to do?

When you fill out an IRA application before rolling over your lump sum, pay close attention to the beneficiary section. It is crucial that you fill this out properly.

Wrong answers can result in devastating taxes on your heirs.

YOUR SPOUSE AS IRA BENEFICIARY

Because an IRA is always held in single-name ownership and cannot be held jointly with your spouse, a husband or wife's claim on it must be through the beneficiary designation on the application. So if the IRA is paid out to anyone other than your spouse (even to your children) that money could be subject to payment of all income taxes due within a relatively short time. Only the spouse can roll over the funds from the IRA rollover and continue to defer all the tax.

> **EXAMPLE**   You list your two children as beneficiaries of the IRA. On your death, your $200,000 IRA rollover account is distributed to them. They each must pay income tax (at their ordinary income tax rates) on the $100,000 distributed to each of them, Thus, the principal is reduced by as much as $60,000 in tax payments.

The tax code recognizes the right of a spouse to roll over a distribution from her deceased spouse's IRA but does not extend that benefit to any other beneficiary.

> **TIP**   Because the courts are taking a much stronger view of the spouse's ownership of his or her spouse's pension benefits in divorce proceedings, your employer will require your spouse to sign off if you elect a lump-sum distribution. Your benefit may be held in your name, but a court could rule that your spouse is entitled to part of the benefit. Therefore there is an implied ownership by your spouse.

Just because you may have completed a comprehensive estate plan doesn't mean you will avoid a sharp tax bite for your heirs. You must name your beneficiaries properly on the IRA application.

> **TIP**   Leaving your IRA to your estate accomplishes little, other than paying the IRA according to the beneficiaries listed in your will.

Let's say you have $500,000 in your rollover account and your wife is beginning to show early signs of Alzheimer's disease. You are worried that she will sink into mental incompetence. So you set up a trust. After your death the $500,000 is paid to the trust, which in turn must pay $130,000 in income taxes on the distribution. These taxes must be paid because the trust, while set up for your wife's benefit, is considered to be a separate and distinct taxpayer. This tax can be reduced. The trustee then assumes control over the funds for her benefit.

Account holders are not required to name a spouse as beneficiary. You could name a child, or any number of children, a charity, or even your university as beneficiary.

> **TIP**   If you are contemplating a divorce, be aware that your spouse could change the beneficiary on an IRA without notifying you. Don't assume that the IRA will automatically be yours on your spouse's death.

If you wish your spouse to be the beneficiary, put that name in the IRA document. By naming your spouse, ownership of the IRA after your death passes on without delay or complication. If you name your estate as beneficiary, the IRA must be handled through the estate. This can lead to needless expense, delay, and complication.

Naming Your Children as Beneficiaries

As close as your children are to you, they can't avoid the income-tax bite. And it is sometimes difficult to leave perfectly equal portions to them because of the intrusion of the income-tax rules. Beneficiaries must pay tax in their own income-tax brackets.

> **EXAMPLE**   You leave your $30,000 IRA to your three children in equal portions. One is unemployed, the other two have successful careers. Since the unemployed child has no other income, he will pay a minimal tax on the $10,000 distribution, while the others will be taxed in much higher tax brackets. After tax, you have not succeeded in making them equal beneficiaries.

The only way to make sure they get equal amounts is to give them different percentages that will compensate them for their tax bill. What you want to compute is their after-tax inheritance.

Naming your children as primary beneficiaries can be an advantage under certain circumstances. But it should be done with great care because when you die your IRA assets irrevocably bypass your spouse. Don't forget that even if your will names your spouse as the beneficiary of your estate, the IRA is governed by the beneficiaries you name in the IRA document.

You should keep in mind two basic tax rules if you do leave your IRA to your children:

1. They are allowed to put their share in a conduit IRA account and then must begin to distribute the assets on a schedule determined by your status when you passed away.

2. They cannot roll over the assets and defer taxation until their own retirement.

This is a strong argument in favor of leaving the account to your spouse, who can roll it over and defer. So you need a compelling reason to leave the IRA to your children or another beneficiary. Here are a few:

1. Your wife will have more than enough assets on your death. There is little point in passing her still more that will be reduced via estate tax on her death. You may find that if your children are in a relatively low income-tax bracket relative to your wife and your wife has adequate sources of income, passing the IRA to your children is possible. However, before naming your children as IRA beneficiaries, you should first explore leaving other assets to them and passing the IRA to your wife. That would allow her to take advantage of the continued tax-deferred buildup of the assets.

2. If your IRA is particularly large, you might want to split it between your spouse and children.

EXAMPLE   You have an IRA rollover account in excess of $1 million. You are 75 years old. Since you must take distributions from the account and pay tax, you decide to leave 50 percent of it to your wife and 10 percent to each of your five children. At 7 percent, your wife can earn $35,000 per year on her share, and since your children have already received an inheritance via the IRA, she can spend IRA principal to increase her annual income. This will reduce her estate over time. The $500,000 given to your children will not be reduced by estate taxes on your wife's death since it is no longer in her estate. By doing this you can make a bequest to your children while providing adequate funds for your wife.

3. If you don't have a family, you can leave your IRA to a charity.
4. You can leave your IRA to a friend, lifetime companion, or any relative.

In most cases, parents can comfortably name their children as beneficiaries.

Once the children are named as beneficiaries it is a personal judgment whether to inform them of the fact. I always lean toward disclosure within the family, although I recognize that this can create problems. If a family is close and acts with good will, disclosure gives you the opportunity to discuss your wishes about the ultimate disposition of the funds.

Often, grandparents would like to make some provision for their grandchildren's college education but don't want to leave the money directly to them. What if the kids don't go to college?

EXAMPLE   You discuss your IRA rollover of $300,000 with your two daughters. After paying income taxes, they will each keep $100,000. You indicate your strong preference for the funds to be used for the college education of your grandchildren. While your daughters aren't bound to your wishes, they agree to do so if at all possible. As an alternative you could pass a fixed percentage of your IRA to your daughter as custodian for your grandchild. Remember, however, that no matter how the grandchild may turn out, the money is his when he reaches the age of majority.

TAX COMPLICATIONS OF THE IRA IN AN ESTATE

If the IRA is paid through your estate, it is subject to estate settlement scrutiny by the attorneys and probate court. Probate is the legal process by which ownership is passed from the deceased person to others. It includes establishing clear title to assets and paying off existing debt. The personal representative is the individual named in the will responsible for carrying this out. Inevitably the services of an attorney are required.

An IRA is a non probate asset if the beneficiaries of the IRA are specifically designated. Also note that if your beneficiary predeceases you, the IRA is paid to the contingent beneficiary, and if you have no contingent beneficiary, to your estate, If the IRA is paid to the estate, the control over the IRA has been given to the estate and must follow the usual probate process. This often takes many months to complete.

Keep in mind that the attorney who probates the estate is entitled to a fee for his or her services, typically a percentage of the estate's assets. You should know that putting a large IRA into an estate will often result in additional legal fees.

If your intent is for the money to benefit your spouse, why make it complicated? If the estate becomes tied in knots due to cross-claims or suit, a clean and timely distribution of the IRA to the spouse will be almost impossible. This on top of the probate expense means that leaving an IRA to your spouse through your estate is often a poor choice.

And this holds true for any other beneficiary you name.

USING THE IRA DOCUMENT TO PASS YOUR IRA TO YOUR HEIRS

When the IRA is left directly to the spouse via the IRA the transfer is quick and direct.

Typically, the personal representative of your estate (usually your spouse) will present your IRA custodian with a copy of your death certificate, affidavit of domicile, and a letter acknowledging transfer to the beneficiary. (The IRA custodian is the bank, brokerage firm, or any other institution holding your IRA.) The custodian should then be free to accomplish the transfer. A lawyer's services are not usually needed, except to furnish these required legal documents. Remember that an IRA is a trust and so has its own terms covering disposition of the assets on your death. Your will need not come into play.

Your spouse will be able to roll over the assets from your IRA into his or her own IRA. After all, he or she is heir to the actual assets, not to their equivalent in cash. Your spouse can use those assets exactly as you did.

Your IRA custodian may allow you to name contingent beneficiaries. That way, if your primary beneficiary dies with you, your custodian can pass the IRA to your contingent beneficiary. People usually name their spouse as beneficiary and their children as equal contingent beneficiaries.

TIP   Your spouse will have to name beneficiaries for her account. She does not have to name your contingent beneficiaries as her own primary beneficiaries. Therefore, do not assume that your IRA will automatically go to your children after you and your wife have passed away. Once the IRA is hers, she is free to name her own beneficiaries.

EXAMPLE   You name your second husband as your primary beneficiary. You name your two children from your first marriage as your contingent beneficiaries. Your second husband has three children from his first marriage. On your death, your IRA passes to him. He names his three children beneficiaries. Your own two children are now disinherited from your IRA.

Unfortunately, the only way to be absolutely sure that the IRA will go to your children is to name them as primary beneficiaries. You could, for instance, name your husband to receive 50 percent of the IRA, with the remaining 50 percent going to your children. Of course, this leaves your spouse less money in the IRA and imposes an income-tax liability on your children.

A better alternative may be to leave the entire IRA to your husband, thus preserving favorable income tax treatment, and give away other assets to your children on your death. When second marriages present inheritance difficulties, a very sharp estate-planning attorney is a must.

NAMING OTHER BENEFICIARIES

IRA rollover accounts make poor estate-planning tools, given the constraints imposed by the income-tax code. And if you happen to be single, beneficiaries will have to wrestle with income tax issues.

Current tax law does not recognize committed lifetime companions as spouses within the tax code, although the tendency in the future will undoubtedly be to address this. Gay couples, for instance, can't take advantage of spousal arrangements in regard to an IRA. If you leave your IRA to your companion, it will be treated under the same rules as any other non-spouse beneficiary.

This is also true if you leave your IRA to a friend or a relative. He must begin taking distributions, the schedule varying again according to the tax rules. Remember, all beneficiaries other than spouses are lumped together as the same type for income-tax purposes. So a friend would have to apply the same tax rules as your children.

CONSIDER A TRUST

Under certain circumstances, establishing a trust may be a good solution.

You have an IRA rollover totaling $600,000. Your son is your only beneficiary. He is not a competent manager of money. Should a trust or other arrangement be established?

Because a trust can set out precisely the rules for both investing and distributing the funds placed in it, it provides a way to extend your wishes beyond your life. Trusts are therefore often used as protective vehicles, sometimes to protect beneficiaries against themselves.

What Is a Trust?

A trust is a fiduciary relationship under which the trustee deals with the property for the benefit of the beneficiary.

Any trust has several aspects:

- A *settlor* or *grantor* is the person with the money who establishes the trust.
- The *beneficiary* is the person on whose behalf the trust is established.
- The *trustee* is the person who takes care of the trust and runs it according to the instructions set out in the . . .
- *Trust document,* which sets forth in writing the terms of the trust under applicable state law.
- A trust is considered to be a separate entity and taxpayer if it is *irrevocable*. A trust for your wife's benefit is a separate taxpayer from your wife. (Although sometimes, the taxes flow through to the beneficiary.)

There are many other characteristics but you can see that the basic goal of a trust is to take the management and control of the trust assets away from the beneficiary and pass it to the trustee for the benefit of the beneficiary.

Trusts can accomplish:

- Management of assets
- Conserving property for beneficiaries
- Minimizing probate costs
- Saving taxes
- Assuring privacy in the transfer of property at death

There are generally two types of trusts: inter vivos and testamentary. An inter vivos trust is created during the life of the grantor. A testamentary trust is established by a will and becomes irrevocable as of the date it is funded.

A revocable inter vivos trust is effective in reducing probate expense, but does not prevent estate taxes. An irrevocable trust is an especially good estate-tax saving device. However, once the assets are placed in the trust they may not be reclaimed by the settlor (the person giving away the assets).

Whether to establish one is always a difficult question. I view trusts as a last resort. Once a trust is funded it is generally an irrevocable decision. Annual expenses to maintain the trust will eat into principal and income. The recipient will have little control over investment strategy.

Yet, if it is obvious that a beneficiary can't handle the money, then a trust should be established.

Establishing a Trust

While do-it-yourself books and software have become increasingly popular, the services of an attorney specializing in estate planning are a must. The attorney will consider your wishes in detail and then show you how a trust can be established to meet those needs. The cost for doing so can run from a few hundred dollars to several thousand if a complete estate plan is required.

The trust document will be drafted by the attorney, setting forth all the terms of the trust, such as when the money will be paid and to whom and under what circumstances.

One of the most important decisions you will make is to name the trustee. The trustee carries a very heavy responsibility, known as a fiduciary role. He or she can be held personally liable not only for errors but for not acting when he or she should. Because of this burden many individuals are reluctant to act as a trustee.

Commercial trust companies therefore exist for this purpose. Your own commercial bank (not a savings and loan) probably has a trust department that can act as a trustee for your trust. Independent trust companies can be considered. There is endless debate about whether institutions or individuals make better trustees. Table 14.1 sets out the basic issues.

You can have two personal friends acting as trustees for your trust. One can focus on investment work and the other on tax and planning issues. Each acts as a cross-check on the other. Then, you can name a trust company as the stand-by trustee should your friend falter. Alternatively, you can name the trust company and a friend as cotrustees. Your lawyer has language to accomplish this.

Unless you have close friends with these skills, however, a corporate trustee is probably your only reasonable choice. While fees and investment returns can be a problem, you can at least be assured

TABLE 14.1 Institution versus Individual as Trustee

Issue	Trust Company	Individual
Continuity	Perpetual	Life of the individual(s)
Potential for misuse	Nearly zero	Possible
Investment results	Average to excellent	Wide variation
Personal attention	Varies widely	Probably high
Fees	Percentage of the assets	None to modest
Trust knowledge	High	Low to high

that the tax and legal requirements for the trust will be met and the funds will be invested regularly,

> **TIP** Pay particular attention to how the trustee can be removed. If you name a trustee and the trustee can't be removed, the trustee can often take the beneficiaries and the trust for granted. The only way to remove the trustee would probably be to institute a legal action. This is a tough way to go.

A trust should be considered if your beneficiary is having severe financial difficulties. If the IRA is paid to a trust for the beneficiary, it may be protected from creditors or a bankruptcy of the beneficiary. You need to check both trust law and commercial law in your state.

Other Possible Arrangements

First, however, explore whether any other arrangement can be made. If a friend can act as an advisor to the trust beneficiary, and the beneficiary agrees, make provisions in your will to pay that friend for rendering investment and financial advice each year. If you have a trusted accountant, broker, or lawyer, explore with him or her how he or she could play a part in working with the beneficiary. While an informal arrangement can always go wrong, most do not and prove excellent ways of helping beneficiaries grow into their new responsibilities.

I want to emphasize that the best course of action is to continually educate the beneficiaries about the IRA account, the investment philosophy used, and the investments in the account. If you have struck a good way of handling your account, don't keep it a secret. Get your beneficiaries into the game. Keep them fully informed about decisions as you make them. Give them a feel for how to handle the account. An educated family is the best response to the beneficiary issue.

Naming a Trust as Beneficiary

In some circumstances you may want to pass the IRA to a trust for your spouse's benefit. This would be especially true if your spouse is incompetent or if you need to be absolutely sure the money eventually reaches your children.

However, combining estate planning with funding for a spouse's retirement-income needs can lead to unintended complication and tax liability. Often, so much effort is focused on saving estate taxes that income taxes are created as a result. For instance, distributing IRA assets into a trust gives away the benefit of tax-deferred buildup of the account value.

Once the trust accepts the IRA, the spousal rights to tax deferral are gone. And the trust must begin taking distributions from the IRA. It does not matter that the trust has been set up for the sole support and benefit of your spouse.

Also, your spouse loses control of the assets, including investment and income decisions. These decisions are now passed to the trustee, who must act under the terms of the trust.

The Revocable or Living Trust

Revocable, or living, trusts have become quite popular estate-planning vehicles. While they generally have no benefit in saving estate taxes, they do avoid probate and help keep the family's affairs out of the public eye since a trust is not subject to probate.

However, naming a revocable trust as beneficiary of the IRA can be costly from an income-tax point of view.

Since a revocable trust, by definition, does not meet the irrevocable requirement that would allow the trust to take distributions from the IRA over many years, the revocable trust must deplete the IRA more quickly than a spouse would. All the income tax must be paid within five years.

EXAMPLE   You name your living (revocable) trust as the beneficiary of your IRA. Your wife is the beneficiary of the trust. You pass away before age 70 1/2. Now the trust must take all the assets within five years and pay the income tax due. Since your IRA had $750,000 in it, your trustee elects equal payments over five years of roughly $180,000 per year to deplete the principal and interest earned from the frozen IRA. Each year income tax is paid on $180,000. Therefore, roughly 40 percent of the money goes to pay income taxes. The trust inherits, net after tax, $540,000. The income that could have been earned from investing tax payments is lost.

Worse, if you were to die after age 70-1/2 and you had begun your required distribution schedule, recalculating your life expectancy every year, your trust would have to take distribution of the entire account in the year following your death. Why? Because you had elected to recalculate your life expectancy, your life expectancy is indeed recalculated—to zero. All the money has to be paid out and the full income tax paid on it.

If you were over 70-1/2 when you passed away and had elected not to recompute your life expectancy each year, your trust would have to take the funds at a rate based on your life expectancy at time of death, reduced by one each year:

EXAMPLE   You pass away at age 73. You had been taking your required distribution each year without computing your life expectancy. Therefore, at age 73, your life expectancy was 14 years (16 years at 70-1/2, minus one each year). So the next year, your trust must withdraw 1/13 of the account, 1/12 the following year, 1/11 the year after that, and so forth. Income tax is paid each year on the distributed amount.

Finally, keep in mind that if a trust is a beneficiary of a deceased employee's lump sum from a qualified employers' plan (but not an IRA), the trust can apply income averaging on the lump sum, but only if the employee was over age 50 before January 1, 1986.

In working on your estate plan, you need to keep these rules in mind. They suggest a reworking of your plan depending on how you begin to take your distributions after age 70-1/2. How you give your money to your heirs can change if they get it all at once or if they will have to take it in annual installments from the IRA.

> **TIP**   Since the IRA is probably the only asset you own that carries such heavy income-tax consequences, and since tax deferral is generally a good idea, you should strive to fund your trusts with other assets that make better planning tools. Stocks, bonds, life insurance can all be used, as well as, of course, cash.

While trusts are acceptable as beneficiaries, they are rarely the best choice for your spouse. However, when leaving your IRA to beneficiaries other than your spouse, a trust can be considered as a viable alternative.

> **EXAMPLE**   You have a $300,000 IRA. Concerned that your son, your only heir, will spend the inheritance foolishly, you decide to establish a trust for his benefit, naming that trust as the beneficiary of your IRA. Upon your death, the trustee invests those assets and disburses them to your son upon his reaching age 35. Although your trust pays income taxes on the distributions from the IRA, this is acceptable because you are certain your son would not have done as well had he been named as outright beneficiary,

SHOULD YOU HAVE A TRUSTEE FOR YOUR IRA?

You may be thinking of giving someone other than your spouse the authority to make investment decisions, for your IRA after your death.

Although you or your spouse could hire a money manager to handle the assets in the account, giving discretion in the nature of a trustee arrangement is impossible. An IRA is a trust held in the name of the individual.

It is a much better idea to draft a durable power of attorney and to have your custodian keep it on file. In this way someone else can legally act for you even if you are incapacitated. But the power of attorney, like all other control you have over the IRA, ceases with your death. You cannot control how the beneficiary, especially your spouse, will invest or otherwise disburse the funds after you are gone. And you need to have your lawyer draft this power of attorney. Some states do not recognize its validity.

SUMMARY

The naming of beneficiaries is a straightforward matter for most people. The spouse is named outright beneficiary with children as contingent beneficiaries.

On the death of the first spouse, the surviving spouse will name the children as primary beneficiaries. In rare cases trusts will be established for the child or children who are incapable of handling the responsibility of a large sum of money. These beneficiary arrangements accomplish the following:

1. No tax is due on the death of the first spouse, either income or estate.
2. No delay is incurred in passing the account to the beneficiary.
3. On the death of the first spouse, the account goes intact to the survivor; investments need not be disturbed or changed.
4. The process avoids legal expense and delay.

We began this chapter with poor Bill Jameson. Bill isn't unique.

Many individuals make a simple solution complicated. Think through the issues, discuss them with your family, and get a good estate-planning lawyer and accountant to help you implement your strategy.

Even if you have a good plan in place, laws, rules, and regulations are in constant flux; a review is a good idea every few years. Such things are not a lot of fun, but they could result in saving many thousands of dollars in unnecessary tax payments.

How to Hold on to Your Money

It's amazing to think of the number of ways in which you can lose money and so, the security of your retirement.

Over the years, I've seen many traps set for unwary investors. From the vantage point of long experience, these snares seem obvious. Yet, I constantly see people—often shrewd survivors in other fields—step willingly into deadfalls and take their faith and fortune down with them.

TWELVE PITFALLS TO AVOID

You can avoid these common investment pitfalls. Once you recognize them as factors that merely activate your fears or your greed, you can sidestep them.

This is a sure thing. This may be the granddaddy of them all. The only time someone will tell you this is when the investment is fraught with risk. Nobody, for instance, talks about Treasury bills as sure things, even though they are as close as you can come to it. But when it comes to buying 20,000 shares of the Brooklyn Bridge at 20 cents per share, out comes, "Don't worry, it's a sure thing." Investment is a risk activity. There are no sure things.

Everybody's buying it. This is an excellent reason for selling it. If everyone's buying it, it is quite possible that almost everyone has already bought it. If they have, who'll you sell yours to? When it comes to investing your money, misery loves plenty of company. It may feel good to be running with the crowd, but it generally isn't profitable, and you'll usually get trampled

I've even recommended it to my mother. If someone has to trot out mother to convince you to buy something, it will almost certainly be a bad investment. Good investments stand on their own merits. They don't need to tug at your heartstrings.

I've got a hot tip for you. Basically, what this means is that the person has inside information—information not yet released to the public that will drive up the price of the stock.

Buying and selling stock based on nonpublic information is a crime in this country, punishable by fines and/or imprisonment. Is it really worth it? And odds are that the hot tip is either not-so-hot or is completely untrue. A really hot tip (read true fact) would come only directly from the company itself, and people in authority don't generally leak information to people you know. Simply put, I ignore "hot tips."

This is where the smart money is going. In all the years I've been investing, I have been unable to define the smart money. I have seen too many dedicated professionals step in the soup to believe that there is an identifiable smart money set.

The closest you can come to it are the officers and directors of a company, who have to report purchases and sales in their company's stock. If six or seven of them are loading up, I guess you could say that the smart money is buying the stock. However, they can be just as wrong as anyone else.

If you don't get it today, you'll miss the opportunity. At times, this can be true. Most of the time, however, this is used as a means to impose selling pressure. If your automatic answer to this ploy is, "I'll pass," you will save yourself a lot of money over the years.

This is a limited opportunity being offered to a select few. The idea here is that you're being blessed and honored with something that you ordinarily wouldn't qualify for, and so you should be both eager and grateful to be involved. It may be a limited opportunity— and the select few might consist of several thousand other prospects.

When opportunities are truly limited and offered to a select few, you can bet that big money is involved, and nobody ever says things like "select few." Pass on these as well.

Let's buy it. After all, how much lower can it go? This is usually said about a stock that has plummeted from, say, $50 per share to $14. The answer is, it can go down a whole lot more. Like to zero. If you buy 100 shares at $14, you've invested $1,400. The stock could go to nothing and you could lose all your money. What difference does it make if it was once $50? Obviously, at $14, something substantial has changed, and it just isn't the same company that it was when the price was $50.

This is even more so when the stock is trading at a very low price. A stock may look very cheap at $1.75, but think about that price this way: $1.75 is also 28 six-cent units. If you think about that stock as trading at 28 units instead of 1.75, you realize that even at $1.75, it can be very expensive if you buy enough of it.

I think the stock is bottoming. Trying to catch a falling stock at the bottom is like trying to catch a falling knife. You usually bleed from the experience. Don't try to pick a bottom. Ever. Period.

There's a shortage of stocks. Whenever this one appears, I look harder at the market to see whether it has made a major top. I think this really means there is a shortage of stocks that are reasonably or cheaply priced. We never hear this until after the market has made a significant advance from bear market lows.

As bull markets progress, new issues flood the market, helping to fill the appetite for common stocks. If you're a corporation interested in raising additional cash, you're going to try to sell your stock at the price most advantageous to your corporation. You'd like to get top dollar for the stock while leaving a bit of appreciation on the table for your shareholder.

There are many new issues from reputable houses that indeed meet the very purpose of the stock market—to raise capital for business—and are legitimate considerations for purchase.

However, when cheap new issues come up in a market at a time people feel a shortage of stocks exist, you have to be very, very careful.

This is the hottest investment within the past five years. The market is a cyclical beast that wanders back and forth between competing investment ideas, with an overall upward bias.

It's human nature to want to be part of a success story. But investing based on yesterday's performance can be dangerous. Once a trend is widely recognized and reported as such, a top may be at hand. This is tricky to judge. Trends, once in place, can persist for a much longer time, and move a lot farther than anyone expects.

The fact that a particular stock may be up 400 percent over the past five years shouldn't mean a thing for you. The question is, what will it do over the next five years?

It's difficult to do well by buying yesterday's winners. You're much better off trying to anticipate a turn, investing in that idea, and then having patience. Your timing can be off, but you'll generally avoid paying too high a price for your investment.

We're entering a new era. Things won't be the same ever again. In 1929 it was felt that stocks had reached a new, permanently high level. The business cycle, it was suggested, had been relegated to the past because of advances in modern business methods.

While there are always differences from one era to another, the basic underpinnings never change. People offer goods and services to make a profit. Fear and greed rule the marketplace. People try to do what is best for them, and try to avoid pain. Just when people felt that junk bonds were permanently changing the investment landscape, the wheel made another turn and they fell from favor.

Always remember that the more things change the more they remain the same. The methods may vary, the products may be different, but human nature and the desire for profit (and avoidance of loss) never changes.

So-and-so recommends it. The never-ending chase for the ultimate investment guru goes on. Over the years, I have seen many good investment seers catch the public's fancy and then fall from grace. It is always difficult to judge how this happens, but typically somebody runs up an outstanding forecasting record. The media pick up on it, and it is widely reported. Then the guru makes a few more outstanding calls, and now carries great weight in the market.

His (or her) calls are reported quickly and followed by many people. Just when it seems he can never be wrong, he makes a serious gaffe and the process begins to unwind. A couple more poor calls follow, and he falls from grace.

Almost any analyst or adviser can enter a period when he has a hot hand. It is impossible to figure out when this will happen. Just as randomly, the hand turns cold. I've seen situations where an industry suddenly comes to life and the stocks roar. Anyone recommending these stocks is known for having a "hot" hand. Often he just happened to be there and the stocks took off. People confuse the action of the stock group with the analyst.

Don't waste your time following the fashionable guru. Stick to basic and fundamental investing principals. Work on your asset allocation. Try to anticipate change. Buy before the crowd gets there. Stick to your strategy and have patience. Listen to people who are known more for long-term consistency than for spectacular prediction.

SUMMARY

Most people think the key to investment success involves picking big winners in the stock market and timing in and out of the market. Actually, the real key is applying a consistent philosophy and strategy over long periods of time. It is really the tortoise and not the hare that wins the investment race.

A big piece of applying that consistency is to avoid the big, gut-wrenching mistakes that force you out of your game plan. Now, you can't always pick a winning stock, and you're not always going to have co-operative markets, but you can work diligently to limit your mistakes. It is my experience that over decades, it is the investors who make the fewest mistakes who find investment success.

An easy way to start down this road is to avoid the more obvious ones. We've discussed a number of them in this chapter, and they're worth listing again for quick reference:

1. There are no sure things.
2. Buying what everyone else is buying will limit your returns.
3. Even mothers get bad advice. Strong investment conviction does not guarantee profits.
4. Hot tips usually aren't.

5. The market is much smarter than any individual or group.

6. Real opportunity welcomes everyone.

7. When something looks cheap, there is a reason why. Know that reason.

8. Don't try to pick bottoms.

9. Don't buy a stock because you think it's in short supply.

10. A hot investment usually turns out not to be.

11. There are constants in the market. New eras must pay homage to the interplay between risk and reward. That never changes.

12. In the end, you and you alone are responsible for your investment returns.

Putting It All Together: A Case Study

It's so easy to get caught up in all the laws, regulations, and rules that it is often difficult to step back from everything in order to make some sense out of the situation. Let's work through a case study for a lump-sum recipient.

This case study is taken from real-life situations. I have purposely hidden the identity of my clients and present this as a composite situation.

CHESTER WARNER

At age 49, Chester and his wife, Sarah, enjoy the fruits of his success at Ajax Engine Manufacturing. Responsible for sales in a territory stretching along a portion of the East Coast, his position as a vice-president is rewarding and interesting. Their oldest child, Mary, has just completed her college degree and Terry is in her junior year at State. They live in their home of 20 years, now worth about $250,000, and they take pride in the relatively small mortgage of $40,000.

Chester has accumulated $100,000, consisting of an old savings plan that he rolled into a new 401(k) and his contributions to the 401(k). With $50,000 in an account with their broker and another $22,000 in IRAs that they began when contributions were deductible, they feel secure and grateful that they have been able to get the kids through college without burdening them with large loans. The company pays all their medical and life insurance expenses, and Chester has just been told that he will earn his first stock options with the company next year, in addition to his salary and bonus of $115,000 per year. He has been with Ajax for 26 years.

Ajax, as a middle-sized American engine manufacturer, has been sorely tested by foreign competition, especially from Japan and Korea. In an effort to streamline and modernize, the new company head has ordered a 15 percent reduction in white-collar staff to reduce overhead and make room for a younger generation of managers. While not unhappy with his performance, the company has offered Chester a severance package if he'd like to pack it in.

$300,000 lump sum from his pension, or a lifetime annuity of $29,000 per year. (since his age and years of service equal 75, the company formula, he qualifies for retirement.)

$115,000, or one year's salary.

Complete medical and insurance coverage for three years.

$50,000 as a special bridge payment to help ease the transition.

Chester likes his position at Ajax and had no plans to leave until normal retirement at age 65. While the package is appealing, he tells his superiors that he has decided to stay on at Ajax. Their response is less than reassuring.

While acknowledging his good work and continued contributions to Ajax, they want him to know that once the reorganization has taken place his position is in danger of being eliminated and they cannot guarantee another position for him. If that happens he might be dismissed without a severance package. Perhaps he should think this over.

Chester feels that Ajax, in addition to treating him with contempt and ingratitude, is engaging in age discrimination. He fumes at Sarah about the unfairness of it all, but what really nags at him is the sheer terror of being cast adrift at 49 with very narrow marketing skills. Who would want him? The whole industry is downsizing. How will he make ends meet? Is he employable? What will they do?

Once the initial shock has subsided, Chester and Sarah realize that no matter their feelings, the handwriting is on the wall. They have 60 days to make a decision. They need to get to work.

> We'll make it easy on Chester and Sarah. We can assume that they have a good investment advisor and a good accountant. If not, we'd have them read the chapter on The Lump Sum Is Not a Do-It-Yourself Project. This will also make it easier on our reader.

The first thing they decide to tackle is their monthly budget. Will they have enough money to live on? If Chester can't find new employment, can their accumulated savings see them through?

Putting together their check register and charge statements for the past two years, they begin adding up their expenses. Every time they come across an expense that they consider a nonessential (the great trip to Hawaii!) or will not recur (Terry's tuition) they put that in a separate column. In this way they isolate the essentials.

Their bare-bones budget appears to be $35,000 per year. Since this is an after-tax figure, they consult the tax tables and find that they'll need about $44,000 per year of pre-tax income, considering the deductions they use for their mortgage interest, property taxes, and so forth. Of course, this doesn't leave room for inflation or any kind of entertainment, but it will get them by for the foreseeable future. Since Terry's final year's expenses will total $10,000, they assume that they'll reduce their savings to $40,000 to pay for it, so they can ignore it as an expense.

How to earn $44,000? If Chester takes the package, he'll get two pieces consisting of taxable and rollover-eligible money:

Taxable:

One year's income	$115,000
Bridge payment	$ 50,000
Total	$165,000

Rollover-eligible:

Pension lump-sum	$300,000
401(k) savings plan	$ 40,000
	$340,000

Chester learns, much to his surprise, that Ajax won't spread out the income and bridge payment; he must take it all this year. Since this will throw his income up to a total of $280,000, his severance package of $165,000 will be taxed at maximum rates, so he'll realize only $105,000 after tax.

They contact their accountant who advises them that Chester isn't eligible for any special income averaging on the two lump sums and that even if he were, the tax would still be quite high.

The accountant then runs a Roth IRA calculation and finds that the tax on $340,000 would be about $140,000 (state and federal ordinary tax rates) leaving about $200,000 for the Roth IRA. Since they need income almost immediately, they decide not to pay the tax—they would lose the income production from the $140,000 paid in taxes. Invested in bonds at 7 percent, for instance, that $140,000 would generate about $9,800 per year income.

Accordingly, the accountant advises Chester to roll over both distributions to an IRA account.

This presents a problem. If they roll over the money how can they use it if they need income? After all, distributions from an IRA for individuals under the age of 59 1/2 are subject to income tax, plus an additional 10 percent tax penalty.

To their relief, they learn that they could, if they had to, begin a periodic income stream from the IRA. And as long as they meet the rules for computing the amount of the income they could avoid the 10 percent tax penalty. Since there is more than one way to compute the income, they ask their accountant for the method that will let them live off the income, without disturbing the principal.

He does the calculations and lets them know that they will have to take about $34,000 per year from the account—all the interest and a little bit more. At least they could cover most of their expenses from the IRA if they had to.

Chester and Sarah realize that the $105,000 after-tax severance pay will see them through for a little more than three years. Since the money has been taxed, they can compare it to their after-tax expenses, which total $35,000. With enforced discipline, the money could last four years.

What then? What if Chester is unable to find work? The prospect for them is frightening. Given their concerns, they visit their broker and express their strong desire to keep the lump sum invested as safely as possible. While they recognize the greater potential in common stocks, they can't face the possibility that their capital could be reduced. They need that safety net.

Their broker advises them that intermediate-term bonds (four to ten years) of good quality (A rated or better) are yielding just under 7 percent. If they can leave the IRA undisturbed for four years, the account will grow to $445,000. At a similar rate of 7 percent, the account will generate $31,000 per year in interest income.

The plan becomes clear:

1. Roll over the two lump-sum distributions to the IRA to preserve the capital from tax.

2. Take the severance and bridge payments and open a companion account. Keep $35,000 in the money market fund for the first year and invest the balance in one- and two-year CD's to have capital ready for each year's expenses. They look at tax-free bonds, but because their income will be so low, they do not find them attractive.

3. Invest the IRA in high-quality bonds in a four- to eight-year bond ladder. All the bonds will pay interest into the account regularly if Chester and Sarah need to begin an income stream from it.

4. Consolidate their $50,000 in savings into the companion account, invested as well in CDs and short-term instruments with a maximum maturity of one year. (They may need money to make a move if Chester's job search warrants it.)

5. He will consolidate his small IRA into his large one.

6. Chester will begin an immediate job search.

They realize that they're being ultraconservative, but Chester's departure from the company is affecting their judgment. In this instance, their need to feel secure prevails over the potential for higher investment returns with increased risk.

After his experience at Ajax, Chester can't possibly imagine giving a new employer his lump-sum distributions.

Implementation

Chester leaves the company and makes a direct trustee-to-trustee transfer of both his distributions to his IRA. The IRA names Sarah as Chester's beneficiary. If Chester dies, the entire account will go directly, without probate, into Sarah's IRA rollover account.

The companion account is augmented with the severance payments, and Chester's broker issues him a checkbook to allow immediate access to the funds as needed.

Since Chester is no longer using payroll withholding on his income, his accountant has him file quarterly estimated tax payments.

Chester's job search begins in earnest. He networks with friends, but this proves futile since the entire industry is downsizing. He prepares a resume and sends it out with little success. Even a professional placement firm can't turn an opportunity for him.

Two frustrating years pass. Chester becomes increasingly irritable and difficult to live with. Once an outgoing and gregarious person, Chester's friends painfully witness his humor melt into bitterness. Sarah understands only too well that the combination of being let go along with idle time is wreaking havoc within him. Only a job will cure the problem.

Out of the blue, they run into an old friend at the supermarket who now runs a small manufacturing company. He could use a marketing rep of Chester's ability. Would he be interested? Chester jumps at the opportunity, and while the job pays only $40,000, there is opportunity to grow if the company does. And he will get his medical insurance from the new company.

A Change in Direction

After six months, Chester feels comfortable enough to make some changes in his investment plans. It is obvious that he is adjusting well at the company, and the business is prospering. He should enjoy some employment stability for the next few years.

He and Sarah visit with their broker and review their accounts. The IRA has grown to $400,000 and the companion account (non-IRA) is now worth about $80,000. At age 53, Chester appears to have a career position at the new company given the sales territory he has developed during the first six months. While he doesn't expect ever to earn much more than $60,000, he knows that he and Sarah have enough to see them through to retirement.

When to retire? The job is a welcome relief from unemployment but not as challenging as Chester's former position. He can take it or leave it. Their broker computes the growth of the IRA at various rates of return and ages (see Table 1). They are trying to see how much money they will have and how much income the account could generate. This will help peg when it is feasible to rely on the accumulated IRA for expenses.

TABLE 1 Growth of a $400,000 IRA at Various Rates of Return

Age	6 percent	7 percent	8 percent	9 percent
53	$400,000	$400,000	$ 400,000	$ 400,000
53	$424,000	$428,000	$ 432,000	$ 436,000
54	$449,000	$457,000	$ 466,000	$ 475,000
55	$476,000	$490,000	$ 503,000	$ 518,000
56	$505,000	$524,000	$ 544,000	$ 564,000
57	$535,000	$561,000	$ 587,000	$ 615,000
58	$567,000	$600,000	$ 634,000	$ 670,000
59	$601,000	$642,000	$ 685,000	$ 731,000
60	$637,000	$687,000	$ 740,000	$ 797,000
61	$675,000	$735,000	$ 799,000	$ 868,000
62	$716,000	$786,000	$ 863,000	$ 946,000
63	$759,000	$842,000	$ 932,000	$1,032,000
64	$804,000	$900,000	$1,007,000	$1,125,000
65	$852,000	$972,000	$1,087,000	$1,226,000

Some pretty big numbers! Chester suggests they try 10 percent and 11 percent returns but their broker suggests that the asset allocation required to get that return would dictate a high percentage of stocks in the account—a risk they clearly are unwilling to assume.

They now look at the interest income the account would generate at the same rates of return (see Table 2).

TABLE 2 Interest Income of a $400,000 IRA Growing at Various Rates of Return

Age	6 percent	7 percent	8 percent	9 percent
53	$24,000	$28,000	$32,000	$36,000
53	$25,440	$29,960	$34,560	$39,240
54	$26,940	$31,990	$37,280	$42,750
55	$28,560	$34,300	$40,240	$46,620
56	$30,300	$36,680	$43,520	$50,760
57	$32,100	$39,270	$46,960	$55,350
58	$34,020	$42,000	$50,720	$60,300
59	$36,060	$44,940	$54,800	$65,790
60	$38,220	$48,090	$59,200	$71,730
61	$40,500	$51,450	$63,920	$78,120
62	$42,960	$55,020	$69,040	$85,140
63	$45,540	$58,940	$74,560	$92,880
64	$48,240	$63,000	$80,560	$101,250
65	$51,120	$68,040	$86,960	$110,340

Age 60 feels comfortable to them, but they are unsure if they will have enough income given the effects of inflation so they assume a 3 percent inflation rate and increase their current expenses by 3 percent per year for seven years. At age 60 they estimate they will need $43,000 to equal today's budget of $35,000. But wait! $35,000 was an after-tax amount. They have to add in taxes since the IRA income taken will be taxed as ordinary income. Assuming a 30 percent tax bracket they estimate they will need $50,000 to $55,000 per year.

To get that return at age 60 without dipping into the principal will mean that they will have to generate an average annual return of around 7.5 percent. If stocks follow their historic return of 10 percent per year and bonds 6 percent per year, a mix of 35 percent stocks and 65 percent bonds appears to be needed to hit the target.

They consult the asset allocation hook chart (see Figure 13.1) and note with relief that a 35 percent stock component doesn't significantly increase the risk in the account over a several-year span.

The plan crystallizes:

1. Invest the $400,000 with $140,000 in common stocks and $260,000 in investment-grade fixed income in the 6- to 10-year area.

2. Continue to invest the companion account in shorter-term municipal bonds to provide tax-free income and liquidity for emergencies and additional expenses.

3. Chester will work until age 60 then begin to tap the IRA for income. The principal will be kept intact and Social Security will provide a pay increase.

4. Since they will then have $700,000 in the IRA in addition to funds in the companion account, they can feel free to spend all of Chester's current income—retirement has been funded.

SUMMARY

Chester and Sarah developed a plan that took into account several different areas.

1. Investment
2. Tax
3. Personal planning

As their circumstances changed, their plan did as well. Their planning always took into account the fact that their circumstances might change and so they took no course of action that couldn't be modified.

Between the ages of 60 and 70-1/2, Chester and Sarah could spend money from the IRA as they needed it. Beginning at 70-1/2 Chester made sure that he was withdrawing at least the minimum amount required under the term-certain method. Eventually, Chester passed away and the IRA was rolled into Sarah's IRA. They used other assets for the trust established before Chester's death.

Sarah continued to enjoy the benefits of the IRA. Eventually, their children came into possession of the account upon Sarah's death and by withdrawing the money over several years they were able to fund their own children's' college education.

Chester's original lump sum funded benefits for three generations of his family. A bit of proper planning and thought about a lump sum can go a very long way.

APPENDIX TWO

A Lump Sum Library

Browse the shelves of any well-stocked book store and you'll find dozens of books on finance and investment. Most are actually quite good, filled with valuable information and tips. Some are of dubious value, and a few probably do more damage than good.

I admire and respect several different sources of information that offer great value year after year. Here's my list of favorite financial, tax, and investment sources.

MAGAZINES AND NEWSPAPERS

Kiplinger's

One of the most underrated magazines in the country. You rarely hear as much about them as you do about Money, but issue after issue, they provide excellent advice for the average and not so average investor. Their subscription rate is a screaming bargain. Pick one up at the newsstand and fill out the subscription card.

Barron's

Barron's is a weekly financial magazine that appears on Saturday. My Saturday-morning visit to the news dealer to pick up my

Barron's (arrives at 11 A.M.) is a weekly ritual. It offers savvy, contrarian advice from some of the best thinkers and advisers around; there is much to muse over with a dash of irreverence and a wealth of economic and market data thrown in for good measure. Don't subscribe or you won't get it until Monday. Pay the cover price and enjoy it over the weekend.

The Wall Street Journal

I can't imagine a publication covering the day-to-day workings of the capitalist system any better than the journal, While *Investor's Business Daily* gives a lot of market action in better form and detail and may be better for traders, no one covers business like the *Journal.* Get home delivery if it is available and enjoy over breakfast.

CNBC/CNNfn/Bloomberg Television

The business newspapers of the air. Day after day, they cover the markets with commentary and reportage. Access to these stations varies on your location, but one should be available. Warning! It's easy to get caught up in the day to day excitement of the markets. Remember that you're a long-term investor—not a trader.

BOOKS

J. K. Lasser's Your Income Tax, the J. K. Lasser Institute, Macmillan USA, published annually.

The paperback version of this indispensable tax guide will run you about $15.00. You can save more than that every time you use it. It covers all aspects of income tax and tax rules, along with estate and financial planning. A must-have for your library.

The Prudent Investor, The Definitive Guide to Professional Investment Management, James P. Owen, Probus Publishing, 1993.

Owen is a managing director of NWQ Investment Management, a large California-based money manager. If you're going manager hunting, this book will guide you through the thickets. A consultant works best, but if you can't find one, Jim's book is the next best thing.

Contrarian Investing, Anthony Gallea and William Patalon III, New York Institute of Finance, 1998.

Bill and I wrote this book to bring the concepts of contrarian investing to a broader audience. I use many of the ideas and concepts in this book to manage our clients' retirement accounts. Even though you may not become a dyed-in-the-wool contrarian, our approach to cutting risk and finding value in the stock market should prove valuable.

Reminiscences of a Stock Operator, Edwin Lefevre, Fraser Publishing Company, 1998

Recommended reading by more professional traders than any other book. Did the notorious Jesse Livermore write it? A real eye-opener written by a Wall Street operator during the wild and woolly early days.

Intermarket Technical Analysis, John Murphy, John Wiley & Sons, 1991

Murphy explores the relationship between various markets in this seminal work. Once you've read it, you'll never see the markets the same way again. Dozens of valuable tips and clues on how to read the markets.

What Works on Wall Street: A Guide to the Best-Performing Investment Strategies of All Time, James O'Shaughnessy, McGraw-Hill, 1998.

O'Shaughnessy studied decades of data on stocks and what stock selection methods worked the best. If you are fashioning your investment strategy, his book is an excellent way to winnow losing systems from winning ideas.

The Wall Street Journal Guide to Understanding Money & Investing, Kenneth Morris and Alan Siegel, Simon & Schuster, 1994.

This is a good overall introduction to the subject. And, in true Journal style, the writing and presentation is accessible to nearly everyone. A book that you'll refer to time after time.

Ernst & Young's Retirement Planning Guide, John Wiley & Sons, 1997.

An in-depth guide to the subject, with worksheets, tips and information on resources and Internet sites. This comprehensive guide explains the basic rules of retirement planning and addresses IRAs and related topics. A bit thin on detailed discussion of several lump sum aspects, but that's OK. You have this book!

APPENDIX THREE

Financial Planning Forms

On the following pages you will find three simple forms that, when completed, will give you an excellent overview of your financial situation.

We all hate to be on a budget, but it is crucial in proper retirement planning to understand clearly how much you spend and how much you can count on for those expenses.

YOUR FINANCES comprises a simple balance sheet that lists all your assets and liabilities. It shows where your assets are and where your debts lie. Use this form to work on debt reduction, consolidation of accounts, and other issues that it may raise. You'll use some of this information to input into the income estimates on the next sheet. This balance sheet will also give you a quick picture of the size of your estate.

ANNUAL SOURCES OF RETIREMENT INCOME helps you estimate your annual retirement income. You can lump various accounts together and apply estimated rates of return to them to pencil out your income sources.

YOUR BUDGET will list all the places you spend money. Use the actual expenses for the year past by going through your checkbook and credit card statements. WARNING! Don't try to estimate these line items. You'll be amazed at how much a guess will underestimate your actual expenses.

Once you've completed one for the year past, complete a second one for the coming year, especially if you're going from employment to retirement. These budget sheets will help you identify spending areas that can be cut to fit into your new retirement income.

At the end of the budget sheet, you'll total your expenses and enter your annual income to arrive at the amount of money you're short, or over, to meet those expenses.

Final comment: Financial planning is something you should do on a regular basis. Try not to make it too much of a chore, since you want to be sure that you do it every six months or every year. If you dread the process, you won't keep up. Better to do something simple that you'll stick with than something sophisticated that you'll never use.

YOUR FINANCES

Amount of

TAX-DEFERRED ANNUITIES $_____
SAVINGS ACCOUNTS $_____
CDs $_____
MONEY MARKET FUNDS $_____
STOCKS $_____
MUNICIPAL BONDS AND MUNI BOND FUNDS $_____
STOCK MUTUAL FUNDS $_____
GOVERNMENT, CORPORATE BOND FUNDS $_____
YOUR IRA ACCOUNTS $_____
SPOUSE IRA ACCOUNTS $_____
KEOGH OR PRIVATE PENSION ACCOUNTS $_____
VALUE OF YOUR HOME $_____
VALUE OF VACATION HOME $_____
OTHER REAL ESTATE INVESTMENTS $_____
401(K) OR OTHER SAVINGS PLAN AT WORK $_____
LUMP SUM DUE TO YOU $_____

Your Debts and Interest Rates on Each

HOME MORTGAGE $_____
VACATION HOME MORTGAGE $_____
HOME EQUITY LINES OF CREDIT $_____
CREDIT CARD DEBT $_____
AUTO AND BOAT LOANS $_____
PERSONAL BANK LOANS $_____
BROKERAGE MARGIN LOANS $_____
LIFE INSURANCE LOANS $_____
OTHER DEBTS $_____

Value of All Your Assets $_____
Amount of Your Debt $_____
   Your Net Worth: (Assets - Debt) $_____

ANNUAL SOURCES OF RETIREMENT INCOME

IRA BALANCES $_____
  Multiply by rate of return   ×_____%
  Annual income $_____
SAVINGS ACCOUNTS $_____
  Multiply by rate of return   ×_____%
  Annual income $_____ $_____
BROKERAGE ACCOUNTS $_____
  Multiply by rate of return   ×_____%
  Annual income $_____ $_____
PENSION HUSBAND $_____
PENSION WIFE $_____
SOCIAL SECURITY HUSBAND $_____
SOCIAL SECURITY WIFE $_____
OTHER INCOME _____ $_____
OTHER INCOME _____ $_____
  TOTAL ANNUAL INCOME EXPECTED $_____

YOUR BUDGET

Actual Annual Expenses

THE HOUSE
    Utilities $ _____
    Maintenance $ _____
    Furnishings $ _____
    Home improvements $ _____
    Rent (if you don't own the house) $ _____
        Home total $ _____
TAXES
    Federal income tax $ _____
    State and local income tax $ _____
    Home property taxes $ _____
    Vacation home property taxes $ _____
        Taxes total $ _____
DEBT SERVICE
    Home mortgage $ _____
    Vacation home mortgage $ _____
    Auto loan #1 $ _____
    Auto loan #2 $ _____
    Credit card debt $ _____
    Home equity line of credit $ _____
    Personal loans $ _____
        Debt service total $ _____
PERSONAL EXPENSES
    Food $ _____
    Clothing $ _____
    Automobile $ _____
    Out-of-pocket medical $ _____
    Charitable contributions $ _____
    Vacations $ _____
    Entertainment $ _____
    Subscriptions $ _____
    Gifts $ _____
    Professional fees $ _____

Miscellaneous $ _____

    Total personal expenses $_____

INSURANCE

    Automobile #1 $ _____

    Automobile #2 $ _____

    Life insurance, husband $ _____

    Life insurance-wife $ _____

    Homeowners $ _____

    Vacation home $ _____

    Medical $ _____

    Total insurance $_____

MISCELLANEOUS

                                    $ _____

                                    $ _____

                                    $ _____

                                    $ _____

_____ $

Total miscellaneous $_____

GRAND TOTAL ANNUAL EXPENSES $ _____

LESS ESTIMATED ANNUAL INCOME $ _____

    Savings $ _____

The author is interested in the reader's questions and comments
Please contact him via e-mail.

gallea@msn.com

Index